Praise for *The Essential Jonathan Edwards*

These primers on Jonathan Edwards's life and thought—his passion for God—provide an excellent glimpse into a life lived unto God. And they help the rest of us slake our thirst for the majesty of our Savior. We owe a great debt to Owen Strachan and Douglas Sweeney for making Edwards and his vision of God so accessible to the rest of us thirsty pilgrims.

THABITI ANYABWILE
Pastor of Anacostia River Church in southeast Washington, D.C.

Everyone says Jonathan Edwards is important. Quite frankly, however, his writing style is pretty dense by contemporary standards, so few pastors and other Christian leaders have invested much time reading him. This new series tackles the problem. Here is the kernel of much of Edwards's thought in eminently accessible form.

D. A. CARSON
Research Professor of New Testament, Trinity Evangelical Divinity School

In *The Essential Jonathan Edwards*, Owen Strachan and Doug Sweeney point with knowledge and excitement to clear and searching sections that illuminate God's truth and search our hearts. In this collection, Edwards is introduced to a new generation of readers. His concerns are made our concerns. This is a worthy effort and I pray that God will bless it.

MARK DEVER
Senior Pastor, Capitol Hill Baptist Church, Washington, D.C.

I am deeply impressed with the vision that has brought together this splendid library of volumes to introduce Jonathan Edwards to a new generation. Owen Strachan and Douglas Sweeney have provided an incredible service by making the often challenging writings of America's greatest theologian accessible for seasoned theologians, pastors, and students alike with *The Essential Jonathan Edwards*. This series is properly titled the "essential collection."

DAVID S. DOCKERY
President, Trinity International University, Deerfield, IL

Jonathan Edwards was a preacher of the Word, a pastor of souls, a philosopher of first rank, and the greatest theologian America has ever produced. In this wonderful new anthology of Edwards's writings, the great Puritan saint lives again. I can think of no better tonic for our transcendence-starved age than the writings of Edwards. But beware: reading this stuff can change your life forever!

TIMOTHY GEORGE
Founding Dean of Beeson Divinity School of Samford University

Let Strachan and Sweeney serve as your guides through the voluminous writings of America's greatest theologian. They have been shaped by his godly counsel and moved by his passion for Christ. By God's grace, Edwards can do the same for you. Start your journey with *The Essential Jonathan Edwards*.

COLLIN HANSEN
Editorial Director of The Gospel Coalition

From a course he taught at Yale and in personal friendship, Doug Sweeney has taught me much about Edwards. Possessing a command of the academic field, he and Owen Strachan nevertheless write this collection with pastoral concern, showing the relevance of Edwards for our Christian faith and practice today. It's a rare combination of gifts and insights that Sweeney and Strachan bring to this task.

MICHAEL HORTON
J. Gresham Machen Professor of Systematic Theology and Apologetics, Westminster Theological Seminary California

Why hasn't this been done before? *The Essential Jonathan Edwards* is now essential reading for the serious-minded Christian. Doug Sweeney and Owen Strachan have written five an excellent and accessible introductions to America's towering theological genius—Jonathan Edwards. They combine serious scholarship with the ability to make Edwards and his theology come alive for a new generation. *The Essential Jonathan Edwards* is a great achievement and a tremendous resource. I can't think of a better way to gain a foundational knowledge of Edwards and his lasting significance.

R. ALBERT MOHLER JR.
President of The Southern Baptist Theological Seminary

A great resource! Edwards continues to speak, and this series of books is an excellent means to hear Jonathan Edwards again live and clear. Pure gold; be wise and invest in it!

JOSH MOODY
Senior Pastor, College Church in Wheaton

You hold in your hands a unique resource: a window into the life and thought of Jonathan Edwards, a man whose life was captured by God for the gospel of Jesus Christ. In these pages you'll not only learn about Edwards, but you'll be able to hear him speak in his own words. This winsome and accessible introduction is now the first thing I'd recommend for those who want to know more about America's greatest pastor-theologian.

JUSTIN TAYLOR
Managing Editor, ESV Study Bible

Jonathan Edwards is surely one of the most influential theologians of the eighteenth century. Now, at last, we have a wide-ranging and representative sample of his work published in an attractive, accessible, and most important of all, readable form. The authors are to be commended for the work they have put into this set and I hope it will become an important feature of the library of many pastors and students of the Christian faith.

CARL R. TRUEMAN
Professor of History, Westminster Theological Seminary

The Essential Jonathan Edwards is a tour de force of theological exploration and pastoral insight. Capturing the marrow of Edwards's life and thought, Owen Strachan and Douglas Sweeney bring us an immensely valuable work that is sure to encourage and enlighten. Whether one is new to Edwards or has long trusted him as a faithful friend, this volume will undoubtedly serve as a welcome companion.

NATE PICKOWICZ
Pastor of Harvest Bible Church, Gilmanton, NH
Author of *Reviving New England* and *Why We're Protestant*

The Essential Jonathan Edwards is a wonderful entryway into the life and work of one who is arguably still America's greatest theologian. Strachan and Sweeney have condensed the best of Edwards's wide-ranging and voluminous works into one large volume, arranged thematically around truth, goodness, beauty, including bookends on Edwards's biography and views on heaven and hell. Highly recommended.

KEVIN J. VANHOOZER
Research Professor of Systematic Theology, Trinity Evangelical Divinity School

Jonathan Edwards is as profound as he is difficult to read, which is precisely why resources like this one are so important. Allow Strachan and Sweeney to introduce you to Edwards's life so that you catch a glimpse of his vision for the glory of God.

KYLE STROBEL
Author of *Formed for the Glory of God* (IVP) and coauthor (with Oliver Crisp) of *Jonathan Edwards: An Introduction to His Thought* (Eerdmans).

If you love America's greatest theologian Jonathan Edwards, then you will love this gem of a book. If you love the Christian faith, the beauty of the gospel, robust God-centered theology, or simply are curious about this Edwards fellow, then you will *really* love this new book. This is Edwards in a nutshell—an inviting introduction that doesn't skimp on substance. I can't recommend it highly enough!

TODD WILSON
Senior Pastor, Calvary Memorial Church in Oak Park, IL

Too many know the name and fame of Jonathan Edwards but remain unacquainted with the man and his theology. This is understandable in light of the complexity of his life, the density of his theology, and the deluge of works published by and about him. Long needed is a book to streamline the gargantuan task and treasure of truly appreciating Mr. Edwards. This is that book! It is more than a biography of his life, and better than a summary of his thought; it is a careful distillation of Jonathan Edwards. These pages provide delightful access to Edwards's genius and will surely generate what he would have hoped—deeper religious affections for Jesus Christ.

RICK HOLLAND
Pastor, Mission Road Bible Church, Kansas City

True pastor-theologians are in short supply today, and this work by Owen Strachan and Doug Sweeney acquaint you with one of history's finest. Few theologians have had a greater shaping impact on my approach to preaching and ministry than Jonathan Edwards, and Strachan and Sweeney deftly guide readers of all levels to the essential elements of Edwards's approach to God and Scripture. Whether you are a new believer who has never heard of Edwards, or an experienced theologian with great familiarity, you'll find much in these pages that stretch your mind and provoke your faith.

J.D. GREEAR
Pastor, The Summit Church, Raleigh-Durham, NC

Jonathan Edwards is a man for our time. I work with twenty-first-century university students and next-generation leaders, yet the treasures that Strachan and Sweeney mine from Edwards leap into our day with immediate accessibility and relevance—for example, Edwards's work to develop a theological aesthetics, a vision of beauty, while a university student. This is exemplary scholarship, and so needed in our day.

JEFF DODGE
Teaching Pastor, Cornerstone Church, Ames, Iowa

What a great book! Strachan and Sweeney have crafted a wonderful volume that demystifies Edwards, making his vision of God, his vivid spirituality, and his sometimes-difficult prose easy to digest and appreciate. *The Essential Jonathan Edwards* is a perfect blend of biography, history, theology, and practical application to the Christian life. I especially enjoyed the theme of heaven that surfaces throughout the book; Christians longing for heaven will cherish its pages.

ROBERT CALDWELL
Associate Professor of Church History

THE

ESSENTIAL

JONATHAN

EDWARDS

———•———

OWEN STRACHAN &
DOUGLAS A. SWEENEY

MOODY PUBLISHERS | CHICAGO

Editors: Christopher Reese and Kevin Emmert
Interior design: Ragont Design
Cover design: Erik M. Peterson

Library of Congress Cataloging-in-Publication Data

Names: Strachan, Owen, author.
Title: The essential Jonathan Edwards : an introduction to the life and teaching of America's greatest theologian / Owen Strachan and Douglas Sweeney.
Description: Chicago : Moody Publishers, 2018. | Includes bibliographical references. | Description based on print version record and CIP data provided by publisher; resource not viewed.
Identifiers: LCCN 2018010163 (print) | LCCN 2018001223 (ebook) | ISBN 9780802496706 () | ISBN 9780802418210
Subjects: LCSH: Edwards, Jonathan, 1703-1758.
Classification: LCC BX7260.E3 (print) | LCC BX7260.E3 S769 2018 (ebook) | DDC
 230/.58092 [B] --dc23
LC record available at https://lccn.loc.gov/2018010163

ISBN: 978-0-8024-1821-0

CONTENTS

PART 4: TRUE CHRISTIANITY

PART 5: HEAVEN AND HELL

Preface

It's the strangest thing: three hundred years after his heyday, Jonathan Edwards is more popular than ever. A man who wore a white starchy wig, ministerial garb, and preached ninety-minute stem-winder sermons on a weekly basis is far more widely read than he was when he lived. Just a decade ago, the "New Calvinism" hit number three on *Time* magazine's list of ideas shaking up the world; in the years that have followed, the church's thirst for deep theology and vibrant spirituality shows no signs of tailing off. Though our culture has undoubtedly secularized since Edwards's day, his ideas, his pulpit legacy, and his God-exalting vision of life endures, and keeps finding a young audience who enthusiastically carries the fire forward.

One of the best ways to spot this recurring trend is in the world of publishing. Of the publishing of books about Edwards, there truly is no end. The leader of them all is none other than Yale University, which produced twenty-six print volumes of the magisterial *Works of Jonathan Edwards* and has since debuted forty-seven more online through the Jonathan Edwards Center at Yale (73 volumes total). This harvest of the Edwardsean word means that there is more primary-source Edwards material available than for almost any other thinker of any era of human history. Beyond his own writing, we've witnessed a flood of books on Edwards hit the market in the late twentieth and early twenty-first centuries, none more consequential than George Marsden's *Jonathan Edwards: A Life*. Iain Murray's *Jonathan Edwards:*

A *New Biography* is no longer new, but has sold steadily since it was first published; John Piper's *Desiring God* is perhaps responsible, as much as any other book, for introducing evangelical readers to Edwardsean theology, particularly from the prism of the intoxicating joy offered all who love Christ.

Many other figures played a role in the church's recovery of Edwards as well—R. C. Sproul, John Gerstner, Harry Stout, and more. Indeed, at the popular level, titles are nearly too numerous to count. Edwards-related publishing is so booming, in fact, that you can—for a pretty penny—buy M. X. Lesser's *Reading Jonathan Edwards*, offering you nearly seven hundred pages of book-listings on the Northampton preacher. It's true—there are books about books on Edwards, and of the door-stopper size!

It's no musty or gloomy thing to participate in this ongoing renaissance in some small way. We both—Owen and Doug—love entering the vast, sprawling world we could call Edwardseana, a land of colonial intrigue, snow-cloaked New England forests, and theistic delights. We plan to do it for the rest of our careers, in fact.

About a decade ago, we got a great opportunity to contribute to the conversation over Edwards's life and theology. It all began with an email from Doug to Owen asking if he was interested in coauthoring a (single!) short biography of Edwards for Moody Publishers, which had reached out to Doug along these lines. At the time, Doug was a professor of church history and the history of Christian thought at Trinity Evangelical Divinity School (he is now a distinguished professor of the same, and director of the Jonathan Edwards Center at the school), and Owen had moved to Deerfield to study under him as a PhD student in Historical Theology. The two of us decided this was not enough vocational overlap, however, and so Doug also supervised Owen at the Carl F. H. Henry Center for Theological Understanding at TEDS *and* the Edwards Center. If you can't tell, Owen's life in this season was decidedly Sweeney-centered, we might say, and full of blessing and happiness because of it. (We will not trouble Doug for his evaluation of the period in question.)

Somehow, amidst research-heavy scholarship, a slate of stimulating Henry Center events, and new babies (the first Strachan child, born in 2008 in Lake Forest, Illinois), the two of us found time to prosecute the project. Through the kind instigation of Dave DeWit at Moody, we took on the five volumes of *The Essential Edwards Collection* (EEC), a distillation of the ideas and existence of a long-gone colonial pastor. The EEC released in 2010 and has found a strong audience ever since. But here we are, ten years later, still working through Edwards's cavernous ideas, still guiding initiates through his high-level thinking, still trying to apply his exhortations to our modern context.

The Essential Jonathan Edwards is an edited version of that earlier project. It is not merely edited, but honed, fine-tuned, and reworked. We want this book to be less of an intro to Edwards—though that goal persists—and more of a one-stop-shop resource on a man who defies easy categorization and simplistic summary. Put more simply: Edwards can be intimidating. We've labored to craft the content of *The Essential Jonathan Edwards* so that it is just that: the essential one-volume resource on Edwards's life and thought. This doesn't mean that the book you're reading is an exhaustive work; it is not. It will, however, give you a walking tour of the man, the myth, and the homiletical legend. Many books offer you a slice of Edwards; we offer you, in just one volume, a multi-course meal that will both inform you and, we pray, inspire you to live zealously for Christ.

This last clause matters. We hope that *The Essential Jonathan Edwards* can play a part, by God's grace, in the extension of the Edwardsean legacy. We have a keen interest in helping normal Christian people like us to learn from and live like Edwards. He was no perfect man (more on that later), but he was a faithful believer who hungered to give God all the glory he could. Whether or not you're in ministry, whether or not you ever enter the pulpit, every believer can emulate him in this respect as he emulated Christ. *The Essential Jonathan Edwards* is written with just that end in mind: not to shoot over people's heads with lofty academic discussion, but to fire the heart and mind to embrace the thrilling experience of a God-centered existence.

We have another aim to declare as well. Since we began working on the first iteration of this project a decade ago, we have seen a major swell of interest in the "pastor-theologian" model of ministry, one exemplified by Edwards some three centuries ago. It was Doug's book *Jonathan Edwards and the Ministry of the Word*, and Doug's legendary doctoral seminar on Edwards, that first lit a fire in Owen for this model of the pastorate—which he now promotes, like Doug, in the classroom as a professor of theology at Midwestern Baptist Theological Seminary. Part of why Edwards is so popular is his conception of the ministry, a conception drenched in glory and driven by a hunger for God's Word. Though our era is marked by a generally diminished pulpit and a growing interest in soft words and culturally palatable doctrines, there is a countermovement afoot. Many younger evangelicals who grew up on fads, stories, jokes, and tips now yearn to enflesh afresh Edwards's model of pastoral work. Conferences, books, and even seminary courses now promote this richer, deeper concept of the shepherd of God's flock, for which we are grateful.

The "big God" whom Edwards promoted is beloved by younger evangelicals, and we are thrilled to see that. We believe that the pages ahead can help readers understand the fullness of the biblical God, a figure who unveils His glory preeminently in the great work of salvation. This same God, however, is no pushover, but brings divine justice to bear on His enemies. It is a tremendous encouragement to Bible-loving Christians that

Christ will return and rout Satan. But we have seen challenges arise to the scriptural account of God since we first began this project. Some today argue for only a God of love and edit out the parts of Scripture that speak of divine wrath. One prominent pastor, addressing Edwards directly, has said this, for example:

> Sin has consequences. We dig a pit of sin . . . and eventually we fall in. We act in malice . . . and eventually it returns to haunt us. We employ violence . . . and eventually it boomerangs back on us. We can call this the wrath of God. The Bible does. But it should not cause us to think that the Father of Jesus is the vindictive and retributive god of Edward's infamous sermon. . . .
>
> What I want to tell you is that God's attitude (spirit) toward you is one of unwavering, unconditional, fatherly/motherly love. You have nothing to fear from God. Let the fear of God be understood as the wisdom which recognizes that reality as God has created it has consequences. But the truth that we live in a consequential universe with a moral arc, does not mean that God views sinners as loathsome spiders. He does not. God looks with unconditional love upon all his sons and daughters . . . even his prodigal sons and daughters. (Zahnd)

This is a recent challenge to God's truth, but also an ancient one. What this author and others attempt to separate the Bible will not allow, and Edwards would not, either. The God of love in Scripture is the same God who protects His covenant people by overcoming their—and His—foes (see Owen's comments in *Always in God's Hands: Day by Day in the Company of Jonathan Edwards,* published by Tyndale Momentum, 2018). We will not find in the sacred text that God treats all people the same; there are the sheep and the goats, the wheat and the chaff, the elect and the reprobate (see Rom. 9, for example). Edwards's "big God" is beloved by many, yet resisted by many others. Now as much as ever, we need to consider afresh Edwards's theology, and especially the biblical vision of God he labored to promote aright.

In these pages, we look to Edwards as a faithful pedagogue, but not a perfect one. His owning of slaves, and his hasty efforts to publicize the revivals he witnessed, stand out as problematic aspects of his legacy—especially the former. We are right to grapple with, and even detest, his legacy as a slaveholder. There is no whitewashing Edwards's conduct here, or his unbiblical theology on this count. It is a part of his program that we lament, and that we do well to interrogate. It is even understandable that some believers will have to fight to read Edwards, knowing his ungodly take on their own humanity. For our part, we obviously would not let Edwards off the hook on these counts, but we would note that we will search church history—even *biblical* history—in vain for perfect leaders (save one). In fact, one can argue that the sins of our fathers mean that we should not leave them aside as we might instinctively wish, but should study them all the more. In doing so, we force ourselves to defy hero worship, assess our own blind spots, and confront our own shortcomings.

Jonathan Edwards has much to teach us today. He calls for pastors to be theologians; he urges Christians to be holy; he pleads with the sleeping to wake up and follow Christ; he exhorts us to see that we are no less pleasure-driven and aesthetically interested than unbelievers. In fact, we have more reason to seek joy and pursue pleasure, for we know the One who made us for Himself and fashioned us for lasting happiness. In a secularizing, "postmodern" age that claims to be fulfilled but seems plunged in perpetual conflict and divisive chatter, Edwards commends the theocentric and joy-centric life. In truth, the two are one, and this discovery will transform the one who makes it.

This is the heartbeat one hears throughout the pages that follow. We show the God-centered life Edwards led, we trace his aesthetic impulse and love for divine beauty and its echoes throughout creation, we argue that he understood the truly good life, we highlight his major pastoral battle and zeal for true Christianity, and we unveil his vivid understanding of the afterlife. We chose these subjects because they are major aspects of his theology and spirituality that every Christian will profit from studying, and because they together build out a full-bore conception of a great and mighty God who delights in forming a people zealous for Himself. We could surely cover other concepts (and do in our other writings), but these rise to the fore—and share a certain harmony—as invaluable for the faithful Christian seeking to gain a bigger, better understanding of their Creator, Lord, and Savior. The same God who exists to make His beautiful glory known is the God who draws us into a life of theocentric pleasure, makes us a true believer, and fits us for eternity, where we fulfill our original doxological mission in full and without interruption. As we can see—and will see in pages ahead—Jonathan Edwards had a unified, God-centric understanding of all things; we want the same for our brothers and sisters.

A quick comment on a final aspect of Edwards that is uniquely helpful for our time. We initially approached Edwards when emerging technologies were just entering the mainstream; Twitter was what a bird did when happy, Facebook was still populated by collegians, and the word *Instagram* made one think of a quickly consumed Pop Tart, perhaps. Blogs that featured content three days a week seemed cutting edge back then. Now, ten years later, we are awash in "digital connection." In our hyperconnected age, it is perhaps easier than ever to lose oneself in small, shallow pursuits. Today as ever, we need *divine connection*. We need Edwards's fixation on the Lord, and also his habits—his practice, for example, of regularly slipping away into nature, on temporary retreats, to commune with God, meditate deeply, and enjoy quiet and beauty. Solitude of this kind—though in short supply in our hyperconnected, privacy-forfeiting age—may seem rather incidental to a thriving spiritual existence, but Edwards and his close spiritual walk with the Lord would suggest to us that it is not.

In sum, Jonathan Edwards has not gone away. He still speaks, still preaches, still inspires and fires and rouses and awakens and perhaps frustrates the reader like few voices in Christian history —or even in human history. He is a nearly peerless expositor of the biblical text and a theologian of the faith (see Doug's recent *Edwards the Exegete: Biblical Interpretation and Anglo-Protestant Culture on the Edge of the Enlightenment*, published by Oxford, 2016). But we also cannot miss that the Northampton pastor lived a godly, though in many ways normal, Christian life. He did not hover over the ground, but he did persevere through many trials, including some of his own making. Edwards summons us today to do the same, to take God seriously, to direct our affections Christocentrically, and to think and act biblically. All this, he shows, is not drudgery, but delight (see Ps. 16:11). For this reason, among others, we note that Jonathan Edwards is not merely still *here*. He is not only, against all the odds, still read and still appreciated; no, the grand vision of God and His matchless grace that Edwards offered is still *essential*.

OWEN STRACHAN AND DOUGLAS SWEENEY
Winter 2018

We dedicate this book to
David Dockery,
in gratitude for his lifetime of support
of serious Christian scholarship and
pursuit of "true religion" in the world.

Foreword

JONATHAN EDWARDS, GOD-ENTRANCED MAN

When I was in seminary, a wise professor told me that besides the Bible I should choose one great theologian and apply myself throughout life to understanding and mastering his thought. This way I would sink at least one shaft deep into reality, rather than always dabbling on the surface of things. I might come to know at least one system with which to bring other ideas into fruitful dialogue. It was good advice.

The theologian I have devoted myself to is Jonathan Edwards. All I knew of Edwards when I went to seminary was that he preached a sermon called "Sinners in the Hands of an Angry God," in which he said something about hanging over hell by a slender thread. My first real encounter with Edwards was when I read his "Essay on the Trinity" and wrote a paper on it for church history.

It had a lasting effect on me. It gave me a conceptual framework with which to grasp, in part, the meaning of saying God is three in one. In brief, there is God the Father, the fountain of being, who from all eternity has had a perfectly clear and distinct image and idea of Himself; and this image is the eternally begotten Son. Between this Son and Father there flows a stream of infinitely vigorous love and perfectly holy communion; and this is God the Spirit. God's Image of God and God's Love of God are so full of God that they are fully divine Persons, and not less.

After graduation from college, and before my wife and I took off for graduate work in Germany, we spent some restful days on a small farm in Barnesville, Georgia. Here I had another encounter with Edwards. Sitting on one of those old-fashioned two-seater swings in the backyard under a big hickory tree, with pen in hand, I read *The Nature of True Virtue*. I have a long entry in my journal from July 14, 1971, in which I try to understand, with Edwards's help, why a Christian is obligated to forgive wrongs when there seems to be a moral law in our hearts that cries out against evil in the world.

Later, when I was in my doctoral program in Germany, I encountered Edwards's *Dissertation Concerning the End for Which God Created the World*. I read it in a pantry in our little apartment in Munich. The pantry was about 8 by 5 feet, a most unlikely place to read a book like the *Dissertation*. From my perspective now, I would say that if there were one book that captures the essence or wellspring of Edwards's theology, this would be it. Edwards's answer to the question of why God created the world is this: to emanate the fullness of His glory for His people to know, praise, and enjoy. Here is the heart of his theology in his own words:

It appears that all that is ever spoken of in the Scripture as an ultimate end of God's works is included in that one phrase, the glory of God. In the creatures' knowing, esteeming, loving, rejoicing in and praising God, the glory of God is both exhibited and acknowledged; his fullness is received and returned. Here is both the *emanation* and *remanation*. The refulgence shines upon and into the creature, and is reflected back to the luminary. The beams of glory come from God, and are something of God and are refunded back again to their original. So that the whole is *of* God and *in* God, and *to* God, and God is the beginning, middle and end in this affair.

That is the heart and center of Jonathan Edwards and, I believe, of the Bible too. That kind of reading can turn a pantry into a vestibule of heaven.

I am not the only person for whom Edwards continues to be a vestibule of heaven. I hear testimonies regularly that people have stumbled upon this man's work and had their world turned upside down. There are simply not many writers today whose mind and heart are God-entranced the way Edwards was. Again and again, to this very day his writings help me know that experience.

My prayer for *The Essential Edwards Collection* is that it will draw more people into the sway of Edwards's God-entranced worldview. I hope that many who start here, or continue here, will make their way to Edwards himself. Amazingly, almost everything he wrote is available on the Internet. And increasingly his works are available in affordable books. I am thankful that Owen Strachan and Douglas Sweeney share my conviction that every effort to point to Edwards, and through him to his God, is a worthy investment of our lives. May that be the outcome of these volumes.

JOHN PIPER
Founder and Teacher of desiringGod.org
Chancellor of Bethlehem College & Seminary

Part 1

Lover of God

Chapter 1

A HAPPY BEGINNING

The man who would stand tall in history began life in a minister's home in East Windsor, Connecticut, a small town on the east side of the Connecticut River and in the central north of the state. The date was October 5, 1703. Jonathan was the fifth child born to the Reverend Timothy Edwards and Esther Stoddard Edwards. Timothy was a gifted pastor and a good father to his family. He took a special interest in Jonathan, for the two of them formed the entirety of the family's male contingent. Jonathan had no less than ten sisters with whom he got along well. Between the busy life of a New England pastor and the bustle of a crowded home, the family led a full and happy life.

Jonathan's parents were devoted Christians. His father was a well-respected minister and his mother's father, Solomon Stoddard, was a pastor in Northampton, Massachusetts, and one of the eminent figures of the Connecticut River Valley. It is difficult to picture today, but in colonial New England some three centuries ago, pastors were the leaders of society. Unlike the current day, when the pastor enjoys less respect in society than in previous generations, these clergy possessed significant cultural influence, watched over churches that included most members of a given town, and understood the pastorate as a sacred calling.

Though they related to their people in various ways, they

were not primarily administrators, folksy storytellers, or isolated intellectuals. They perceived themselves to be shepherds over God's flock, those who were responsible for the survival and flourishing of God's people. Preaching constituted the means by which such nourishment flowed from God to people, as did careful church oversight involving church discipline and observation of the sacred ordinances (baptism and the Lord's Supper). With such a spiritual diet, the colonists of New England were equipped to live in a hard world of taxing labor, frequent sickness, and early death.

In a society that highly respected preachers and called them to a high standard, Solomon Stoddard was a titan. His congregation was huge, he was a theological authority, and he possessed the bearing of a statesman. To say that Jonathan was born into the line of preachers, then, is no small claim. More accurately, he was born into New England royalty, and he was expected from a young age to pursue the Lord, the ministry, and the application of his considerable gifts in his life's work. He was raised in the church and was trained to view it as the theater of the supernatural, the arena in which God's glory shone through the proclaimed Word and the poured-out Spirit. The pastor was at the center of this divine drama. To the perceptive young mind of Jonathan Edwards, his father possessed the ability as a minister to move his people and draw them close to the Lord through preaching. Visits to Grandfather's church in Northampton would only have magnified such an observation as the little boy observed the gathering of hundreds on a weekly basis for worship under Stoddard's magisterial direction.

YOUNG JONATHAN'S SERIOUSNESS

Between the boy's natural gifts and his impressive lineage, it seemed clear to many that young Jonathan had a date with a pastoral destiny in the near future. In time, and with much training, he would meet his destiny and take the office of colonial pastor to a height unknown by either father or grandfather. He would not do so, however, without considerable preparation for his future ministry. In colonial America, this meant academic study from an early age—six in Jonathan's case. At an age when children today barely know the alphabet, Jonathan began the study of Latin under the tutelage of his father, who supplemented his pastoral income by tutoring boys preparing for college. Jonathan mastered Latin and progressed to Greek and Hebrew by age twelve. His intellectual ability was matched by his irrepressible spiritual fire. He later reflected that in this period:

> I, with some of my schoolmates joined together, and built a booth in a swamp, in a very secret and retired place, for a place of prayer. And besides, I had particular secret places of my own in the woods, where I used to retire by myself; and used to be from time to time much affected. (*Works* 16, 791)

Though Jonathan had not at this time cried out for salvation, he was clearly engaged in religious activity—activity prompted, no doubt, by the example of his godly parents. At this point in his life, however, Christianity was more an exercise to be performed than a faith to be experienced. Though he did speak of emotional stirrings when spiritually engaged, it seems that a true work of grace had not yet inhabited his heart and saved his soul. The young Edwards was quite serious about Christianity but had not yet tasted the miracle of conversion.

Jonathan's seriousness extended into areas that were ignored by others of his age. Well before he wrote his famous sermon "Sinners in the Hands of an Angry God," he showed an early sensitivity to the reality of death. In a cheerful letter to his sister Mary, written in 1716 when just twelve, Jonathan reported:

> There has five persons died in this place since you have been
> gone . . . Goodwife Rockwell, old Goodwife Grant, and Benjamin
> Bancroft, who was drowned in a boat many rods from shore,
> wherein were four young women and many others of the other sex,
> which were very remarkably saved, and the two others which died
> I suppose you have heard of. (*Works* 16, 29)

Residents of colonial New England were more accustomed to the frequency of death than we are today. Yet we glimpse a particular awareness of the realm beyond this one in Jonathan's letter. His tone is not dark or foreboding, but he clearly understands the nearness of death. Raised by his father and mother to acknowledge and confront difficult realities, Jonathan was able from a young age to look deeper and clearer into his world than peers who sought simply to pass the time.

THE SCHOLARLY LIFE BEGINS

When the time came to attend university, the natural choice was the Connecticut Collegiate School, known to us today as Yale University, located in New Haven, some fifty-four miles from East Windsor. In 1716, when Jonathan entered a branch of the school in Wethersfield, his class consisted of twelve other young men. The teacher was his cousin, Elisha Williams. The course consisted mainly of reading, memorization, written work, and recitations. The emphasis in the 1700s was more on rote learning and recital than on discussion and lecture. The course of study could be grueling, and students spent many hours in small rooms and hard chairs memorizing their texts.

Jonathan's capacity for logical thought, clear writing, and sharp analysis of an argument developed during this time. In Wethersfield and later New Haven, the young Edwards also indulged his great appetite for theology during his years at Yale, reading classics such as the Puritan William Ames's *The Marrow of Theology*, and other texts that shaped his thinking.

Jonathan's four years at Yale were full of hard work and contemplative intellectual formation. Reading, reflection, and writing would be integral to his life for the remainder of his days. Though a young man with few responsibilities, he devoted himself to the cultivation of his mind. "I am sensible of the preciousness of my time," he wrote his father in 1719, "and am resolved it shall not be through any neglect of mine, if it slips through without the greatest advantage" (*Works* 16, 32). His devotion paid off in September 1720, at the end of his bachelor's degree, when Jonathan graduated as the valedictorian of his class. He delivered a valedictory address in Latin and prepared himself for the next phase of his education, a master's degree, then the highest academic degree attainable.

Jonathan was now a man. In his young life, he had accomplished much and impressed many. He had charted an excellent course for himself and had honored his parents and tutors. Yet he had not tasted the beauty of living for God in repentant, joyful trust. His life was full and good, his mind was sharp, but the dawn was yet to break. In coming days, a strange and wonderful light would shine in Jonathan's heart, transforming a young, scholarly, religious student into a God-intoxicated man.

Following Edwards

A Well-Led Home

Jonathan Edwards's full and happy life did not come out of a vacuum. He grew up in a home that cultivated faith, just as a gardener cultivates healthy plants. He was raised in a home that was devoted to the Lord through the leadership of his father and mother. With the help of his wife, Jonathan's father trained his children to embrace the realities of life in a fallen world and to prepare their souls for the world beyond. When the husband exercises spiritual leadership in this way, and works together with his wife to raise his children in Christian faith, his children will learn to confront hard truths, to take spiritual things seriously, and to pursue the Lord with passion. Though this spiritual preparation might seem unimportant compared to other things, it is in fact the greatest gift that parents can provide their children.

The Importance of Worship to the Family

The Edwards family made worship a fundamental priority. Though not all fathers are pastors like Timothy, all dads can lead their families in worship. Parents can set a pattern for their children in which worship is not an obligation or a chore, but an exciting, life-transforming privilege. The church of God would greatly benefit today from parents that celebrate worship and church involvement like Timothy and Esther Edwards did.

Prioritizing Education

Like the Edwardses, our parenting should also give priority to the educational formation of our children. This will involve emphasizing the importance of a Christian worldview that prizes the life of the mind and that embraces diligent study of numerous fields. No matter what our children go on to do in life, they can honor the Lord by approaching learning with discipline and passion. Enthusiastic parental support for education from an early age will set them on a course to do so.

Chapter 2

THE JOYS OF NEW BIRTH

After earning his bachelor's degree, seventeen-year-old Jonathan Edwards plunged into his master's degree. Though he wanted to go into the ministry, he was too young to be a pastor and he thought it wise to further cultivate his mind. Edwards's continued preparation equipped him to be a pastor who could handle the difficult intellectual challenges of his day. This approach was common in the 1700s, as future pastors sought rigorous preparation for the demands of pastoral ministry. If they were to be leaders of church and society, authorities in a wide variety of fields, able teachers of the Word, they needed excellent academic preparation. The pastor-theologians, as they are called, sensed the high calling of the pastorate and shaped themselves accordingly. Thus for Jonathan, the master's degree was an essential step in preparing for God's work.

"WRAPT UP TO GOD IN HEAVEN": CONVERSION

In his master's work, Jonathan found that he had more time to mull over the Bible he was studying. Always a contemplative person, he enjoyed meditating on Scripture. One day in the spring of 1721, Edwards pondered 1 Timothy 1:17 (KJV): "Now unto the King eternal, immortal, invisible, the only wise God, be honour and glory for ever and ever. Amen." In the course of this spiritual exercise, one of thousands experienced in his life to this point, something happened. While silently walking along, a thunderclap struck in Jonathan's heart. He later said of that instance:

> As I read the words, there came into my soul, and as it were diffused through it, a sense of the glory of the divine being; a new sense, quite different from anything I ever experienced before. Never any words of Scripture seemed to me as these words did. I thought with myself, how excellent a Being that was; and how happy I should be, if I might enjoy that God, and be wrapt up to God in heaven, and be as it were swallowed up in him. (*Works* 16, 792–3)

This sensation of being "swallowed up" in God erupted into a fresh love for Jesus Christ:

> From about that time, I began to have a new kind of apprehension and ideas of Christ, and the work of redemption, and the glorious way of salvation by him. I had an inward, sweet sense of these things, that at times came into my heart; and my soul was led away in pleasant views and contemplations of them. And my mind was greatly engaged, to spend my time in reading and meditating on Christ; and the beauty and excellency of his person, and the lovely way of salvation, by free grace in him. (*Works*, 16, 793)

Though he never formally said it, this was Jonathan's conversion experience. He had grown up with Scripture and had been study-ing it academically for years. He knew it very well and attempted to obey its moral and spiritual guidelines. As important as knowl-edge and obedience are, neither can save the soul and transform the heart. One must acquire what Jonathan later called the "true sense" of God for conversion to take place:

> A true sense of the divine and superlative excellency of the things of religion; a real sense of the excellency of God and Jesus Christ, and of the work of redemption, and the ways and works of God revealed in the gospel. There is a divine and superlative glory in these things; an excellency that is of a vastly higher kind, and more sublime nature than in other things; a glory greatly distinguishing them from all that is earthly and temporal. He that is spiritually enlightened truly apprehends and sees it, or has a sense of it. He does not merely rationally believe that God is glorious, but he has a sense of the gloriousness of God in his heart. There is not only a rational belief that God is holy, and that holiness is a good thing, but there is a sense of the loveliness of God's holiness. There is not only a speculatively judging that God is gracious, but a sense how amiable God is upon that account, or a sense of the beauty of this divine attribute. (*Works* 17, 413)

Jonathan attained this "true sense" while he walked the campus of Yale, pondering the first chapter of 1 Timothy. He suddenly realized in a personal way the majesty, excellency, and greatness of Jesus Christ. He became for Edwards the fountain of beauty and the purpose of life. Once ten thousand miles away, now He was near.

Jonathan would never again study God abstractly. From this moment on, he would enjoy Him. He would seek to know the Lord, a journey that involved the full capacity of his mind, emotions, and soul. Jonathan's life would not be easy from this point forward, and he sometimes doubted his salvation, but his commitment would never fade.

THE SWEETNESS OF MEDITATION
AND THE REALITY OF HEAVEN

A year passed in Jonathan's life, one filled with academic work and tutoring of undergraduate students at Yale. In the summer of 1722, though immersed in his studies, Jonathan was called by an English Presbyterian congregation in New York City—a city then housing about ten thousand residents, many of whom engaged in the booming sea trade. He agreed to serve as pastor of the little church, which had divided over its previous pastor. In the course of Edwards's year in New York, the congregation healed its wounds and called the former minister, James Anderson, back to the pulpit.

Though his stay in the city was brief, Jonathan's passion for the Lord only intensified while in New York. He thought much about heaven and later reflected on his contemplation: "The heaven I desired was a heaven of holiness; to be with God, and to spend my eternity in divine love, and holy communion with Christ. My mind was very much taken up with contemplations on heaven, and the enjoyments of those there; and living there in perfect holiness, humility and love." Jonathan's delight in heaven sometimes overwhelmed him as:

> The inward ardor of my soul, seemed to be hindered and pent up, and could not freely flame out as it would. I used often to think, how in heaven, this sweet principle should freely and fully vent and express itself. Heaven appeared to me exceeding delightful as a world of love. It appeared to me, that all happiness consisted in living in pure, humble, heavenly, divine love. (*Works* 16, 795–6)

For many Christians, heaven is a matter-of-fact reality, the logical end to the Christian life. Jonathan, however, sought to look deeply into the life to come. He knew from Scripture that heaven was a place of perfect holiness, a "world of love." Jonathan knew that while unceasing holiness and happiness prove evasive on this earth, heaven promised the believer absolute purity and joy. If young Jonathan had a faraway look on his daily walks by the Hudson River, it was because he was thinking of another place.

Jonathan knew that heaven was not a fairy tale mystery. For Jonathan, the unseen mysteries of the faith, including heaven, were no less real than earthly life. Earthly life was merely a shadow of that to come. In his quest to live well for the Lord, the young Christian focused on the realm where He resided.

HOLY LIVING AND THE RESOLUTIONS OF ACTION

As he pondered weighty matters like heaven, Jonathan kept a record of his thoughts. Over the course of his life, he compiled over fourteen hundred reflections on doctrine, philosophy, Scripture, and other intellectual interests. Called the "Miscellanies," these reflections feature the young thinker's perspectives on the apocalypse, the workings of the mind, science, and scriptural passages, among many other subjects. Jonathan also kept a diary at times, recording the activities and key events of his daily life. He loved to study and to think about his life and world. But he was not lost in the clouds. Jonathan excelled at putting his contemplative faith to practice. His deep thinking did not weaken his decision-making and his capacity to act. No, it fueled it.

At the same time that Jonathan was meditating on heaven, he assembled for himself a list of spiritual "resolutions" by which to live. His resolutions, seventy in number and compiled over several months, laid out definitive ways in which Jonathan could put his passion and theology into practice. The young man who sought to meditate deeply tried with similar zeal to live "holily," as he put it.

The first resolution centered on the glory of God and the duty to reflect it:

Resolved, that I will do whatsoever I think to be most to God's glory, and my own good, profit and pleasure, in the whole of my duration, without any consideration of the time, whether new, or never so many myriads of ages hence. Resolved to do whatever I think to be my duty, and most for the good and advantage of mankind in general. (*Works* 15, 795)

Living for God in pursuit of beauty and joy did not mean a leisurely, airy existence. It meant action that resulted in "God's glory" and Jonathan's "own good." Though he certainly practiced his faith in a fallen way, as all Christians do, Jonathan sought to use all his ability to give God all the glory. This meant a fusion of faith, thought, and action all directed to a doxological end.

Jonathan's aims were not rooted in pride, but they were certainly broad. As a young man, he charted a plan for his life. His sixth resolution vowed that he would live with vigor: "Resolved, to live with all my might, while I do live." History often pictures Edwards as a dry scholar. But he was not a weak or wimpy man. He possessed purpose and energy. He lived a spiritually ambitious life marked by purposeful, focused labor. His resolutions, made when he was very young but remembered throughout his life, fueled all of this activity.

The disciplined Christian life was for Jonathan saturated by the gospel. Resolution eighteen made this clear: "Resolved, to live so at all times, as I think is best in my devout frames, and when I have clearest notions of things of the gospel, and another world." If his intellect, status, or spiritual achievements loomed large in his mind, Jonathan knew that his focus would shift. He would live to be admired or to become famous or to be envied. Such ungodly ambitions would drive his decisions and lead him away from the Savior. If he lived with the gospel in view, though, he would remember his depravity and the grace of God. He would center all of his life and activity on honoring his Savior and on living a life reflective of the gospel. Instead of drifting away from the truth, he would stay the course.

Early in his life, Jonathan sought to twist his whole being into a tool in the hands of God. He wanted to constantly grow as a Christian. Resolution thirty captured this desire: "Resolved, to strive to my utmost every week to be brought higher in religion, and to a higher exercise of grace, than I was the week before" (*Works* 16, 755). Jonathan knew that if he did not pursue the Lord, he would not grow as a believer. Though he set a rigorous pace, he positioned himself to experience the full blessings of life as a Christian. He desired a life that constantly bore spiritual fruit, just as a tree bears physical fruit in seasons of health. Jonathan knew that the Lord would use such a life in this world for significant ends.

In mapping out his resolutions, Jonathan realized before turning twenty what it takes many people a lifetime to discover: living for God matters more than anything else. In order to accomplish this aim, Jonathan mapped out a plan for his life that would shape his brief time on earth. Because he lived in this way, his life drew the favor of God. In time, it lit up colonial New England like a comet in the night.

Following Edwards

The Power of Meditating on Heaven and God's Truth

Jonathan often meditated on the reality of heaven. Though the scriptural doctrine of heaven is shrouded in layers of mystery, and we possess little material by which to figure out what life in the new heavens and earth will look like, Jonathan serves as a model for us in his attempt to set his thoughts on his eternal home. Just as Jonathan stoked the passions of his heart by meditating on heaven, so too can Christians today reflect on the wonderful truths of the Christian faith. We may not express ourselves as Jonathan did, and we may not experience the level of emotion that he did, but we all can lift ourselves up out of the doldrums of daily existence by peeking into the realities of the gospel.

As we drive to our job, or work around the home, or go to school, we can memorize a biblical verse and meditate on it. As we turn over scriptural truths in our minds, we will see them in a fresh light. The Bible will come to life when we view it as a life-transforming gift from a loving Creator (Ps. 119). The person and work of Jesus Christ will shine with glory when we contemplate the hugeness of our sin problem (Rom. 3). Heaven won't be so mysterious, for example, if we think about how God will rule us in perfect love there (Rev. 21–22). If we would take snatches of our day and devote them to reflection as Jonathan did, we would find a deeper and more satisfying walk with Christ that would redeem not only our time, but also our hearts and minds.

Meditation Followed by Action

One might be worried that if one goes through with all of this meditating, we'll lose our place in the real world—maybe it sounds like we're suggesting that Christians should walk through life on an airy cloud. While that does sound comfortable, we really want to know the quiet satisfaction of thinking on God. But we also hope to encourage a life of practical action. The first, in fact, fuels the second. The more we think about the deep things of the faith, the more we'll love God, and the greater our desire for holiness and spiritual action will be. Just like Jonathan, who drew up his steps for holiness and action in his "Resolutions," we too can set some spiritual goals for ourselves. We don't need to be legalistic about these goals, and we don't even have to write them down. But we could sketch out some scriptural attitudes and actions that we need to cultivate—the fruit of the

Spirit, for example (Gal. 5:22–23)—and lay out some guidelines for ourselves by which to develop these attitudes. Doing so is not legalistic; it's wise, and godly, for the authors of Scripture constantly did this in their letters and writings to the people of God. It will help us to remember the sort of life that we seek as a Christian and will turn us away from sin in moments when we feel like we have lost our way.

Chapter 3

THE TRIALS OF A YOUNG MAN

Jonathan had pursued high-level academic work for some time before his graduation from his master's program at Yale in September 1723. It was common for students who had attained this honor to deliver a shortened version of their major paper to the campus community at commencement. Jonathan had worked on the matter of individual salvation, specifically on the way that God justifies sinners through faith in His Son. Some in Jonathan's day had questioned the necessity of this central tenet of the Reformation and many disagreed with the young scholar's position. Reading his thesis in Latin, per the academic custom of the day, Jonathan boldly asserted that justification by faith meant that

> God receives the sinner into his grace and friendship for this reason alone, that his entire soul receives Christ in such a way that righteousness and eternal life are offered in an absolutely gratuitous fashion and are provided only because of his reception of Christ. . . . We maintain that Christ is the complete Savior and not merely the partial author of our eternal salvation. Because of these considerations we deny that a sinner is his own redeemer and mediator. (*Works* 14, 61)

Jonathan's master's work placed him squarely in the camp of orthodox Protestantism. Some in his day challenged the idea that a sinner had to be saved solely by divine grace, asserting that people, in effect, completed their salvation by good works. Christ had partially achieved redemption through His death, but needed the obedience of His followers to see them through to the other side. Jonathan, however, argued with force that "Christ is the complete Savior," having offered His perfection to mankind "in an absolutely gratuitous fashion." Jonathan's study of the Bible had convinced him that God had to be the initiator and agent of salvation because mankind was so lost as to be helpless before God. The greatness of God's power made possible the extent of God's love.

Though he possessed the ability to think for himself and to probe doctrines that other people accepted but thought little about, Jonathan desired from an early age to hold fast to the tenets of orthodox Christianity. He thought innovatively (as will be seen in later chapters) and never made himself a slave to tradition, but he never challenged tradition for the sake of doing so. Jonathan searched the Scriptures, learned from his teachers, and strove to be faithful. This frequently meant that he upheld and defended historic views of doctrine. While others of similar abilities chased the latest doctrinal trends, Jonathan displayed from an early age a resolute desire to adhere to what the Bible taught. Though some of his Yale peers and tutors challenged the tradition on the matter of salvation, Jonathan courageously defended the orthodox view. The young Christian showed no allegiance to popular opinion. He was a man of his own mind, and his mind was fundamentally calibrated to stay true to the wisdom of the Word.

IN SEARCH OF EMPLOYMENT

Soon after graduating from Yale, Jonathan took a preaching assignment in Bolton, Connecticut, near Hartford. After agreeing to settle in the newly formed town, Jonathan found that the church could not support him, either by salary or with a parsonage in which to make his home. Though his father had arranged the call, it fell through. An offer to serve as senior tutor at Yale came soon after. These were hard times for Jonathan. He was well prepared for the work of pastoring and yearned to do it, yet his desire had been frustrated in Bolton. He thus moved back to New Haven for the work of overseeing Yale's forty students in their studies. To one who had just left the college, this seemed a strange providence. But Jonathan trusted the Lord's will and began his work with zeal.

SICKNESS OF THE BODY BUT NOT THE SOUL

Jonathan was a hard-working tutor. He tried diligently to balance the responsibilities of teaching and administration at the small, understaffed college. In the midst of his heavy load, Jonathan ran into a wall that he frequently hit in his adult life. He overworked himself as a young tutor and fell very sick in September 1725. The young tutor had a great deal of mental energy and wanted to honor his employers, but simply could not because of his sickened body.

Jonathan was not and never would be a physically robust person. He did not pity himself, though. He determined by his strong will to taste the Lord's goodness by applying his mind to study God's character. He later wrote of this period:

> In this sickness, God was pleased to visit me with the sweet
> influences of his spirit. My mind was greatly engaged there on
> divine, pleasant contemplations, and longings of soul. I observed
> that those who watched with me, would often be looking out for
> the morning, and seemed to wish for it. Which brought to my
> mind those words of the Psalmist, which my soul with sweetness

made its own language, "My soul waiteth for the Lord more than they that watch for the morning: I say, more than they that watch for morning" [Ps. 130:6]. And when the light of the morning came, and the beams of the sun came in at the windows, it refreshed my soul from one morning to another. It seemed to me to be some image of the sweet light of God's glory. (*Works* 16, 798–9)

In times of difficulty, Jonathan went back to the Lord. He meditated on Psalm 130 and found refreshment in the Lord and His sovereignty over his life. Jonathan's focus on the Lord and His goodness enabled him to thrive in his season of trial. He waited on the Lord, thinking about Him while huddled in blankets by the fire, seeking to recover his strength. The days stretched into weeks, and the weeks wore on, but Jonathan did not need the absence of hardship to make him happy—only the presence of the Lord.

Though his body struggled for vitality, and his tasks went undone, Jonathan tasted the beauty of living for God by focusing on God and His goodness as revealed by the psalmist. The problem of physical weakness would return throughout his life due to his relentless work ethic and frail constitution. Despite this challenge, Jonathan tried hard in seasons of difficulty to redeem them and to make them seasons of growth.

THE CALL OF A LIFETIME

It took months for Jonathan to recover from his illness. While healing, he received an offer to preach temporarily in Glastonbury, a small town near Hartford. Jonathan preached for several weeks and once again felt a fire in his bones. His tutoring duties picked back up, however, and his labor in New Haven continued into the summer. The young tutor tired of his vocation, though he plugged away at it until another call came. This one would alter his course forever.

In 1726, Solomon Stoddard, Jonathan's grandfather, needed a pastoral assistant. The people of Northampton had long known Stoddard as a "river god," one of the most powerful figures of the Connecticut River Valley. Northampton, though holding only around eleven hundred residents, was a bustling town featuring homes built close to one another in case of attack. Now in his eighties, Stoddard had labored for decades in the town, winning the respect not only of his congregation but his region. His days as a pastor would soon run their course, a fact that caused the town to seek out Jonathan for the training position. The people of Northampton knew Jonathan well. He had won respect and acclaim throughout the colonies for his intellect, his intense devotion to the Lord, and his promise in light of his familial heritage. In November 1726, the congregation voted him in as assistant to Stoddard. The work was challenging, as the church included hundreds of townsfolk, but Jonathan learned quickly, worked hard, and already had several years of preaching behind him. From 1726 to 1728, he preached once on Sunday and taught once on a weekday. In February 1727, the church ordained Jonathan to the ministry. His grandfather led the service. It must have been a poignant scene for both grandfather and grandson. The precocious young boy who grew up in his grandfather's shadow had become a leader of God's people. The stage was set for Jonathan's future assumption of the Northampton pastorate. Still, he lacked one thing.

THE DRAMA OF YOUNG LOVE

Jonathan loved the life of the mind. He could be bookish and isolated, but he had another side, a side that is easy to ignore in studying his career. Though occupying an eminent ministerial position, Jonathan was just twenty-three at this point in his life. He knew the attraction of the fairer sex, and he sought a spouse.

His interest centered on a young New Haven woman named Sarah Pierpont.

A pastor's daughter, Sarah had first caught Jonathan's attention when he worked as a tutor at Yale. Though young by today's standards, Sarah exhibited a faith and dignity that drew Jonathan like a moth to a flame. The pen that produced eloquent theological treatises later in life served a different purpose in this period as Jonathan, passionately in love, penned some of his most famous lines when reflecting on Sarah:

> They say there is a young lady in New Haven who is beloved of that almighty Being, who made and rules the world, and that there are certain seasons in which this great Being, in some way or other invisible, comes to her and fills her mind with exceeding sweet delight, and that she hardly cares for anything, except to meditate on him—that she expects after a while to be received up where he is, to be raised up out of the world and caught up into heaven; being assured that he loves her too well to let her remain at a distance from him always. There she is to dwell with him, and to be ravished with his love and delight forever. Therefore, if you present all the world before her, with the richest of its treasures, she disregards it and cares not for it, and is unmindful of any pain or affliction. She has a strange sweetness in her mind, and singular purity in her affections; is most just and conscientious in all her actions; and you could not persuade her to do anything wrong or sinful, if you would give her all the world, lest she should offend this great Being. She is of a wonderful sweetness, calmness and universal benevolence of mind; especially after those seasons in which this great God has manifested himself to her mind. She will sometimes go about from place to place, singing sweetly; and seems to be always of joy and pleasure; and no one knows for what. She loves to be alone, and to wander in the fields and on the mountains, and seems to have someone invisible always conversing with her. (*Works* 16, 789–90)

Like anyone, Jonathan could appreciate beauty when he saw it, and he thought that this pastor's daughter was lovely. One can easily imagine him drifting into romantic contemplation while preparing a lesson at his desk in New Haven or a sermon in Northampton. Her face would come to mind, and for a moment, the abstractions of philosophy or theology were forgotten, lost in a world where a woman of "wonderful sweetness" walked closely with her "great God." Sarah's beauty had tapped the romantic side of Jonathan, but her character and her faith elicited his highest praise. Sarah did not want to live for this world. In Jonathan's idealistic expression, "you could not persuade her to do anything wrong or sinful." Unlike many girls her age, Sarah was not led by her passions. As Jonathan saw her, she possessed "a singular purity in her affections," a love for God that transcended other concerns. In Sarah, Jonathan had found a person like him, one so wrapped up in God that she could not be described without reference to Him.

Though Jonathan's language displays the drama of young love, it also reveals that the love Jonathan felt for Sarah possessed a strongly theological character. Here was a woman "ravished" with God's "love and delight" who loved "to wander in the fields and on the mountains," talking with God. The poetry of the passage provides a way to understand how Jonathan and Sarah found one another. Both of these young Christians walked in their own world, devoting themselves to the Lord. When they met and fell for one another, it was as if they met in distant fields that no one else could see. They soon discovered that the path they walked was the same.

MARRIED LIFE BEGINS

On July 28, 1727, the spiritual companionship between Jonathan and Sarah took shape in a marriage ceremony in New

Haven. After the celebration, the couple traveled to Northampton, where they settled in a parsonage in the heart of the little town. Jonathan led a busy life, often spending over twelve hours of the day in his study, and Sarah busied herself with a wide variety of economic and domestic responsibilities. By all accounts, the couple enjoyed much happiness and closeness. For his part, Jonathan was established in his pastoral work and the head of a happy home. His grooming for this ministry was complete. As his grandfather ailed, Jonathan grew stronger. He burned to preach the Word of God to the people of God. The call to the pulpit approached. His life's consuming work would soon begin.

Following Edwards

The Duty of Courage

Jonathan's courageous defense of justification by faith alone challenges Christians of the current day to contend for biblical truth. In the case of his Yale address, Jonathan actually opposed fellow Christians. Chapter 5 will show how Jonathan pursued correct doctrine for the health of his flock and the evangelization of the lost. In this chapter, though, we see that Jonathan publicly opposed false doctrine that Christians might not fall into error. His master's address, then, was not a sermon for his people, but a tract for doctrinal faithfulness. It defined the boundaries of Christian orthodoxy for the colonial churches. Jonathan set an example for believers of his day and of those to come in defending the faith. Where cardinal doctrines of the faith suffer attack, and Christians begin to lose sight of their doctrinal foundation, believers must respond. As Paul instructed in his letter to Timothy, his young apprentice: "By the Holy Spirit who dwells within us, guard the good deposit entrusted to you" (2 Tim. 1:14). In the current day, Christians must "guard" the "deposit" of biblical faith just as Timothy did centuries ago.

The Passion of the Redeemed Heart

Historians and college students often conceive of Jonathan Edwards as a dour, grim-faced theologian who cared for little except thunderous preaching that left people quaking in their boots. In reality, Jonathan was a passionate, tender man who in early manhood yearned with all his being for a wife. When beautiful Sarah first caught his eye, Jonathan fell under a spell. In his deep mind, theology had to share space with romance. His experience corrects our understanding of him and encourages us to seize the good things of life and enjoy them. Contrary to what we might think, Jonathan lived a deeply vigorous and emotional existence in which he embraced the powerful feelings and joys of life. He sought them out, and when they came, he did not shy away from them but breathed them in like air from the ocean. In our day, we should do the same. We should not simply *know* the faith and its inherent goodness, but *taste* it. We should not shy away from emotion, passion, or joy, but should celebrate these things as gifts from God that keep us from being automatons.

This applies to romance as much as anything else. In a world gone mad with lust and the desire for transcendent experience, Christians should be clear that we do not advocate an ascetic, joyless existence, but that we in fact have found the most pleasurable pursuit of them all. Becoming a Christian does not kill delight; it intensifies it. As some have said, we should out-live the world, displaying the transformative reality of the gospel in the way we work, study, eat, and love.

Chapter 4

BEHOLDING THE GOD OF GRACE

In 1727, Northampton and surrounding towns felt the earth move beneath them. An earthquake struck the New England colonies, shocking residents who had heard of such phenomena but rarely experienced them, and sparked some measure of revival in the area. On February 11, 1729, the town felt a different kind of tremor when Solomon Stoddard, the "pope" of the surrounding country, passed away. Two days later, the church memorialized Stoddard in a burial service. Leaving little place for sentimentality, Jonathan preached a sermon in Stoddard's honor entitled "Living Unconverted under an Eminent Means of Grace." He exhorted his hearers to repent of their sins, no matter how long they had been a member of the Northampton church. In this initial move, Jonathan took the helm of the congregation with a firm grip, setting the tone for his ministry that characterized it until its end.

STRENUOUS LABOR, HUMBLING RESULTS

Jonathan worked incredibly hard as a young head pastor, leading him to collapse in a matter of months. Throughout the spring of 1729, Jonathan stayed at home. He had again driven himself with such passion that he damaged his health. If the young pastor's sense of urgency allowed him to accomplish much, it also drove him into the ground at times and hindered his ministry. If this would seem like the error of a young man, Jonathan repeated this mistake throughout his life. In the midst of this self-inflicted trial, Jonathan celebrated his second anniversary and the first birthday of his child, Sarah. She was the first, but not the last. Ten more would eventually join the family.

EXALTING DIVINE GRACE

Between 1730 and 1734, the year a great revival broke out in Northampton, the Edwards family enjoyed several relatively quiet years. Jonathan devoted himself to the craft of sermonizing, the care of his congregation, and the cultivation of his young and thriving family. The intensity that occasionally drove Jonathan to exhaustion aided in the production of masterful sermons whose fame soon spread throughout the colonies. Spending thirteen hours daily in the study gave the preacher a substantial block of time with which to work. Because Jonathan concentrated by the minute, and did not whittle his time away in idle pursuits, he was able to compose sermons of great insight and spiritual benefit. In one of his most famous sermons from this period, "God Glorified in Man's Dependence," preached in July 1731, Edwards outlined the dimensions of divine grace:

> The redeemed have all from the grace of God. It was of mere
> grace that God gave us his only begotten Son. The grace is great in
> proportion to the excellency of what is given. The gift was infinitely
> precious, because it was of a person infinitely worthy, a person of
> infinite glory; and also because it was of a person infinitely near
> and dear to God. The grace is great in proportion to the benefit we
> have given us in him: the benefit is doubly infinite in that in him

we have deliverance from an infinite, because an eternal, misery, and do also receive eternal joy and glory. The grace in bestowing this gift is great in proportion to our unworthiness to whom it is given; instead of deserving such a gift, we merited infinitely ill of God's hands. The grace is great according to the manner of giving, or in proportion to the humiliation and expense of the method and means by which a way is made for our having the gift. He gave him to dwell amongst us; he gave him to us incarnate, or in our nature; and in the like through sinless infirmities. He gave him to us in a low and afflicted state; and not only so, but as slain, that he might be a feast for our souls. (*Works* 17, 203)

One finds in these poetic words a passion to communicate the greatness of God's grace. Jonathan used the repetition of words—"infinitely" and "infinite" occur six times in close proximity—to drive home a particular concept in his hearer's minds. Here, he sought to stretch his congregation's understanding of grace. As the fiery preacher saw it, many in his day made too little of grace. In focusing heavily on what a person's will could accomplish, one ended up cheapening the power of divine grace. As Jonathan conceived of grace given by God, however, it was, like its source—awesome. Where some might have pictured it as a sweet and gentle stream from which to drink as one saw fit, Jonathan saw God's grace as a tide of goodness that overwhelmed the sinner. God, if He were truly divine, could not be small; grace, if it were truly grace, could not be weak.

GOD AS THE END OF ALL THINGS

God was the source of grace. In Jonathan's mind, though, He was not a means to an end. He *was* the end. In conversion, one did not profess faith in God and then move on. As Jonathan understood Him, God was a sovereign, a mighty ruler, a figure too glorious to take in, even with eyes of faith. Those who met God in salvation, then, did not move on to better things after their conversion. In their new birth, they had found the Lord of the universe and the goodness they had always sought, as shown in another elegant section of "God Glorified":

> God himself is the great good which they are brought to the possession and enjoyment of by redemption. He is the highest good, and the sum of all that good which Christ purchased. God is the inheritance of the saints; he is the portion of their souls. God is their wealth and treasure, their food, their life, their dwelling-place, their ornament and diadem, and their everlasting honour and glory. They have none in heaven but God; he is the great good which the redeemed are received to at death, and which they are to rise to at the end of the world. The Lord God is the light of the heavenly Jerusalem; and is the "river of the water of life" that runs, and "the tree of life that grows, in the midst of the paradise of God." The glorious excellencies and beauty of God will be what will forever entertain the minds of the saints, and the love of God will be their everlasting feast. The redeemed will indeed enjoy other things; they will enjoy the angels, and will enjoy one another; but that which they shall enjoy in the angels, or each other, or in any thing else whatsoever that will yield them delight and happiness, will be what shall be seen of God in them. (*Works* 17, 208)

The force of Jonathan's speech, with God functioning as the subject of successive sentences, drew the attention of his hearers to the awesomeness of God. Seen through eyes of faith, the Lord is great, and high, and holy. His people feed on His greatness and bask in His transcendence even as they draw comfort from His immanent presence. For Edwards, life is not about one's selfish interests and heaven is not about one's prefabricated paradise.

Earthly life and heavenly life alike revolve around the greatness of God.

THE WORD OF LIGHT AND TRUTH

Jonathan discovered the glory of God in a personal way through the study of His Word. In his famous sermon "A Divine and Supernatural Light," preached in August 1733, Edwards detailed how a person came to understand the beauty of the Bible. When one reads the Scripture with faith,

> A true sense of the divine excellency of the things of God's word doth more directly and immediately convince of the truth of them; and that because the excellency of these things is so superlative. There is a beauty in them that is so divine and godlike, that is greatly and evidently distinguishing of them from things merely human, or that men are the inventors and authors of; a glory that is so high and great, that when clearly seen, commands assent to their divinity and reality. When there is an actual and lively discovery of this beauty and excellency, it will not allow of any such thought as that it is a human work, or the fruit of men's invention. This evidence that they that are spiritually enlightened have of the truth of the things of religion, is a kind of intuitive and immediate evidence. They believe the doctrines of God's word to be divine, because they see divinity in them; i.e., they see a divine, and transcendent, and most evidently distinguishing glory in them; such a glory as, if clearly seen, does not leave room to doubt of their being of God, and not of men. (*Works* 16, 415)

The Bible served as the means by which one could unearth the "beauty and excellency" of the Lord. In reading the teachings and stories of Scripture, one found a "divine and godlike" quality that distanced the sacred text from all other books. The contents of

Scripture contained a "distinguishing glory" that marked it as the very Word of God to mankind. Edwards did not see the Bible as a static collection of timeless truths and moral maxims. He viewed the Scripture as a living thing. It pulsed with life; it shone with beauty; it bore the glory of God.

This last facet of Edwards's understanding of Scripture relates directly to the way he lived. Jonathan did not practice a weak faith filled with doubt and worry about the irrationality of belief and the mystery of God. As Jonathan saw it, faith was reasonable—that is, it made sense—and doubt was irrational. The Bible accounted for this confidence. The Spirit had spoken through the Word to Jonathan's heart, performing a surgery of the soul and mind such that Jonathan's synapses fired from a position of faith. As he put it in "A Divine and Supernatural Light," the divine nature of the Word "does not leave room" for doubt. If studied with trust, it reorients a person's world such that one sees that God is fundamentally true and right. As a result, believers can live and speak with great boldness.

"A Divine and Supernatural Light" shows us that Jonathan operated from a position of experiential trust in the Lord. Jonathan had not tamed the Word of God such that he could extract from it what he liked and believe what he preferred. The beauty of God's living Word had captured Jonathan. His convinced mind and captivated heart formed the foundation from which all his exhortation and teaching sprang. The majesty and beauty of God, communicated in His Word, beckoned to all, offering every person the opportunity to experience the transforming power of trust.

MEDITATION AND THE FRUSTRATING STRUGGLE TO MORTIFY SIN

Edwards thought it important to meditate on these truths. He often enjoyed riding and walking in nature, where he would think, pray, and relish the natural beauty of unspoiled New England. One can conjecture that these excursions provided a good deal of the contemplation that fueled the pastor's expansive preaching and teaching. Time in nature meant rest, relaxation, and refreshment. Without such times, it is doubtful that Edwards would have accomplished all that he did or communed as deeply with the Lord as his brief retreats made possible.

Edwards's efforts bore tremendous fruit. The young pastor knew his share of dark days, however. No person can evade faithless thoughts and sinful appetites, no matter how strong their faith may be. Years after Jonathan penned his monumental sermons, he reflected on this period in his life, noting that amidst the highs of spiritual growth, it contained no small amount of struggle with sin:

> Often, since I lived in this town, I have had very affecting views of my own sinfulness and vileness; very frequently to such a degree as to hold me in a kind of loud weeping, sometimes for a considerable time together; so that I have often been forced to shut myself up. I have had a vastly greater sense of my own wickedness, and the badness of my heart, than ever I had before my conversion. It has often appeared to me, that if God should mark iniquity against me, I should appear the very worst of all mankind; of all that have been since the beginning of the world to this time; and that I should have by far the lowest place in the world to this time; and that I should have by far the lowest place in hell. When others, that have come to talk with me about their soul concerns, have expressed the sense they have had of their own wickedness by saying, that it seemed to them, that they were as bad as the devil himself; I thought their expressions seemed exceeding faint and feeble, to represent my wickedness. (*Works* 16, 801–2)

Students of Edwards need to mark these words. We should not view him as a super-Christian. The Northampton pastor modeled a faithful Christian life of great depth and joy, but he was a man, and a sinner, just like the rest of the race. This passage captures this reality. Though Edwards does not spell out specific sins in which he indulged, he makes clear that he fought a great fight against his own indwelling sin, a fight that he sometimes lost.

Whether faced with pride, arrogance, jealousy, self-sufficiency, or other personal weaknesses, Edwards recognized that the stuff of "vileness" moved in his bones. He preached great sermons and ministered powerfully to his family, church, and society. But he also hurt his wife, wronged his children, and spoke bitterly against his church. He sinned, just as every Christian does. He tried to work hard without complaining, but he surely did complain. He yearned to stop pride in its tracks, but he sometimes could not. His days as a pastor in Northampton brought great blessing and encouragement, but they also brought struggle, pain, and the profoundly humbling realization that "if God should mark iniquity" on his account, he would not stand, but would fall into an eternity of darkness and destruction from which no person could emerge. As a young pastor, the beauty of living for God mingled with the pain of living in sin. This pain did not overwhelm him, but neither did it leave his side. Jonathan's life was like that of every Christian. It was a struggle, a fight for faith, that did not rest until his death.

FAMILY LEADERSHIP

In a difficult period, the natural rhythms of life and family brought Jonathan refuge from despair, as they so often do. From the time they arrived in Northampton, the Edwardses watched as their family steadily grew. Sarah came along in 1728, Jerusha in 1730, and Esther in 1732. In coming years, Mrs. Edwards gave birth to eight more children—Mary (1734), Lucy (1736), Timothy (1738), Susannah (1740), Eunice (1743), Jonathan Jr. (1745),

Elizabeth (1747), and Pierrepont (1750). In the midst of a packed calendar, the Edwardses produced nothing less than a tribe. Though families in this era often grew quite large, the Edwards home seems as filled with happiness as it was with children. Jonathan and Sarah each exuded dignity and authority, but they also easily won the affection and loyalty of their children.

As his father had done, Jonathan provided tender spiritual leadership for his children. On the weekends, Edwards catechized his charges, and led them in a special time of singing and prayer on Saturday night in preparation for the spiritual feast of the next day. On weekday mornings, Jonathan read a chapter in the Bible and then commented briefly on the text, according to his protégé Samuel Hopkins. Once the day began, Edwards took up his pen and dove into the life of the mind, writing sermons and treatises and reading books. He frequently interrupted his work, though, for interaction with his children, "to treat with them in his Study, singly and particularly about their . . . Soul's Concerns," always being "careful and thorough in the Government of his Children." In response, his children "reverenced, esteemed and loved him" (Sweeney, *Jonathan Edwards and the Ministry of the Word*, Chapter 2, 10). Edwards was not a perfect father, but the record of his family life shows that he did not selfishly shut himself off from his loved ones. As important as his work was to him, it seems that his children took first priority. Their later flowering testifies to this. The girls married well and had numerous children who became Christian leaders and important social figures. The boys distinguished themselves as pillars of their communities and the broader New England region. The lives of successive generations suggest that the Lord blessed the Edwards home for its fidelity to Him.

Following Edwards

Prioritizing Rest and Balance

In a hard-driving world, Christians should mark the way that Jonathan worked himself to debilitation time and again during his career. Some of us, of course, have the opposite tendency, but others struggle just as Jonathan did to approach their work and responsibilities in a balanced way. When one becomes too driven in the area of primary duty, all other areas of life will suffer: family, friends, church involvement, evangelism, and more. It is wise to rest and to pace oneself. Furthermore, it is humble to do so. Though it may not seem to be motivated by pride, overworking sometimes reveals a desire to control the world such that one cannot be happy unless all is in immediate order. Though it seems strange in a very busy age, resting can often glorify the Lord since it expresses humility and a recognition of God's sovereignty. If we would seek to emulate Edwards in his work ethic, we also should seek a more balanced life than he achieved, for the good of ourselves and our families and, ultimately, for the glory of God.

The Duty to Fight Doubt

A proper understanding of God, one based in the Bible, will equip the Christian to fight doubt. Satan is an active agent in our lives, and he will attempt to lead us to doubt God frequently over the course of our existence as Christians. How essential, then, that like Jonathan we drink deeply from the Word for the purpose of strengthening our faith. The more we hesitate to spend time in Scripture, the more we will struggle to find assurance in moments of doubt. The more we meditate on Scripture, though, the more we will lay hold of firm confidence and dispel doubts when the enemy sends them. Pastor Tim Keller's *The Reason for God* and other apologetics books will buttress our study of the Bible by pointing out reasonable answers to questions about the Christian faith.

With such resources, we can ward off doubt and despair and conform our mind to the Scripture so that it will grow strong and sure (as Romans 12 assures us will happen). This is essential, because Satan will tempt us not only to doubt God intellectually, but also to doubt the progress and existence of our faith. At times, we will feel like Edwards, and wonder if we truly have any faith at all. We will taste the bitterness of sin after we speak unkindly to our spouse, or fail to care for a dear friend, or compromise our ethics at school or work, or gossip about peers, or revel in pride when in the company of people we dislike. We will justly feel shame after such sins, and we must carefully repent of them, but we must also avoid an ungodly sense of melancholy and despair that robs us of effectiveness in the faith.

We could say it this way: we should learn to doubt our doubts, and be skeptical about skepticism.

Chapter 5

THE EXTRAORDINARY WORK

The early 1730s were a period of calm in the life of the Edwards family. Life was busy, and the family welcomed several children into the world in this period, but Jonathan found large blocks of time to think, write, and care for the needs of his congregation.

In the winter of 1734, everything changed. Jonathan had long preached for revival in his sermons. He sought to draw his people, many of them nominal Christians, to faith in Christ. Suddenly, without warning, the preaching of the young pastor lit a spark. Edwards preached a series of sermons on true Christianity and the scriptural truths that produced it. The series bought a spiritual harvest not seen in Northampton for decades. This spark spread to a flame, and left little Northampton basking in a spiritual revival. Edwards's pastoral strategy worked to a degree he did not expect and could not have imagined. Soon, Christians from all corners of the world were writing to the thirty-one-year-old pastor, wondering why and how this providence had struck the Massachusetts countryside.

A NARRATIVE OF ONE TOWN'S SALVATION

It is worth quoting Edwards at length to reveal the drama of this story. Writing to a friend in Boston in May 1735, Edwards made a number of observations that best summed up the origins of the revival. This letter, later revised into a book, tells a fascinating story of one community's spiritual revival:

> In the April following, anno 1734, there happened a very sudden and awful death of a young man in the bloom of his youth; who being violently seized with a pleurisy, and taken immediately very delirious, died in about two days; which (together with what was preached publicly on that occasion) much affected many young people. This was followed with another death of a young married woman, who had been considerably exercised in mind, about the salvation of her soul, before she was ill, and was in great distress in the beginning of her illness; but seemed to have satisfying evidences of God's mercy to her, before her death; so that she died very full of comfort, in a most earnest and moving manner warning and counselling others. This seemed to contribute to render solemn the spirits of many young persons; and there began evidently to appear more of a religious concern on people's minds. (*Works* 4, 147–8)

Theological debates also swept through the land in this era, leaving some wondering about their true spiritual state. In this setting, Edwards recounted,

> Many who looked on themselves as in a Christless condition, seemed to be awakened by it, with fear that God was about to withdraw from the land, and that we should be given up to heterodoxy and corrupt principles; and that then their opportunity for obtaining salvation would be past; and many who were brought a little to doubt about the truth of the doctrines they had hitherto been taught, seemed to have a kind of trembling fear with their doubts, lest they should be led into bypaths, to their eternal undoing: and they seemed with much concern and engagedness

of mind, to inquire what was indeed the way in which they must
come to be accepted with God. There were then some things said
publicly on that occasion, concerning justification by faith alone.
(*Works* 4, 148)

The heightened awareness of death and increased interest in
the person of Christ mingled to produce a great hunger for God
that soon manifested itself in force in Northampton. In December 1734,

> the Spirit of God began extraordinarily to set in, and wonderfully to
> work amongst us; and there were, very suddenly, one after another,
> five or six persons who were to all appearance savingly converted,
> and some of them wrought upon in a very remarkable manner.
>
> Particularly, I was surprised with the relation of a young
> woman, who had been one of the greatest company-keepers in the
> whole town. When she came to me, I had never heard that she
> was become in any wise serious, but by the conversation I then
> had with her, it appeared to me that what she gave an account
> of was a glorious work of God's infinite power and sovereign
> grace; and that God had given her a new heart, truly broken and
> sanctified. I could not then doubt of it, and have seen much in my
> acquaintance with her since to confirm it. (*Works* 4, 149)

Edwards wondered to himself what this startling conversion
would bring. Would some of this young woman's friends react to
this development by disparaging him and cursing God? Would
they turn their back on the church even more now that it had
taken one of their own? The results proved just the opposite. In
contrast to his fears, the young pastor found that

> the event was the reverse, to a wonderful degree; God made it, I
> suppose, the greatest occasion of awakening to others, of any thing

that ever came to pass in the town. I have had abundant opportunity to know the effect it had, by my private conversation with
many. The news of it seemed to be almost like a flash of lightning,
upon the hearts of young people all over the town, and upon many
others. Those persons amongst us, who used to be farthest from
seriousness, and that I most feared would make an ill improve-
ment of it, seemed to be awakened with it; many went to talk with
her, concerning what she had met with; and what appeared in her
seemed to be to the satisfaction of all that did so. (*Works* 4, 117)

In the end, the revival exerted a powerful influence on the people
of Northampton. In such a close environment, news of the revival spread like thunder across the plain. To Edwards's eyes, the
town changed, and became a center of worship:

> There was scarcely a single person in the town, either old or
> young, that was left unconcerned about the great things of the
> eternal world. Those that were wont to be the vainest and loosest,
> and those that had been most disposed to think and speak slightly
> of vital and experimental religion, were now generally subject to
> great awakenings. And the work of conversion was carried on in
> a most astonishing manner, and increased more and more; souls
> did as it were come by flocks to Jesus Christ. From day to day, for
> many months together, might be seen evident instances of sinners
> brought out of darkness into marvellous light, and delivered out of
> an horrible pit, and from the miry clay, and set upon a rock with a
> new song of praise to God in their mouths [cf. 1 Peter 2:9 and
> Ps. 40:2–3]. (*Works* 4, 150–51)

From Edwards's account, it appears that something unique
and rather extraordinary did occur in Northampton in the mid-
1730s. His summary of the revival makes only the briefest mention of the sermonic content that prompted the awakening. This

humble omission, however, does obscure the true cause of the event. Edwards had preached a series of lectures on justification and the new birth in the fall of 1734. His preaching to his congregation differed from his earlier treatise on justification and salvation that he delivered at Yale in 1723. There, Edwards preached defensively, to contend for the traditional Protestant understanding of justification in a public setting. In 1734, the pastor preached offensively. He wished to clarify the substance of saving faith in Jesus Christ for his congregation so that they might find salvation.

Edwards believed that certain members of his flock had either deceived themselves about their spirituality or had misunderstood the nature of saving faith and the new birth due to unbiblical teaching on the doctrine of justification by faith alone, and he thus set out to win them to a vibrant understanding of this teaching that would nourish Christians and rescue unbelievers. Edwards maintained that it is faith in Christ alone that

> justifies, or gives an interest in Christ's satisfaction and merits, and a right to the benefits procured thereby, viz., as it thus makes Christ and the believer one in the acceptance of the Supreme Judge. 'Tis by faith that we have a title to eternal life, because 'tis by faith that we have the Son of God, by whom life is. (*Works* 19, 158)

As articulated here, faith in Christ had the crucial effect of uniting Christ and the believer, once separated by a chasm of sin and unbelief. This was a crucial point. His sermons on justification helped, he thought, "to establish the judgments of many in this truth" and also "to engage their hearts in a more earnest pursuit of justification" (795).

Engage hearts he did. Through these sermons, many unbelievers came to saving faith, leaving the chains of sin and misery behind, and many Christians found fresh assurance of their salvation, leading them to live more joyfully and obediently. There were surely some false conversions and unfulfilled hopes in this season, but the revival that began in Northampton and swept throughout the Connecticut River Valley in the mid-1730s accomplished much for God's kingdom.

Edwards modeled godly shepherding in his preaching on saving faith. He knew that he was responsible for the spiritual well-being of his people and that this role necessitated that he publicly articulate biblical truth for the health of his people and also for the salvation of some who thought themselves converted. For Edwards, truth and doctrine were not minor matters, mere footnotes of the Christian faith that believers arranged as they saw fit. If he and his fellow ministers tinkered with these truths, Christians would grow weak and worldly. Their minds would grow confused, their hearts weak, and men and women would spiritually suffer even as God lost the glory due to Him. If churches held fast to truth, however, and preached it passionately and vigorously, Christians would flourish and stand firm in their faith. They would taste the rich blessings of theological confidence and spiritual hope. Unbelievers would see this distinctive way of life and question their beliefs and behaviors. Though embattled, the church and its members would remain faithful and fruitful. God, observing and orchestrating these events from His throne, would gain glory.

DOCTRINE AS A MEANS TO JOY

Edwards yearned to produce true Christians in his town and to see the faith of those Christians flourish and multiply. He preached and prayed and exhorted toward this end. He did not seek to change the emotions of his flock, nor did he wish merely to equip his people to win theological arguments or memorize a body of doctrine. Edwards labored to communicate truth to his people so that their souls might brim with passion and love for God. Doctrine, then, was a means to love, the factory of passion, the genesis of joy. The Lord rewarded this emphasis. He placed His hand on the little town and its neighbors, marking it for the ages as an example of what the Word moving through a church can accomplish when the Spirit moves with it in a mighty way.

THE REVIVAL DECLINES

The revival soon waned in intensity, though Edwards observed positive effects of his preaching throughout the late-1730s. However, in March 1737, a catastrophe struck the Northampton church. During a service, the decrepit church gallery collapsed, causing people sitting on the second floor to land on the people in the pews below. Somehow, none of the parishioners lost their lives in the accident, and the church resolved to redouble efforts to build a new meeting house. These plans, which had languished for some time, led to the dedication of a new building on Christmas Day of December 1737.

The order of seating in the new building caused Edwards some discomfort, however, as the building's designers had arranged the pews according to the accumulated wealth of their patrons. Jonathan grew quite angry over this and voiced his displeasure to the church, though his denunciations achieved little. This pattern would repeat itself numerous times in the coming years, with the intensity of dialogue soon reaching a pitch that only separation would quiet. Jonathan possessed impressive powers of articulation, but he sometimes struggled with matters of personal communication and tended on occasion to speak harshly when a gentler tone would have sufficed. Like many of us, Edwards's strengths were also his weaknesses. His ability to nuance an argument and state it with great authority helped to persuade many readers of the soundness of his writings. Yet these same qualities sometimes escalated congregational debates that were unworthy of the proportions they reached. Further displeasure resulted from the suicide of Edwards's uncle and church communicant, Joseph Hawley, in 1735, and from the excommunication of a church member, Abigail Bridgman, for drunkenness in July 1739. The exhilaration of 1734 seemed to have given way to frustration and disappointment in the latter half of the 1730s and the early months of 1740.

WHITEFIELD PAYS A VISIT

The clouds lifted when the young evangelist George Whitefield touched down in Northampton. The young Whitefield was a natural force for the gospel. He preached with a power few of his era could claim. He had it all—eloquence, a booming baritone, passionate piety, scriptural knowledge, and a deep sense of the drama of the gospel. Whitefield had preached to tens of thousands by this time, though he was only twenty-six years old. Hundreds of people from America and England had responded to his call to conversion, making Whitefield the first trans-Atlantic celebrity. In this era, when religion ruled the roost, a wildly successful evangelist like Whitefield routinely stole the headlines of local newspapers. For his part, Whitefield did not oppose such publicity. A talented publicist, he embraced media coverage of his evangelism, and sought to use it to push the gospel even further into the consciences of colonial citizens.

Whitefield employed his capacity for organization by contacting Edwards on his second trip to the colonies in 1740. Though Edwards was young and had not published a great deal at this point, he already had a reputation as a leading pastor and promoter of revival in his region. Whitefield desired permission to preach at Edwards's church. Edwards responded warmly to Whitefield: "I have a great desire, if it may be the will of God, that such a blessing as attends your person and labors may descend on this town, and may enter mine own house, and that I may receive it in my own soul" (*Works* 16, 80). Edwards knew that such a visit could bring with it powerful results and declared his excitement openly to Whitefield: "I hope this is the dawning of a day of God's mighty power and glorious grace to the world of mankind." The expectation of Whitefield's visit gave Edwards hope that revival would visit Northampton once more.

The eminent ministers met on October 17–19, 1740, in Northampton. Whitefield preached movingly in four separate sermons, affecting the congregation in visible ways. Even stoic Jonathan could not contain tears of joy upon hearing the gospel of Christ proclaimed with such electric feeling. The two men enjoyed fellowship during Whitefield's stay in the Edwards home and forged a lasting friendship. Edwards went so far as to rebuke Whitefield after hearing the young, passionate speaker denounce certain colonial pastors for lack of emotion and zeal for the gospel. Though Edwards shared his friend's concerns, he sought to refine Whitefield's public method. He succeeded in doing so, a testimony to the evangelist's respect for the preacher.

THE FRUITS OF WHITEFIELD'S PREACHING

In later months, Edwards wrote to his friend, giving him a report of the results of Whitefield's visit to Northampton. "I have reason to think that a considerable number of young people, some of them children, have already been savingly brought home to Christ. I hope salvation has come to this house since you was in it, with respect to one, if not more, of my children" (*Works* 16, 87). Edwards then shared a desire to know a similar anointing on his own ministry. Pray for me, he said, "that I may become fervent, as a flame of fire in my work, and may be abundantly succeeded, and that it would please God, however unworthy I am, to improve me as an instrument of his glory, and advancing the kingdom of Christ."

In the visit of the young evangelist, Edwards had glimpsed a life stamped by zeal for the gospel. George Whitefield worked tirelessly to advance the message of salvation, retiring late to bed and rising early in the morning in order to talk with as many people as he could. Even after leading many to the Savior, Jonathan Edwards desired to grow as an evangelist. In his mind, he had not "arrived" as a faithful Christian. He knew that he would never perfectly consecrate himself to his ministry. Yet he pressed on toward the high calling of faith, working hard to bolster his preaching and his Christian witness. His efforts would soon pay off—in an even more dramatic fashion than the earlier revival. As his letter indicated, after Whitefield's visit, Edwards freshly committed himself to communicating the glory and drama of the gospel to his people in his weekly sermons. As he did so, his preaching reached greater heights. Many more townspeople experienced the new birth. The Great Awakening, begun several years earlier, soon reached its peak as the words of the Northampton pastor gripped his congregation with a force only divine unction can account for.

Following Edwards

Humility Rather than Jealousy

If a Christian today can take any "secret" from this period of Edwards's life, it is this: to pursue in a simple but concerted way increased conformity of the heart and mind *to* Christ for the purpose of increased spiritual harvest *for* Christ. Edwards demonstrated no jealousy or competitiveness with Whitefield, sins into which he could easily have fallen due to Whitefield's success as an evangelist. Instead, Edwards seems to have been sharpened

and encouraged by Whitefield's example. Sadly, Christian friendship often faces the challenge of jealousy, a sin that Christians
rarely talk openly about. For his part, Edwards seems to have
avoided jealousy over Whitefield's ministry. We are reminded of
the need to fight jealousy in our own lives, particularly in matters that we care about. It is one thing to feel little jealousy over
things that do not matter to us; it is quite another to demonstrate
humility when others have precisely what we desire.

Loving and Esteeming the Local Church

Christians need to remember that doctrine is not only to be defended, as Edwards did in his Yale address, but to be offered as
a feast of faith, as Edwards did in his evangelistic preaching. In
particular, the good news of salvation, including the idea of justification, need not be seen as a mere set of beliefs, but as a means
to passionate trust in the Lord. Believers can act practically on
such a conviction by esteeming the gospel-centered teaching
and preaching of the local church. Taking the sermon seriously
is a great way for a Christian to begin to actually enjoy doctrine.
If one would approach the sermon and the Sunday service not
as a spiritual doctor's appointment, a rote exercise, but as a feast
of spiritual food, one would attain maturity and joy previously
unthinkable for a less serious-minded Christian.

Each week, Edwards tried to lay out just such a meal for
his people. He had eaten richly himself during the week as he
prepared his message. If Christians would emulate Edwards's example, whether as a pastor or a layperson, they would acquire a
great love for truth, much as one acquires a taste for fruits and
vegetables after years of hot dogs and nachos. As Christians,
we must train ourselves both to love rich teaching and to leave
doctrinal junk food behind. For more on this sort of living, see
Thabiti Anyabwile's book *What Is a Healthy Church Member?*

Chapter 6

THE UNSEEN UNDERWORLD

In the spring and summer of 1741, Jonathan Edwards delivered the sermon that etched him into the history books for centuries to come. "Sinners in the Hands of an Angry God," as it became known, turned Northampton and the Connecticut River Valley upside down and sent a message of ultimate reality through the colonies that echoes to this day. Nearly three hundred years after Edwards first preached it, it remains the most famous American sermon, and perhaps the most famous sermon of all time.

It all began on a hot summer day in 1741 in little Enfield, Massachusetts (now in Connecticut, about thirty-one miles south of Northampton), when Jonathan stepped into the pulpit and began expounding on Deuteronomy 32:35 (KJV): "Their foot shall slide in due time." Though his tone was calm, his words were full of thunder. In sentence after dreadful sentence, Edwards laid out the torments that awaited unrepentant sinners in the afterlife, describing them with such force that one could almost see the fiery pit as the sermon unfolded. Beginning as he so often did with the relation of God to the sermon's subject, Edwards observed that God

> is not only able to cast wicked men into hell, but he can most easily do it. Sometimes an earthly prince meets with a great deal

of difficulty to subdue a rebel, that has found means to fortify himself, and has made himself strong by the numbers of his followers. But it is not so with God. There is no fortress that is any defense from the power of God. Though hand join in hand, and vast multitudes of God's enemies combine and associate themselves, they are easily broken in pieces: they are as great heaps of light chaff before the whirlwind; or large quantities of dry stubble before devouring flames. We find it easy to tread on and crush a worm that we see crawling on the earth; so 'tis easy for us to cut or singe a slender thread that anything hangs by; thus easy is it for God when he pleases to cast his enemies down to hell. What are we, that we should think to stand before him, at whose rebuke the earth trembles, and before whom the rocks are thrown down? (*Works* 22, 405)

Edwards had long sought to develop his writing style, to make it simultaneously pungent and precise, rich and enveloping. He wanted his words to communicate transcendent concepts and ideas. In "Sinners in the Hands of an Angry God," he demonstrated that he had found his voice.

As in "A Divine and Supernatural Light," Edwards's words in "Sinners" brought his hearers to another place. His language and logic were relentless. He turned his subject like a diamond, just a few degrees with each description to catch the attention of his hearers. This was no mere intellectual exercise, however, no storytelling time. Edwards preached to save the souls of his hearers. The earth opened up as Edwards mixed illustrations, doctrinal statements, and plain exhortation to illuminate the true nature of hell, the realm where flames devour and men's souls are continually anguished. An awful majesty loomed over this terrible scene, for God ruled over hell, Edwards declared, a figure of fury toward all who had rejected Him. Unlike the deity fixed in many minds, Edwards taught his hearers that God was no buddy in the sky, but a ferocious conqueror of all who had defied Him. If massive "rocks" were "thrown down" in God's presence, how could human sinners expect to stand before the holy Lord of heaven and earth?

THE POWER OF SATAN

Another figure loomed large in the supernatural world that Edwards depicted, a shadowy, sinister figure who desired to destroy everyone he could:

> The devil stands ready to fall upon them and seize them as his own, at what moment God shall permit him. They belong to him; he has their souls in his possession, and under his dominion. The Scripture represents them as his "goods," Luke 11:21. The devils watch them; they are ever by them, at their right hand; they stand waiting for them, like greedy hungry lions that see their prey, and expect to have it, but are for the present kept back; if God should withdraw his hand, by which they are restrained, they would in one moment fly upon their poor souls. The old serpent is gaping for them; hell opens its mouth wide to receive them; and if God should permit it, they would be hastily swallowed up and lost. (*Works* 22, 406–7)

In Edwards's mind, the figure of Satan existed as a very real presence, a powerful force for evil. Commanding minions who obeyed his every whim, Satan stood ready to devour lost souls, "gaping for them." The scene is akin to a modern horror film of the darkest sort and accords with biblical accounts of Satan (see 1 Peter 5:8, for example). According to Peter and other biblical authors, Satan does not conduct his work of terror from a position of weakness. Though he is bounded by the will of God (see Job 1), Satan roams over all the earth, observing it, and roaring with bloodlust. He zeroes in on those who give themselves over to sin, feeding their hunger for evil until he secures their damnation. As they suffer his torments, he watches over them, gleeful, victorious, roaring with pride, hungry for more. His thirst for souls is never sated, and until Christ returns to earth and defeats him in the last battle, he will not cease to destroy men, women, and children from every corner of the world.

THE HOPELESSNESS OF THE SINNER

When Edwards preached "Sinners," the weight of this description and others caused many in the audience to weep and wail and even scream in terror. The preacher proclaimed that God and Satan stood close at hand to the unrepentant sinner, waiting for the right moment to unleash wrath and destruction on them. The wicked, Edwards declared in no uncertain terms, had no friend, no savior. The dark lion waited to pounce; the majestic sovereign stayed his hand for the moment, but would swing it like a hammer in due time. Having sketched these roles, Edwards then focused on the condition of the sinner, urging that

> Your wickedness makes you as it were heavy as lead, and to tend downwards with great weight and pressure towards hell; and if God should let you go, you would immediately sink and swiftly descend and plunge into the bottomless gulf, and your healthy constitution, and your own care and prudence, and best contrivance, and all your righteousness, would have no more influence to uphold you and keep you out of hell, than a spider's web would have to stop a falling rock. (*Works* 22, 410)

Edwards diagnosed the presumptuousness of the unredeemed human heart in words designed to scorch away its natural narcissism:

Were it not that so is the sovereign pleasure of God, the earth would not bear you one moment; for you are a burden to it; the creation groans with you; the creature is made subject to the bondage of your corruption, not willingly; the sun don't willingly shine upon you to give you light to serve sin and Satan; the earth don't willingly yield her increase to satisfy your lusts; nor is it willingly a stage for your wickedness to be acted upon; the air don't willingly serve you for breath to maintain the flame of life in your vitals, while you spend your life in the service of God's enemies. God's creatures are good, and were made for men to serve God with, and don't willingly subserve to any other purpose, and groan when they are abused to purposes so directly contrary to their nature and end. And the world would spew you out, were it not for the sovereign hand of him who hath subjected it in hope. (*Works* 22, 410)

The Northampton preacher recalibrated the presuppositions of his hearers. Many of them, he supposed, believed that God represented some sort of benevolent father who sought only to serve people and make them happy. The earth, made by God, and all that was in it, then, existed solely to please and gratify human beings. Man, fundamentally, was right, and knew what he deserved and should have. He had a natural right to grace and could justifiably curse God if such did not come to him. Against such a depraved mindset, Edwards offered a vision of God in which God was holy, sovereign, the possessor of self-determinacy, and the just recipient of worship and service. Edwards removed man from the place he naturally claimed, the throne of God, and restored God's proper rulership. His words exploded the presumption of the human heart by showing that human beings only lived and breathed at all because of the divine will, the "mere pleasure" as he later put it, of the Lord. Like gravity to a stone, the weight of God's justice drove sinners to the hell they deserved, with only God's goodness staying this irresistible force.

THE AWESOME MERCY OF CHRIST

Having laid out in great detail the agonies of hell and the frailty of human existence, Edwards summoned his hearers to the mercy of Christ. His sermon had dashed their false hopes and exploded their arrogance. Now, the preacher exhorted "everyone that is yet out of Christ, and hanging over the pit of hell, whether they be old men and women, or middle aged, or young people, or little children, now hearken to the loud calls of God's Word and providence." Speaking with great urgency, Edwards stated that "God seems now to be hastily gathering in his elect in all parts of the land; and probably the bigger part of adult persons that ever shall be saved, will be brought in now in a little time," a pronouncement that captured the sense of drama and immediacy that the young pastor felt. With a final warning, Edwards called to his hearers to seize eternal life while they still could:

> Therefore let everyone that is out of Christ, now awake and
> fly from the wrath to come. The wrath of almighty God is now
> undoubtedly hanging over great part of this congregation: let
> everyone fly out of Sodom: "Haste and escape for your lives, look
> not behind you, escape to the mountain, lest you be consumed"
> [Gen. 19:17]. (Works 22, 418)

When Edwards ended the sermon, people cried out audibly for salvation. The master craftsman had made a deep impression on his hearers. He preached his message without relish or pomposity, and opened up the spiritual realm for all to see. Edwards's sermon captured the biblical reality that a vast battle between God and Satan rages for the souls of mankind. Many people responded to this new vision with repentance born of fear and gratefulness to the Savior, Jesus Christ, whose atoning death and resurrection made possible the forgiveness of sins, the satisfaction of God's wrath, and the attainment of eternal life in heaven with God. This, after all, was Edwards's aim: not to merely scare his people or share frightening stories, but to cause them to look honestly on their sin and their deserved fate, and then to joyfully flee to Christ, the sinner's substitute, for salvation.

DISCERNING SAVING FAITH

The good effects of Edwards's preaching continued throughout the summer as the pastor preached "Sinners in the Hands of an Angry God." He saw numerous people profess faith in the new birth and witnessed a spirit of reverence and awe spread throughout his congregation. Even with such observably positive results, however, a group of Protestant pastoral colleagues spoke against the revivals Edwards led, decrying them as mere "enthusiasm" that would pass in short order. Edwards took care to respond to the awakening's detractors, delivering an address at Yale's commencement in September 1741 entitled "Distinguishing Marks of a Work of the Spirit of God." In this nuanced yet vigorous defense of the revivals, Edwards laid out a theology of conversion, detailing the marks of a redeemed heart alongside "signs" that neither proved nor disproved the claim of conversion.

First, Edwards covered the neutral marks that could not conclusively provide evidence of either a true or false work of God in His people. "A work is not to be judged of," wrote Edwards, "by any effects on the bodies of men; such as tears, trembling, groans, loud outcries, agonies of body, or the failing of bodily strength" (*Works* 4, 230). Positive signs included love for Christ, opposition to Satan, reverence for God's Word, and love for God and man. The address illuminated the Christian's experience of these signs. In reflecting on the way that the Holy Spirit produces love for God in the hearts of the truly converted, Edwards explained that the Spirit "works in them an admiring, delightful

sense of the excellency of Jesus Christ, representing him as 'the
chief among ten thousands, altogether lovely' [Song of Solomon
5:10, 16], and makes him precious to the soul" (*Works* 4, 256).
The Spirit causes intense delight in the heart of the Christian as
He "makes the attributes of God as revealed in the Gospel and
manifested in Christ, delightful objects of contemplation; and
makes the soul to long after God and Christ, after their presence
and communion, and acquaintance with them, and conformity
to them; and to live so as to please and honor them." This love
flowed into the daily life of the Christian as the Spirit "quells
contentions among men, and gives a spirit of peace and goodwill,
excites to acts of outward kindness and earnest desires of the salvation of others' souls; and causes a delight in those that appear
as the children of God and followers of Christ" (*Works* 4, 256).

"Distinguishing Marks" displays a pastoral theology of the
richest sort. The text goes beyond a defense of the revivals and
delves into far deeper matters involving the nature of Christianity. Edwards could write soaring treatises about philosophical
matters or theological quandaries, but he was fundamentally a
pastor who wanted to help his congregation figure out the Christian life.

MAKING CHRISTIANITY CLEAR

Although his address at Yale began as an apology, it soon turned
toward a biblical picture of the converted life. As with so much
of the preacher's writings, theological description bled over into
exhortative meditation. Edwards was not immune to a snarky exchange, as future years would make clear, but in his hands, even
a self-defensive polemic against his detractors could become a
contemplation of the glories of Christ and the beauty of living
for Him through the Spirit. Edwards never sought simply to
describe, but to awaken. The exercise of carefully studying the

marks of rich Christian living naturally leads the heart to yearn for such character. In "Distinguishing Marks," one picks up the scent of fresh, vivid faith, a discovery that leads one to hunger for that which is described.

A STORMY SEASON OF MINISTRY

The early 1740s brought considerable encouragement to Edwards as he observed positive results from his preaching and leadership of his church. The mid-1740s, however, proved challenging for the preacher, now recognized as the leader of the "New Lights," the enthusiastic promoters of evangelical revival. His congregation, seemingly transformed during Whitefield's visit and the subsequent preaching of Jonathan, grew lax in their faith and failed to respond passionately to much of Edwards's pulpit ministry. Edwards approached his work with deadly seriousness and interpreted this laxity as a personal responsibility. He responded by ramping up the rhetoric of his sermons, chastising his congregation over and over for their spiritual laziness.

In 1744, Edwards attempted to discipline a number of young men in his church who had gotten hold of a midwives' manual depicting matters of pregnancy and then acted in sexually suggestive ways to a number of young girls. The behavior was sinful by any standard, but Edwards approached it as a watershed moment for his flock, believing that he had to publicly condemn the act from the pulpit, doing so even as he sought to discipline the young men. The affair went badly, and the youths rebelled against their pastor. Edwards could not reconcile with them, which left a bad taste in many mouths.

Edwards picked this testy period to begin conversations about an increase in his pastoral salary. The process lasted for no less than three years and involved many publicly embarrassing moments for the pastor. Though an eminent minister and the product of a revered family, Edwards had to fight tooth and nail for his raise, and he had to promise after receiving the increase that he would not again raise the matter. Edwards did live at a high standard in comparison with his parishioners, but he also worked in an era in which pastors led their communities and occupied a loftier social position than today. Nonetheless, he showed an ill-tempered spirit at times and did not always make the process of negotiation an easy one.

CONTINUED DEFENSE OF THE REVIVALS

Circumstances improved when he published the *Treatise Concerning Religious Affections* in 1746. The text expanded on the work Edwards had done in his "Distinguishing Marks" address at Yale in 1741. The book incited some controversy, but has proven to be a classic work in the field of pastoral theology. It acted as a further affirmation by Edwards of the veracity of the Great Awakening and demonstrated his continued belief in the reality of conversion produced through evangelistic preaching. When visited by the Holy Spirit, the encounter of conscience and content created saving faith in Jesus Christ. Though some still denounced this method of sermonizing, Edwards defended it until his death. Preaching for him was not merely about forming strong character or delving deeply into a passage. Edwards aimed at transformation. For that, only the gospel would do.

FURTHER CONTROVERSY

Controversy flared again in 1747 when Edwards publicly pressed a young man, Thomas Wait, to marry a girl, Martha Root, whom Wait had impregnated. One senses the tension of the ordeal in a brief, sparse letter from Edwards to a fellow minister involved in the council adjudicating the matter: "The number of the chosen council is but small," Edwards wrote in taut prose, "and if some should fail, the design might fail" (*Works* 16, 222). The design did fail. Wait refused to marry Root, bringing further embarrassment to Edwards and leaving him wondering about the extent of his pastoral influence. Edwards's attempts to model and to exert a holy example upon his church and town had at times succeeded, as seen in the revivals his preaching produced. At other times, however, his efforts failed, and he often felt personally responsible.

Like any Christian, the pastoral leader and literary luminary of colonial New England knew his trials, both personally inflicted and externally caused. Unfortunately, several more visited him before the contentious decade of the 1740s ended, including one that robbed him of two of his dearest friends in the world.

Following Edwards

Beyond Mere Belief

Edwards was able to live with great seriousness and passion because he knew where he did not want to go and where he did not want other people to go. He studied hell and often remembered what God had saved him from. He did not simply think about where he was going after death; he thought about where, but for the grace of God, he would surely have gone. This contemplation fueled his passion for the Lord and drove him to live a serious and purposeful life. Because Edwards looked deeply into the reality of eternal torment, he was equipped to live a life of great spiritual intensity that pointed countless people away from hell and toward heaven.

One certainly doesn't need to be a pastor to exert this kind of influence on peers, friends, and family. Christians of all kinds can model interest in the afterlife. We need simply to take God, His Word, and heaven and hell seriously, and then to transfer that seriousness to a pattern of life that motivates people to consider unseen things that seem otherworldly but will soon become reality.

The Duty of Examination

Edwards's work to examine his life and his church members' lives for the marks of conversion sets a great example for Christians and churches today. On a regular basis, we should take stock of our spiritual lives. In our churches, we should emphasize the marks of conversion so that people know what it means to be a Christian. Edwards's writings on this subject are some of the best for understanding the redeemed life. Believers of all backgrounds can help fellow church members to find assurance and conviction by studying and talking about the biblical marks of conversion. Many people today waver in their faith because they have little understanding of the spiritual fruits. Studying this subject will lead both to conviction over patterns of sin and fresh assurance for believers that their contradictory behavior does not necessarily signal unbelief, but rather the need for fresh dependence upon the Spirit.

Chapter 7

A WILDERNESS ERRAND

THE STORY OF DAVID BRAINERD

While Edwards loved each of his children and spent much time with them, Jerusha, the second child, shared her father's passionate faith and enjoyed a special closeness with him. Of all the Edwards offspring, Jerusha responded most to her father's teaching and even as a teenager showed a desire to offer a sacrificial witness to the lost around her.

It was not surprising that she got along particularly well with a young visitor to the Edwards household in 1747. David Brainerd, a Yale graduate and a missionary to the Indians in Stockbridge, Massachusetts, came to the home after falling terribly ill during his missionary work. Brainerd had made Edwards's acquaintance while a student at Yale. A devout person, Brainerd impressed Edwards with his seriousness, though Edwards worried from their first meeting about the young man's melancholy disposition and lack of personal balance. He maintained contact with Brainerd during the missionary's time among the Indians of Stockbridge and served as a counselor to the gifted but often-depressed Brainerd.

Brainerd's ministry had started off rockily. He labored to communicate with the Indians to whom he evangelized, had no

English-speaking friends around him, and struggled to build ad-
equate shelter and find sufficient food. Months passed, and the
young Christian made little meaningful contact with the Indians.
Yet he preached the gospel time and again, attempting to make
clear the most basic matters of the Christian faith to a people
who had little natural connection with the message. Brainerd repeatedly despaired and wrote in his diary of a desire to leave the
work. When seemingly at his lowest point, however, light broke
out. Multitudes of the Indian people expressed interest in the
gospel. Soon, many professed belief in it to their family members
and became observably faithful to the Bible. The change was as-
tounding. Brainerd's heart soared. After a long season of struggle,
the Lord had smiled on his work and drawn dozens of lost people
to Himself.

BRAINERD'S ILLNESS

In the process of ministering to the Indians of Stockbridge,
Brainerd had often abused his body by not sleeping enough and
eating too little in order to evangelize. The results proved disastrous, and in the fall of 1746, Brainerd set out from Stockbridge
to rest at the home of family. He did not complete the journey,
but collapsed in the home of a friend and sponsor, Jonathan
Dickinson, and remained there for several months. After his time
there, Brainerd moved from home to home, never fully recover-
ing, until he landed at the Edwards's home in May 1747.

Brainerd's health improved under the excellent care of Sarah
Edwards and others. The Edwards home was always open to
needy people with whom the Edwards had acquaintance, and
Jonathan personally gave large sums of money to needy people
in his church and town. He had a burden to help others, though
he rarely, if ever, mentioned such deeds. He and Brainerd enjoyed much conversation and fellowship together. He loved to

hear Brainerd pray, for the young man exhibited fervent piety and sound theology.

MENTORING THE FUTURE GENERATION

Edwards saw Brainerd as one to mentor. Edwards mentored a large number of young men in his pastoral career, informally training a corps of theologically minded pastors and Christian leaders from his home in Northampton. Though his house was already filled with numerous inhabitants, including children and slaves, Edwards made training the next generation of pastors a priority and invited future pastors and theologians to stay with him and use his impressive library for a season of study and learning. The mind boggles to know how Jonathan accomplished this goal in the midst of family life, church oversight, and writing, but he did. At meals, in snatches of conversation while working in his study, while riding for exercise, Jonathan kindly reached out to numerous young men and imparted wisdom and a vision of ministry to them. The Lord honored these efforts. Years after Jonathan's death, numerous churches across New England benefited from skilled pastor-theologians who trained under the Northampton pastor.

THE SHAMEFULNESS OF SLAVERY

It should be noted that Edwards was able to accomplish as much as he did in part because he bought into the viability of slavery. This is a massive stain on the reputation of a great Christian man. Though Edwards did treat his slaves well, and though he believed in and taught about the spiritual equality of all people before the Lord, he failed to adequately apply spiritual truth to his everyday life. Even so faithful a Christian and so biblically concerned a believer as Edwards had his blind spots—some of them, like slavery, shameful in great measure. Those of us who celebrate his legacy must square with this offensive aspect of his life even as we remember others of more positive character.

There is some additional complexity to Edwards's legacy on this point. As Kenneth Minkema has shown, Edwards came to believe that the Atlantic slave trade was unjust. In the 1740s, he voiced his disapproval of it in public (Minkema, 36). Edwards sometimes preached—movingly—on the liberating power of God, and his words could not have failed to perk the ears of slaves within his hearing. It is clear that Edwards saw problems in colonial slavery, and also that he saw himself as responsible for the well-being of slaves in his home. He called himself to be a "good master" and to teach his charges the ways of Christ, unlike those who who gave their slaves "neither food nor clothing" and left them "naked and famishing" (Minkema, 40). Nonetheless, though he came to criticize the slave trade, he never embraced an abolitionist position, and he did not reach a point where he freed all his own slaves.

It is a tragedy that more Christians who shared Edwards's love for the Bible had similar blind spots. Though the Exodus account clearly indicts slaveholding and presents the true God as a liberator of harshly treated, wrongly oppressed people, and though the New Testament offers no justification of anything close to the slave trade and condemns the man-stealing upon which slavery is based (1 Tim. 1:10), many Christians failed to make good on this teaching. They followed their culture and its trendy thinking over the Scripture. They thought it was fine to own slaves, provided one treated them well—basing this view on a prejudiced read of Ephesians 6:5, which in no way enfranchises chattel slavery. Thankfully, numerous followers of Edwards would advance the nascent antislavery trajectories of his thought. Jonathan Edwards Jr., for example, became a leading abolitionist figure, as did others who studied with Edwards. This does not mitigate the problems already identified; it does show us that there was horsepower within Edwardsean theology for the kind of revolutionary change that eventually, after a long and awful conflict featuring untold human suffering, came to pass.

BRAINERD AND JERUSHA

Brainerd and Edwards enjoyed a happy season of mutual enrichment until Brainerd set off for Boston in the summer to improve his health through horseback riding. Brainerd did not travel alone. Jerusha Edwards rode with the young missionary, keeping him company and watching over his health. The two likely talked for hours, enjoying conversation about spiritual things, gazing at the countryside, enjoying companionship with a like-minded person. As they traveled, David's condition worsened. Once in Boston, Brainerd abruptly neared the edge of mortality. He suffered from tuberculosis, and his doctors informed him that he could die at any moment. He rested for weeks in the city, with Jerusha constantly by his side.

In late July, Brainerd had recovered enough strength to return to Northampton. Not even thirty years of age, he possessed the body of a much older man, and had to travel slowly to Edwards's home. Once the party reached their destination, Brainerd sank into bed, rarely rising through the late summer and early fall. He edited the diary he had written as a missionary, talked at length with Jerusha, and spent time with Jonathan, his mentor. Though this was a happy season, Brainerd's hour drew near.

In early October, David and his friends knew that death was not far away. Over the next few days, the missionary said his goodbyes. His words to Jerusha were poignant: "Dear Jerusha, are you willing to part with me? I am quite willing to part with you: I am willing to part with all my friends: I am willing to part with my dear brother John; although I love him the best of any creature living: I have committed him and all my friends to God, and can leave them with God" (Marsden, 326). The statement testified to Brainerd's profoundly spiritual orientation. He lived with the realities of the spiritual world on his mind. As with Edwards, God was close at hand for Brainerd.

Brainerd's next word to Jerusha showed deep affection for his spiritual companion. "[I]f I thought I should not see you and be happy with you in another world, I could not bear to part with you. But we shall spend an happy eternity together!" (Marsden, 326). Two days later, on October 9, 1747, he breathed his last, leaving Jerusha, Jonathan, and the Edwards family heartbroken.

JERUSHA'S DEATH

Several months later, the family continued to recover from Brainerd's passing. In February 1748, Jerusha also fell deeply ill. After a week of suffering, the young woman died in the arms of her family. Edwards was grief-stricken. Jerusha was "generally esteemed the flower of the family," as the pastor told a friend (Marsden, 325), and the family felt a "melancholy absence" after losing her (*Works* 16, 245). Edwards memorialized his daughter in a moving sermon. Jerusha had been "remarkably weaned" from the world and frequently "declared in words, showed in deeds" that she was "ever more ready to deny herself, earnestly inquiring in every affair which way should most glorify God" (Marsden, 328). Jerusha's death and conflicts with his congregation cast a shadow over most of the 1740s, and Jonathan struggled at times to stoke his heart. The sweet things of life could become the saddest. This reality yielded another irony, however: it was often in these hardest of hard times that the kindness of the Lord became most apparent.

THE LEGACY OF DAVID BRAINERD

Edwards memorialized his spiritual son Brainerd in *An Account of the Life of the Late Reverend Mr. David Brainerd*, published in 1749 after Edwards finished a biographical essay on Brainerd and the editing of the missionary's journals. He published the text for the ages, hoping it would stir up Christians of present and future generations to embrace missionary work. Brainerd's diary captured the marrow of difficult evangelistic labor even as it presented the reader with a challenging portrait of a life consecrated to the Lord.

Brainerd exhibited, Edwards wrote, "such an illustrious pattern of humility, divine love, discreet zeal, self-denial, obedience, patience, resignation, fortitude, meekness, forgiveness, compassion, benevolence, and universal holiness, as neither men nor angels ever saw before." This man "was a minister of the Gospel, and one who was called to unusual services in that work, whose ministry was attended with very remarkable and unusual events," for he "was the instrument of a most remarkable awakening" (*Works* 7, 90). Edwards's effort to honor Brainerd and perpetuate his legacy paid off in abundance. Modern missionary experts credit *The Life of David Brainerd* with sparking the modern missions movement, which has led to the sending of thousands upon thousands of missionaries to every corner of the globe.

A TRYING HOUR

Edwards's time with Brainerd lifted his spirits for a period as the two enjoyed deep friendship. When Brainerd and Jerusha passed away, however, Edwards grieved for an extended period. His difficulties, however, would not pass for some time. In a shocking turn of events, Jonathan Edwards's congregation fired him in 1750. The magnitude of this event requires some brief background explanation.

Edwards's grandfather, Solomon Stoddard, had instituted a controversial policy in the Northampton church during his tenure as pastor. Observing his society shift away from interest in Christianity, but wanting people to remain connected to the church, Stoddard came to believe that he should offer the Lord's Supper to all who attended the service, regardless of whether they professed and demonstrated faith in Christ as Savior. This decision placed Stoddard in disagreement with many evangelical ministers who had followed historical trends in allowing only believers to take of the bread and the cup per certain passages of 1 Corinthians 10 and 11 (see especially 10:16–17). Stoddard, however, saw the Lord's Supper as a means of evangelism. In participating in the holy rite, he argued, people would come face to face with the reality of Christian faith. They might well respond by receiving Christ as their savior for the first time.

Jonathan had long disagreed with his venerated grandfather, yet he did not want to ruffle feathers unnecessarily. He sought to step carefully in changing the policy of the church on admission to the supper. He waited for over two decades before introducing the matter to his congregation, at which point he argued forcefully for his view that only believers ought to take communion. Jonathan believed that allowing unbelievers to partake of the elements invited the Lord's judgment upon them and the minister who served them. He had published his view the year before in 1749 in a careful but characteristically forceful manuscript entitled *An Humble Inquiry in the Rules of the Word of God, Concerning the Qualifications Requisite to a Compleat Standing and Full Communion in the Visible Christian Church*. Edwards thought at the time that the church would follow his lead and change their doctrinal position on the matter. As he wrote to a friend, "I am not sure but that my people, in length of time and with great difficulty, might be brought to yield the point as to the qualifications for the Lord's Supper, though that is very uncertain" (*Works* 16, 283).

EDWARDS'S EJECTION

Whether naïve or just optimistic, Edwards's hopes were soon dashed when his handling of a difficult matter raised a storm in the church. Edwards refused to admit a young man without testimony of salvation to membership, causing many to oppose him. The church and Edwards engaged in a protracted public struggle over the matter, with both sides expressing frustration. Edwards was not permitted to hold a conversation with his congregation that would have allowed him to clarify his decision regarding the young man's membership. Bad turned to worse, and on June 22, 1750, the greatest preacher America has ever known was ejected from his church.

Edwards and his family were stunned. Though Edwards did not shy away from strong leadership that led at times to controversy, the family did not expect so late in life to lose their ministry and all that came with it—their home, their reputation, and their future in Northampton. Jonathan enjoyed a tremendous reputation among colonial pastors. His firing caused him great embarrassment and wrenched him from an established pattern of writing, preaching, and leading that he had carried out for decades. Yet Edwards believed strongly in the providence of God, and he trusted the Lord to lead him through this trial. In his last sermon as the pastor of the Northampton church, he concluded his tenure with a word full of pathos to the people he had so long shepherded:

> Having briefly mentioned these important articles of advice, nothing remains; but that I now take my leave of you, and bid you all farewell; wishing and praying for your best prosperity. I would now commend your immortal souls to him, who formerly committed them to me; expecting the day, when I must meet you again before him, who is the Judge of quick and dead. I desire that I may never

forget this people, who have been so long my special charge, and that I may never cease fervently to pray for your prosperity. May God bless you with a faithful pastor, one that is well acquainted with his mind and will, thoroughly warning sinners, wisely and skillfully searching professors, and conducting you in the way to eternal blessedness. May you have truly a burning and shining light set up in this candlestick; and may you, not only for a season, but during his whole life, and that a long life, be willing to rejoice in his light.

The sermon closed with this:

And let us all remember, and never forget our future solemn meeting, on that great day of the Lord; the day of infallible decision, and of the everlasting and unalterable sentence, Amen. (Kimnach, 240–1)

Pastoring to the end, Jonathan Edwards concluded his career in Northampton.

FINDING A NEW WORK

At age forty-six, Edwards found himself out of work. The irony of this situation would have been rich if it were not so bitter. This was a tough time for Edwards. Though the previous fifteen years had brought considerable hardship and challenge to him, he continually rededicated himself to serving the Lord. Talented and focused as he was, Edwards could not avoid suffering. He could, however, face suffering from a confident belief in God's goodness and power that enabled him to fight his way to joy in a fallen world.

Edwards's situation weighed on his mind, however, for he had a large family to feed. He filled the Northampton pulpit, ironically, but could not do so indefinitely. He also preached in other locations, including Boston; Middletown, Connecticut; and Longmeadow, Massachusetts. In February 1751, though, Edwards found his next calling: he took over the Stockbridge Indian Mission in Massachusetts. Edwards had long supported missionary causes, and he had helped to fund this mission, sending Brainerd to evangelize in the area. The little village of Stockbridge had raised enough funds to build a church and several schools. The missionary efforts in the town had gone well, with over 175 Mahican and Mohawk Indians being baptized. Edwards and his family hoped to continue the good work and moved into town, side-by-side with the Indians whom they sought to evangelize. The new work had begun.

RECLAIMING STOCKBRIDGE

Fifty miles west of Northampton on the Massachusetts border, Stockbridge was a frontier town, small but full of factions, including one containing members of Edwards's extended family, the Williamses. The Williamses were small-town elites who ran things and made life difficult when they were not in charge. They initially made life incredibly challenging for Jonathan as they ran schools for Indian children but with little concern for the physical and spiritual welfare of the students and their families. Edwards was not immune to certain racist attitudes and actions (as noted, he held slaves over the course of his adult life), but he also showed clear concern for people whom others neglected. Over a period of months, Edwards bravely fought the Williamses, ultimately winning control of the school. He did so not to win power for its own sake, but to help the Indians, to educate them so that they could learn the faith and participate in colonial society.

In this incident, one sees some of Edwards's strongest virtues: courage, conviction, devotion to the spiritual good of others, and a willingness to persevere in a just cause. Jonathan brought great blessing to the Indians and the town of Stockbridge by his courage. He stood up to the ill-minded power brokers of the town and watched as the Lord honored his efforts by granting him victory in the feud.

A CONTEXTUALIZED MINISTRY

The controversy took much of Edwards's time and energy and shows how sin and selfishness can end up consuming large amounts of time for Christians. The missionary, though, did not lose sight of his primary calling. Jonathan devoted himself to reaching the Indians. He contextualized his message for them, preaching expository messages in stark, simple language that made the fundamental claims of Christianity abundantly clear. Compare the following excerpt from a sermon on 2 Peter 1:19 to Edwards's previous preaching in Northampton:

> You see how it is [in] the spring. When the sun shines on the earth and trees, it gives 'em new life, makes the earth look green. It causes flowers to appear and give a good smell.
>
> So it is in the heart of a man when the light of God's Word shines into it. Wisdom and knowledge in religion is better than silver or gold and all the riches of the world.
>
> The light, when it shines into the heart, is sweeter than the honey, and the gospel will be a pleasant to you when you come to understand it. (Sermons, 110)

Edwards wisely tailored his message to his audience. He knew that if he tried to preach in the same style that he deployed in Northampton, his message would not connect with his hearers. Thus, he contextualized his preaching, using simple phrases, relevant analogies, and direct language. The above sermon is set against the backdrop of nature, the world in which the Indians lived and easily understood. Edwards was not merely a master wordsmith, but a wise evangelist, employing all of his abilities to reach the particular people under his watch.

THE DAWN OF A NEW SEASON

The Edwards family had successfully resettled. Under Edwards's leadership, the family adapted nicely to life on the frontier. Times were sometimes tough, and life was certainly harder than it had been in Northampton, but Jonathan and Sarah continued to nurture their large family and to lead them well spiritually. Even under the constant threat of attack from hostile Indians, the family prospered. When reports of approaching warriors reached the town, Jonathan and Sarah took what measures they could and trusted the Lord with the results. Such scares occurred frequently in the settlement. It was not safe, to be sure, but it was home. In one sense, Stockbridge is a fitting metaphor for all of Edwards's life—and beyond this, for the life of all Christians in a world in which believers must necessarily be strangers in a strange land.

Following Edwards

Mentoring the Next Generation

The way in which Edwards mentored a young and dying David Brainerd presents an excellent model for contemporary Christians. Whether we target missionaries or young moms, construction workers or professional athletes, all Christians can mentor someone and lead them to spiritual maturity. Jonathan trained a large group of pastors and theologians over the years. Though our target group may differ, we will find abundant blessings if we simply make the time to train young Christians in the faith. Our mentoring need not be fancy or creative; we could simply read a helpful theological book together and discuss it. In the course of doing so, we can share the wisdom we've gained in our own Christian walk. The effects of such engagement are difficult to quantify, but investment in even one person's life can make a tremendous spiritual difference. Indeed, it would be wonderful if entire churches caught the mentoring vision and created a culture of discipleship. This would contribute to unity and maturity on a previously unseen scale.

Making the Most of Difficulties

The way in which Edwards responded to his firing is a model for all Christians who find themselves in grievous circumstances. Terrible things can happen to faithful Christians, including the loss of a job, the onset of a disease, and difficult family situations. In such circumstances, we should embrace Edwards's model, and make the best of our situation. In his case, Jonathan used his firing as an opportunity to evangelize an unreached people and write important theological texts. All this after the most embarrassing moment of his life! If Edwards can make the most of his awkward situation, so can we. When we find ourselves in such moments, then, we must rededicate ourselves to prayer and to the will of God and seek a place of service to the Lord. It may be that, like Edwards, the Lord desires us to do significant work for His kingdom that we would not otherwise have discovered on our prior path. How important it is not to consider only our difficulties, but to consider the will of God that is moving through our difficulties and that ultimately will bring good to us and glory to Him (Rom. 8:28; 31–39).

Chapter 8

THE PASSING
OF A GREAT MAN

THE FREEDOM OF THE WILL

To many, Stockbridge seemed to represent a dead end for Edwards's ministerial career. Ironically, the relative quiet of the New England frontier allowed the pastor to carve out several master works. From 1751 to 1757, Edwards wrote a series of texts that established him as America's greatest theologian. The first of these was *The Freedom of the Will*, a response to some theologians who argued that those who emphasized the sovereignty of God in salvation construed God as a puppet master and humanity as a race of automatons. This group essentially believed that any attempt to preserve God's power in the sphere of salvation resulted in the loss of human freedom. Edwards disagreed.

Edwards believed in the sovereignty of God over all things, including salvation. His conviction came from a careful reading of texts like Romans 9 and Ephesians 1. Yet, at the same time, Edwards believed that underneath the sovereignty of God, humanity possessed considerable agency that cooperated with the divine will to accomplish the purposes of God. Against robotic control of humans on one hand, and absolute freedom that rendered God a weak deity on the other, Edwards struck a balance between the two extremes with his position, commonly called *compatibilism*. This view, Edwards argued, adhered to the biblical picture of the divine and human wills in events like the exodus of Israel from Egypt (see Ex. 7–15). The human will acted freely in choosing its course in life, just as Pharaoh hardened his heart and chose not to release the Israelites on several occasions (see Ex. 9:34, for example). Though God was ultimately sovereign over all things, He worked out His sovereignty in such a way that humans did not live as robots but made real choices as free agents in the world.

In 1754, Edwards published these views in his book *The Freedom of the Will*. The text represented the fruit of years of thinking on the matter. In page after page, the pastor-theologian relentlessly refuted the logic of his opponents and presented numerous scriptural passages supporting his view. In one section, Edwards wrote,

> And if that first act of the will, which determines and fixes the subsequent acts, be not free, none of the following acts, which are determined by it, can be free. If we suppose there are five acts in the train, the fifth and last determined by the fourth, and the fourth by the third, the third by the second, and the second by the first; if the first is not determined by the will, and so not free, then none of them are truly determined by the will: that is, that each of them are as they are, and not otherwise, is not first owing to the will, but to the determination of the first in the series, which is not dependent on the will, and is that which the will has no hand in the determination of.
>
> And this being that which decides what the rest shall be, and determines their existence; therefore the first determination of their existence is not from the will. The case is just the same, if instead of a chain of five acts of the will, we should suppose

a succession of ten, or an hundred, or ten thousand. If the first act be not free, being determined by something out of the will, and this determines the next to be agreeable to itself, and that the next, and so on; they are none of them free, but all originally depend on, and are determined by some cause out of the will: and so all freedom in the case is excluded, and no act of the will can be free, according to this notion of freedom. (*Works* 1, 173–4)

The passage—and the book more generally—is intellectually weighty. Many readers have grappled with it. The essential idea here and in the bulk of the text is this: freedom of the will, rightly defined, means that we can do whatever we want to do. All of our actions, then, proceed directly from our wills.

Those who opposed Edwards's position argued that he had bound the sinner's will such that the sinner could not choose what he desired (namely, God) but instead chose what he did not desire (unrighteousness). Edwards thought this response quite wrong. The key problem with a sinner, Edwards argued, is that though the human will is free, the sinful heart is corrupt, and thus leads mankind to naturally choose sin over righteousness. This act of choosing is free, because the will freely chooses, but the human heart is still bound with the chains of sin and thus can only choose God when the Holy Spirit regenerates the heart and causes it to know and love God.

ORIGINAL SIN

Freedom of the Will sold well and continues to exert theological influence to this day, as do other of Edwards's later works. *Original Sin* (pub. 1758), written in this era and published after Edwards's death, offered a bracing apologetic for the traditional Puritan view of the natural human condition as inherently "depraved," or sinful. Some in Edwards's day argued instead that the human will was inherently good. Against this position and its adherents, Edwards contended that all humans demonstrated, from birth, a "tendency" to sin, regardless of whether this tendency manifested itself in public or private sins. No one had to be taught to sin, but everyone sinned naturally and continually. "A propensity to that sin which brings God's eternal wrath and curse (which has been proved to belong to the nature of man) is evil," Edwards wrote,

> not only as it is calamitous and sorrowful, ending in great natural evil; but it is odious too, and detestable; as, by the supposition, it tends to that moral evil, by which the subject becomes odious in the sight of God, and liable, as such, to be condemned, and utterly rejected and cursed by him.
>
> This also makes it evident, that the state which it has been proved mankind are in, is a corrupt state in a moral sense, that it is inconsistent with the fulfillment of the law of God, which is the rule of moral rectitude and goodness. That tendency, which is opposite to that which the moral law requires and insists upon, and prone to that which the moral law utterly forbids, and eternally condemns the subject for, is doubtless a corrupt tendency, in a moral sense. (*Works* 3, 129)

Here, Edwards made the case that sin was evil not simply because it created harmful conditions, but because it offended a holy God. All humans sinned and transgressed God's "rule of moral rectitude and goodness." The argument is simple, but devastating. If human nature is inherently good, why do all people display a "corrupt tendency"? Where else does the tendency for sin come from but the fall of Adam and Eve, the original sin? Through this act all became sinners, as Edwards read Romans 3 to argue. Whether one judged the matter by plain observation or biblical testimony, Edwards claimed, one could not avoid the reality of original sin in the hearts of mankind. Though many continue to disagree with Edwards's central contention, *Original Sin* is still referenced in the current day as a sure-footed guide to questions about fallen human nature and personal suffering in the world.

LIFE'S PURPOSE AND VIRTUE'S IDENTITY

Edwards completed two other important books while in Stockbridge. The first, *Dissertation Concerning the End for Which God Created the World* (pub. 1765), tackled the heady question so often debated: why does the world exist? Edwards provided a God-centered answer to the question in a voluminous text:

> In the creature's knowing, esteeming, loving, rejoicing in, and praising God, the glory of God is both exhibited and acknowledged; his fullness is received and returned. Here is both an *emanation* and *remanation*. The refulgence shines upon and into the creature, and is reflected back to the luminary. The beams of glory come from God, and are something of God, and are refunded back again to their original. So that the whole is *of* God, and *to* God; and God is the beginning, middle and end in this affair. (*Works* 8, 531)

According to Edwards's theological calculations, all that exists does so for the glory of God. Human beings carry the unique ability to not merely please God through their existence, but to do so through conscious joy in their Creator. Whenever people seek to live according to the Scripture for the purpose of glorifying the Lord, they effectively send back—or "remanate"—the original "emanations" of God's goodness. To live for God, then, is to be a mirror and a conscious actor in the drama of divine magnification. Edwards's view invested even the most mundane existence with cosmic significance. All who lived could participate in this work of "remanation" and enter into the great story of God's creation. God and man could draw near to one another and share the great work of magnifying the glory of the Lord. This was not merely a theological proposition, but a narrative for life.

Edwards defined virtue, a hot topic in his day, along these lines in the companion to *Dissertation*, a book entitled *The Nature of True Virtue* (pub. 1765). Against some who defined virtue in secular terms, believing it to be a matter of choosing good over lesser options, Edwards framed the matter with characteristically God-centered dimensions. True virtue "most essentially consists in benevolence to Being in general." This "Being" was God, though in Edwards's system the term referred also to all of God's glorious creation. This virtue proceeded from an unselfish disposition that Edwards called "disinterested benevolence." Instead of seeking one's own glory, the virtuous person "being as it were under the sovereign dominion of *love to God*, does above all things seek the *glory of God*, and makes *this* his supreme, governing, and ultimate end" (*Works* 8, 559). The one who sought the glory of God would naturally be a virtuous, others-centered person. Though many people could perform isolated acts of benevolence, only the one focused on honoring God could perform the sweetest act the world could know: living kindly and sacrificially in service to the One who had Himself given His people all things. The chief gift, of course, was the Son of God, Jesus Christ, whose self-giving nature overturned the curse of death and sent a shock of glory throughout the universe that will ripple into eternity.

AN UNTOUCHED LITERARY LEGACY

Edwards had crafted these works throughout his time in Northampton and Stockbridge. He had written them in his mind and transferred portions to paper when he could. Though he did not live to see the positive impact of these important texts, he managed to finish a body of literature unlike any other ever produced by a pastor. It may well be that the world will never know another figure like Edwards, who stands alone in American church history as so significant a writer and thinker. Ironically, the posthumous publication of Edwards's most significant writings testifies eloquently to the concept of "disinterested benevolence." Seeking to redeem every moment for the glory of God, Edwards failed to publish most of these important treatises before his death. He thus failed to taste any significant reward for his efforts. This was not Edwards's purpose, of course. He sought simply to glorify his God with his mind and share his insights with God's people. As Edwards taught his readers, the Lord's gifts to his saints are not ends in themselves, but are "streams of glory" to be reflected back to heaven through the conscious attention of one's mind and heart. If one truly wished to follow Edwards's teaching, one would not ultimately praise the man or his talents. One would thank the Lord.

A FRESH CHALLENGE

The work at Stockbridge proceeded without major interruption until 1757, when the Edwards family received yet another shock. The trustees of the College of New Jersey, a fledgling Christian institution, sought Jonathan for the school's presidency, a post vacated by the death of Edwards's son-in-law, Aaron Burr, father of the famous dueler. Edwards was initially inclined to reject the offer, but as he conferred with friends and trusted colleagues, his mind began to change. After a formal council of advisors encouraged him to take the post, Edwards accepted, though not without some resignation.

As noted previously, Stockbridge had afforded Edwards many opportunities to produce important texts, a situation the

theologian was loath to give up. He had more books in the pipe-
line, including a project that covered the history of redemption
and would likely have emerged as one of the most important
books in Christian history. Though a college presidency appealed
to many of Edwards's instincts, he also struggled to give up his
missionary work. In addition, Edwards did not want to initiate
the laborious and extended process of relocation so late in life
with so large a family. He consented to the offer, however, writing a friend to request prayer in a tone that expressed a mixture
of trepidation and humility. "I desire, Sir," he wrote to Gideon
Hawley of Stockbridge, "your fervent prayer to God that I may
have his favor and assistance in this great and arduous [task], for
which I am so insufficient of myself" (*Works* 16, 738).

On February 16, 1758, the College of New Jersey, later
Princeton University, installed Edwards as its president. He
settled into the presidency in his first few weeks, working from
the expansive president's home next to Nassau Hall, the college's
academic building. He made initial contact with his students
when he met with a group who wished to ask him theological
questions. The meeting went nicely, as the students warmed to
Edwards's capacious intellect and personal concern. The presidency was off to a good start. Edwards lived alone in this month,
as he had traveled to Princeton without his family so that they
could prepare for the process of moving.

THE END OF A LIFE

A week after he became president of the college, Edwards underwent an inoculation for smallpox, a dreaded disease in his day.
Inoculations caused some controversy in the 1750s. They were a
risky venture, but some physicians, including the Philadelphia
doctor William Shippen, had proven their ability to safely treat
patients. After receiving much counsel on the matter, Edwards

decided to take the inoculation. Soon after the procedure, however, he found himself unable to swallow liquids. The disease consumed his body over a period of agonizing weeks while he battled starvation and fever with all the strength his thin frame could muster.

As the sun rose on March 22, 1758, Edwards knew that he would soon die. He called his daughter Lucy to his side and offered his final words. "Dear Lucy," he said in halting tones,

> It seems to me to be the will of God that I must shortly leave you; therefore give my kindest love to my dear wife, and tell her, that the uncommon union, which has so long subsisted between us, has been of such a nature, as I trust is spiritual, and therefore will continue forever; and I hope she will be supported under so great a trial, and submit cheerfully to the will of God. (Marsden, 494)

Before requesting a plain funeral, the loving father of ten addressed his children:

> And as to my children, you are now like to be left fatherless, which hope will be an inducement to you all to seek a Father, who will never fail you. (Marsden, 494)

Soon after, Edwards's breathing slowed, his heart stopped, and the pastor walked into his everlasting rest.

THE END OF AN UNCOMMON UNION

Sarah received the news a few days later while ill herself. Exhausted and stricken with grief, she found strength to write a few lines to her daughter Esther. Her words offer testimony to her confidence in God, even in the presence of almost unbearable grief:

A holy and good God has covered us with a dark cloud. Oh that we may kiss the rod [of reproof], and lay our hands on our mouths! The Lord has done it. He has made me adore his goodness, that we had him so long. But my God lives; and he has my heart. Of what a legacy my husband, and your father, has left us! We are all given to God: and there I am, and love to be. (Marsden, 495)

Without Jonathan, her rock and her love, Sarah struggled bravely to lead her family, but the task was too much. She fought illness and sleeplessness into the fall, when she contracted dysentery. On October 2, 1758, she passed away, joining her husband in heaven.

Having lost both of their parents, the Edwards children soldiered on. Trained by godly parents, they went on to live fruitful Christian lives as homemakers, mothers, statesmen, theologians, and politicians. Succeeding generations of the family produced more of the same, leaving a familial legacy that is to the present day untouched by any other American family. The Lord honored his faithful servant by blessing Jonathan's family for generations to come.

THE LEGACY OF JONATHAN EDWARDS

The life of Jonathan Edwards was monumental. It was a life lived for the glory of God. Though a pastor, theologian, and college president, Jonathan Edwards was fundamentally a follower of the Lord Jesus Christ. He accomplished much in his life, much that this text has celebrated, but all that he did began and ended with his sincere devotion to the Lord. Wherever he was, in whatever situation he found himself, whether a studious schoolboy or a towering intellectual, a chastened ex-pastor or an esteemed college president, Jonathan tenaciously pursued the Lord. He did so because he believed that he could only find lasting joy, taste true beauty, and know real forgiveness by worshiping the majestic God of the

Bible. His life, like his faith, was dramatic, for Jonathan realized more than most that he did not live in a small and insignificant little world, but in a realm between heaven and hell where one served either God or Satan. Through dogged study of the Bible and regular meditation upon its realities, Edwards entered into the great battle for souls on the side of the Lord. He knew great trial in his life, and he struggled with sin all of his days, but he never stopped seeking the reward set before the saints of God.

Edwards's life is a living example to all the children of God in the current day, to put aside the things that hinder our faith and distract our focus. Though we may not serve as pastors, every believer can serve the local church devoted to Jesus Christ with all of their heart in whatever role God gifts them for. Though we may not possess a prodigious intellect, we can use our minds to study the Word and apply it to all of life. Though we may not articulate the faith with fresh insight and stirring language, we share the gospel and lead souls to Christ. It is not genius that the Lord seeks after, but faith. This Jonathan had; this we must have as well, in order that like him, we may one day meet the sovereign Lord of all the earth and bow before him in worship that will never cease.

A LIFE LIVED FOR GOD

There is much to celebrate about the life of Jonathan Edwards. As we have seen in our brief survey of his life and thought, Edwards wore many hats in his day. He was a uniquely talented pastor and scholar.

We have briefly covered some of the philosophical contributions Edwards made. Masterpieces like *Freedom of the Will*, ironically penned in a fortified enclosure in the New England wilderness, established Edwards in his day as America's foremost philosopher. Over 250 years later in an age that boasts a much livelier academic climate, no American has surpassed Edwards in this field.

We have looked extensively at Edwards's sermons. Regardless of background or conviction, one cannot help but marvel at Edwards's preaching. As he honed his writing style, Edwards became a masterful preacher, able to simultaneously enlighten the mind, sear the heart, and stir the soul. The sermons that produce this effect, often spanning ten to twenty single-spaced pages of text, pack more punch than many full-length books. To put it succinctly, Edwards was one of the most able preachers of Christian history.

We have also observed Edwards's ability as a theologian. His work in texts like *Distinguishing Marks* sets him apart as a skillful, biblically oriented thinker. In a number of areas—salvation, holiness, and the afterlife, among others—Edwards distinguished himself as a rigorous and insightful theologian. He made his mark in this role, we might note, in the context of pastoral ministry.

As the story of Edwards's life has unfolded, we have also seen other roles Edwards filled in his busy life—husband, father, college president, mentor. We have seen that Jonathan Edwards was a uniquely gifted man who accomplished a great deal in the time given him by the Lord. The Northampton pastor was a choice servant of God.

In seeking the essence of Edwards, though, we have argued that he was, at his core, nothing more than a Christian man. This is not to minimize him. We have in fact taken pains to explore his multidimensionality and to benefit from it. But we have suggested that Edwards's identity centered in his Christian identity. Jonathan Edwards was fundamentally a Christian man. He lived for the glory of God. Throughout his life, he woke each morning with a thirst to magnify the Lord who had saved his soul from hell and given him eternal life. His days were filled with activity toward that end. If we do not understand anything else about

Jonathan Edwards, we should understand that. He was a Christian—not a super-Christian, not a man who walked an inch off of the ground, but a believer in the Lord Jesus Christ who fought the same fight we do and loved the same God we love.

If we would home in on the essence of Edwards, we would do well to home in on the essence of his faith. The pastor lived a great life because he worshiped a great God and savored that reality each day that he lived. In his mind, God loomed large over the great and small things of life, directing them according to an all-wise providence. He was not limited or weak. He was magnificent, and He gave his creation the opportunity to taste the goodness of life lived for Him. He had spoken to humanity in His Word, enabling all who yearned after a savior to find Him in the revelation that disclosed the person and work of Jesus Christ. At its core, Edwards's existence centered around a personal God who offered atoning salvation to a fallen race through His inspired Word. So too must ours, for our justification and our delight.

The life and thought of Jonathan Edwards calls us to emulate him today. Living in a very different world, with unique challenges and opportunities, we have the same ability to seize life for the glory of God. We who love and worship Jesus Christ will find Him just as satisfying in our modern era as Edwards did in his own day. May we learn from his example, glean his wisdom, and above all, devote ourselves to pursuing our great God on a daily basis just as Jonathan Edwards, lover of God, did so many years ago.

Following Edwards

Living Life for God's Glory

Early on, Jonathan Edwards discovered the meaning of life—to joyfully glorify God. In fulfilling this end, Christians should take stock of their gifts. What natural strengths and abilities do we have? Once we have studied the Word, prayed about this question, and sought responses from our pastors and fellow church members, we should then ask, Where can I use these gifts for God's glory? What can I do with the life I have to "remanate," or reflect, glory back to God? What can I do to proclaim the gospel in this world? How can I advance God's kingdom? Who can I reach? These and similar questions, asked in concert with Bible study and wise counsel, will lead us to use our lives well.

Dying Well

As we seek to live well, so should we seek to die well. Like Edwards, we must seize our season of death as a last opportunity to glorify our Lord. In our final act, we must hold fast to our faith and testify to those around us that we do not prepare for our termination, but our release.

Though we do not know when the last hour will come, we can constantly prepare for it, just as Jonathan did. In fact, if we do so, we will find that living well and dying well are really the same thing for a Christian. To live well *is* to prepare to die and to stand before our Savior with a clear conscience. Without morbidity, but with a continual sense of confidence in the Lord and His plan, let us live with every ounce of strength, every atom of our being, for the glory of God. Let us follow in the steps of Jonathan Edwards, faithful witness, devout Christian, lover of God.

Part 2

Beauty

Chapter 9

THE BEAUTY OF GOD

What is the starting point of Christian faith? When you wake up and begin your morning study of the Bible, what are you seeking to find out? Or, to go back in time a bit, why did you begin to study the Bible in the first place?

The starting point of religion or spirituality for many today is the individual and his or her subjective feelings. What do I want? What do I need, in a spiritual sense? How can religion, and whatever superpower lies behind it, serve me and meet my desires? In short, what can I get from this deal? Sadly, even Christians are not immune to these questions.

Though biblical spirituality certainly addresses and responds to the heart cries of lost sinners, its starting point is nothing other than the living God. From the awe-inspiring opening of Genesis 1:1—"In the beginning, God"—to the cataclysmic ending of Revelation 21:22—"in the city . . . is the Lord God the Almighty and the Lamb"—the Bible declares without interruption or apology that God is the starting and ending points of true religion. As portrayed in the Bible, God does not bow to man. Man, lost and helpless, bows to God.

Jonathan Edwards seized upon this central truth early in his life. When he was a young, budding scholar at Yale University, he suddenly discovered in his daily meditation on the Scripture "a sense of the glory of the divine being" that transformed his life (*Works* 16, 492). Reflecting later on this chrysalis moment, Edwards preached that with genuine faith "There is not only a speculatively judging that God is gracious, but a sense how amiable God is upon that account, or a sense of the beauty of this divine attribute" (*Works* 17, 413). When a sinner comes to understand the graciousness of God, and the majesty of His character, they see with piercing clarity that "There is a divine and superlative glory in these things; an excellency that is of a vastly higher kind, and more sublime nature than in other things; a glory greatly distinguishing them from all that is earthly and temporal" (*Works* 17, 413). In this chapter, we examine the center of Edwards's theology, the Lord God, who formed the first link in a cycle of beauty that begins with creation and runs its course to heaven.

THE STARTING POINT OF THEOLOGY

When the young Yale tutor pushed past the muddle of everyday life and became aware of God's ineffable character, it was as if scales fell from his eyes. The theater, the cosmic drama, of God's reign over the world came into view, and Jonathan stood transfixed. He saw heaven and hell, man and Satan, in clearer view than ever before. But above all, Jonathan saw the Lord. He knew then that God was no abstract deity, but was a personal being whom all creation could not contain. In his sermon "God's Excellencies," preached in 1720, the same year of his spiritual breakthrough, Jonathan considered the qualities of God that robed Him in splendor. He prefaced his analysis with a warning of his unworthiness for the task:

> What poor, miserable creatures, then, are we, to talk of the infinite and transcendent gloriousness of the great, eternal, and almighty Jehovah; what miserable work do worms of the dust make, when

they get upon such a theme as this, which the very angels do stammer at? But yet, although we are but worms and insects, less than insects, nothing at all, yea, less than nothing, yet so has God dignified us, that he has made [us] for this very end: to think and be astonished [at] his glorious perfections. And this is what we hope will be our business to all eternity; to think on, to delight [in], to speak of, and sing forth, the infinite excellencies of the Deity. He has made us capable of understanding so much of him here as is necessary in order to our acceptable worshipping and praising him, and he has instructed us, and taught us, as little ignorant babes and infants, and has helped our weak understanding by his instructions; he has told us what he is, has condescended to our poor capacities and described himself to us after the manner of men: as men, when they teach children, must teach them after their manner of thinking of things, and come down to their childish capacities, so has God taught us concerning himself. (*Works* 10, 417–18)

The one who spoke of God, in Edwards's mind, did so as a created, lowly being, a "worm of the dust." This is a striking beginning for the study of God. One did not discuss the Lord as an abstract concept. One begins the study of theology lying in the dust beside the prophet Ezekiel, heart pounding, eyes straining to shut out the piercing glory of God (Ezek. 1:28–2:10).

Beginning his study of God with the Word of God, Edwards, like Ezekiel, raised himself from the ground and began to speak of what he saw. God's beauty had numerous facets and required all of man's senses to comprehend it. Edwards identified seven attributes that demonstrated God's excellency, or beauty. Edwards's descriptions of these are worth quoting at length. One should ponder them slowly and meditatively, for they provide rich food for one's spiritual nourishment.

ETERNALITY AND SELF-EXISTENCE

The first of these was longevity and independence of existence. Edwards strove to wrap his mind around the reality that God had always existed. He wrote,

> [I]t is necessary that that which hath a beginning must have some cause, some author that gave it a beginning, but God never had a beginning; there was none before him, and therefore none that gave him his being. He thanks no one for his being; doth not, nor ever did depend upon any for it, but receives his being from himself, and depends alone on himself. Neither doth he thank anyone for anything he enjoys: his power, his wisdom, his excellency, his glory, his honor, and [his] authority are his own, and received from none other; he possesses them and he will possess them: he is powerful and he will be powerful; he is glorious and he will be glorious; he is infinitely honorable, but he receives his honor from himself; he is infinitely happy and he will be infinitely happy; he reigns and rules over the whole universe, and he will rule and do what he pleases, in the armies of heaven and amongst the inhabitants of the earth. Poor nothing creatures can do nothing towards controlling of [Him]; they, with all their power conjoined, which is but weakness, can't deprive Jehovah of any of these things. He was just the same, in all respects, from all eternity as he is now; as he was, infinite ages before the foundations of the world were laid, so he is now and so he will be, with exactly the same glory and happiness uninterrupted, immovable and unchangeable, the same yesterday, today, and forever. (*Works* 10, 419)

As Edwards saw Him, God dwelt in a realm of glory untouched by time and age, dependent on nothing for His timeless existence. Theologians use the term *aseity* to describe the utter independence and power of God. God "thanks no one for his being," as Edwards put it. His existence is underived. He is altogether powerful, needing no one, never aging, never changing, never growing weary. From the beginning of time until the end of the universe, God exists.

One of the central ironies of the Christian life is that the more we come to learn about God, the more awesome He appears. No matter how high-powered one's mind may be, He is the "immovable and unchangeable" one, a timeless figure from a realm outside our own. Finite creatures simply cannot comprehend His duration of existence, hard as we try. The more we understand, the more we realize how little we truly know.

GREATNESS

God's greatness, or exalted status, stands beside His length of existence as a second element of His excellency. Over every living thing, Edwards preached, stands God:

> God is infinitely exalted above all created beings in greatness. This earth appears to us as a very great thing. When we think of the large countries and continents, the vast oceans, and the great distance between one country and another, the whole, together, appears very great and vast; but especially doth the great universe surprise us with its greatness, to which, without doubt, this vast earth, as we call it, is less than any mote or dust, that ever we saw, is to the whole earth; but how shall we be surprised when we think that all this vast creation, making the most of it we can, is infinitely less, when compared with the greatness of God, than the least discernible atom is to the whole creation! (*Works* 10, 419)

Over all the heights of the universe stands the Lord God. There is no point of comparison between God and all else, wrote Edwards; He "is infinitely exalted above all." God has no end, and one cannot map out His coordinates. He is vast and mysterious, greater than the greatest things we can imagine. His scope speaks to His majestic beauty.

LOVELINESS

The third attribute that shows God's beauty is His loveliness or splendor. Edwards used picturesque images to describe God's bountiful loveliness:

> The beauty of trees, plants, and flowers, with which God has bespangled the face of the earth, is delightful; the beautiful frame of the body of man, especially in its perfection, is astonishing; the beauty of the moon and stars is wonderful; the beauty of [the] highest heavens is transcendent; the excellency of angels and the saints in light is very glorious: but it is all deformity and darkness in comparison of the brighter glories and beauties of the Creator of all, for "behold even to the moon, and it shineth not" (Job 25:5); that is, think of the excellency of God and the moon will not seem to shine to you, God's excellency so much outshines [it]. And the stars are not pure in his sight, and so we know that at the great day when God appears, the sun shall be turned into darkness, shall hide his face as if he were ashamed to see himself so much outshined; and the very angels, they hide their faces before him; the highest heavens are not clean in his sight, and he charges his angels with folly. (Works 10, 421)

While a pastor in Northampton, Edwards loved to take long walks or ride his horse through the stunning New England countryside. Though he relished the outdoors, he knew that the beauty of the earth was nothing but a passing shadow compared to the beauty of God. The shining stars and the brisk Northampton nights, though grand, were still "not pure in his sight." Even the very realm of the Lord, "the highest heavens," pale in comparison to Him. God's beauty is perfect, and all appears unclean in comparison.

POWER

The fourth attribute that displayed the beauty of God was His power. Over the most powerful people of the earth, God reigned as King:

> When he pleases, one king must die, and who he pleases must reign in his room; armies conquer or are conquered according as he will have it: "The king's heart is in the hand of the Lord, and he turns them as the rivers of water" [Proverbs 21:1]. Thus he holds an absolute and uncontrollable government in the world; and thus he has done from the beginning, and thus he will do to the end of all things. Neither is his dominion confined to the children of men, but he rules the whole creation. He gives commands to the seas, and has appointed them bounds which they cannot pass; "which removeth the mountains, and they know it not who overturneth them in his anger; which shaketh the earth out of its place, and the pillars thereof tremble; who commandeth the sun and it riseth not; who sealeth up the stars, which maketh Arcturus and Orion, and the chambers of the south; who doth great things past finding out; yea, wonders without number" [Job 9:5–7, Job 9:9–10]. (*Works* 10, 422)

Edwards summarized this material by noting,

> What a vast and uncontrollable dominion hath the almighty God. The kings of the earth are not worthy of the name, for they are not able to execute their authority in their narrow bounds, except by the power and assistance of their subjects, but God rules most absolutely the whole universe by himself; kings rule, perhaps

sometimes for forty years, but God's kingdom is an everlasting
kingdom, and of his dominion there is no end. Well, therefore,
may he be said to be the blessed and only potentate, King of
Kings, and Lord of Lords. (*Works* 10, 422)

Against the self-importance of earthly rulers, Edwards asserted
the sovereignty of the God of the Bible. Kings thought that
they governed with unchallenged authority, but Edwards's God
"rules the whole creation," "gives commands to the seas," and
oversees "most absolutely the whole universe by himself" while
He advances His "everlasting kingdom." The Lord controls the
hearts of men but is Himself "uncontrollable." The power of this
God is itself a work of beauty, an aesthetic performance. In the
hurricane's squall, the shuddering of the earth, the eruption of a
volcano, we glimpse the force that formed this world and rules
over it until the end of the age.

WISDOM

The fifth element of God's excellence and beauty is His wisdom.
Edwards turned again to the best of human beings to compare
them to God:

> The wisest of men, how little do they know, how frequently are
> they deceived and frustrated, and their wisdom turned to foolish-
> ness, their politic designs undermined; but when was the time
> that God's wisdom failed, that he did not obtain his end, although
> all the bleak army of hell are continually endeavoring to counter-
> work him? When was it that God altered his mind and purpose, or
> took a wrong step in the government of the world? (*Works* 10, 423)

Edwards revealed that God's purposes are not frustrated. What
He plans according to His stores of wisdom, He does. The earth

and all who live in it take their cues from Him. He is quite unlike even "the wisest of men," who cannot help but see "their wisdom turned to foolishness" and their "politic designs undermined." God may face resistance to His plans, but only for so long as He tolerates it. No man can stand before Him, and no one can resist His will (Rom. 9:19).

Edwards believed strongly in the infallibility of God, His inability to make an error or mistake of any kind. God's infinite knowledge undergirded this trait:

> Solomon was sensible that there was need of uncommon and extraordinary wisdom to rule such a kingdom as he had; but what wisdom, what vast knowledge and infinite penetration must he have, who has every being in the world to rule and govern; who rules every thought, and every purpose, every motion and action, not only of angels and men, but of every creature, great and small, even to every little atom in the whole creation, and that forever and ever? What infinite wisdom and knowledge is necessary and requisite in order to this! But this God doth; this he hath done and will do. All the changes and alterations that happen in all the world, heaven and earth, whether great or never so small, he knows it altogether, even to the least insect that crawls upon the earth, or dust that flies in the air, and it is all from his disposal, and according to his eternal determination. (*Works* 10, 423)

Edwards compared the Lord to Solomon, the wisest man who ever lived. Solomon, Edwards noted, used his intelligence and discernment "to rule such a kingdom as he had," but God "rules every thought, and every purpose, every motion and action" of all that will ever live and breathe on the earth. To reign wisely, Solomon collected whatever knowledge he could; God, however, possesses all the knowledge of the world without sending so much as a solitary angel from heaven to report back. In Edwards's simple phrase, "He knows it altogether." The knowledge of God extends over and into all things. The Lord is by definition not a limited, finite being like a human. He knows all and exercises complete control over all. If it were not so, Edwards's words indicate, He would not be God.

HOLINESS

The sixth quality of God that rendered Him beautiful in the mind of the Massachusetts theologian was His holiness. "Now God is infinitely holy," Edwards declared,

> and infinitely exalted therein, above the holy angels and all creatures; there is not the least tincture of defilement or pollution in the Deity, but he is infinitely far from it: he is all pure light, without mixture of darkness; he hates and abhors sin above all things, 'tis what is directly contrary to his nature. This, his great holiness, has he made known to us by his justice, truth, and faithfulness in all his dispensations towards us, and by the pure holiness of his laws and commands.
>
> Holiness used to be for a distinguishing attribute between the God of Israel and other gods, Daniel 4:8, "But at last Daniel came in before me, whose name is Belteshazzar, according to the name of my God, and in whom is the spirit of the holy gods"; and so in the next verse, "because I know the holy gods is in thee." Likewise, in the eighteenth verse, "the Holy One" is a name that God seems to delight [in]. 'Tis that attribute which continually ravishes the seraphims, and causes them continually to cry in their praises, without ceasing, "holy, holy, holy." This is the sound with which the highest heaven, the palace of God, perpetually rings, and [it] will ring on earth in the glorious times that are hastening. (Works 10, 423–4)

Above the greatest, purest beings one could conceive, the Lord shone in the mind of Edwards and the world beyond "in the splendor of his holiness" (Ps. 96:9). Using one of his favorite metaphors, Edwards preached that the Lord "is all pure light, without mixture of darkness." As with so much of Edwards's discussion of the Lord's attributes, moral and ethical description mingles with aesthetic and physical description. The Lord's appearance relates directly to His works even as His works relate directly to His appearance. He does that which is of the light, and He Himself is the light. His character, like His person, radiates. His holiness is the spark that illuminates the heavens and the earth.

GOODNESS

The seventh and final attribute described by Edwards as a part of God's overarching excellence was His goodness. This attribute consisted primarily of a blend of kindness and justice that God frequently manifested to the world:

> God is infinitely exalted above all created beings in goodness. Goodness and royal bounty, mercy, and clemency is the glory of earthly monarchs and princes, but in this is the Lord, our God, infinitely exalted above them. God delights in the welfare and prosperity of his creatures; he delights in making of them exceeding happy and blessed, if they will but accept of the happiness which he offers.
>
> All creatures do continually live upon the bounty of God; he maintains the whole creation of his mere goodness: every good thing that is enjoyed is a part of his bounty. When kings are bountiful, and dispense good things to their subjects, they do but give that which the Almighty before gave to them. So merciful and so full of pity is God, that when miserable man, whom He had no need of, who did Him no good, nor could be of any advantage to

Him, had made himself miserable by his rebellion against God, He took such pity on him that He sent His only Son to undergo his torment for him, that he might be delivered and set free. And now He offers freely, to bestow upon those rebels, complete and perfect happiness to all eternity upon this, His Son's account. There never was such an instance of goodness, mercy, pity, and compassion since the world began; all the mercy and goodness amongst creatures fall infinitely short of it: this is goodness that never was, never will, never can be paralleled by any other beings. (*Works* 10, 424)

Edwards compared the potent goodness of God with the goodness of the most powerful earthly figure, the king. His comparison showed how much greater God was than even the most majestic emperor. The king could show bounty, mercy, and clemency, but all his goodness paled before the supernatural kindness of the Lord.

In Edwards's conception, God's goodness meant that "he delights in making" His people "exceeding happy and blessed." The highest expression of this goodness was the crucifixion of the Son of God. In the death of Jesus Christ, God showed His kindness and love to sinners on a scale only infinity could contain. "There never was such an instance of goodness, mercy, pity, and compassion," Edwards asserted, for "this is goodness that never was, never will, never can be paralleled by any other beings." No one else could qualify to take on the sins of mankind, bear the wrath of God, and cleanse the guilty but the Son of God. One could spot God's goodness in countless forms throughout the world—whether in His general care for mankind or His special care for His people—but nowhere in greater measure than in the death of Jesus Christ.

The beauty of God was, in the eyes of Edwards, a multifaceted diamond, a precious collection of attributes in their purest form: self-existence, greatness, loveliness, power, wisdom, holiness, and goodness. Over all the earth and all the created order stood this Lord, beautiful for the perfections of His person. Edwards discovered these perfections in Scripture and thus began his spiritual life and theological thought from a God-centered starting point.

MAKING GOD'S BEAUTY KNOWN

Because of His majesty, unfolded in the seven attributes examined above, the Lord properly delighted in Himself and the mere presence of His own beauty. Before one discussed creation, Christ's incarnation, the church, or heaven, one had to realize that God's self-sufficiency, His perfect fullness and majesty, rendered Him the only figure in existence who could justly glory in and be satisfied by Himself. Edwards articulated this foundational point in his *Dissertation Concerning the End for Which God Created the World*, where he argued that

> God's love to himself, and his own attributes, will therefore make him delight in that which is the use, end and operation of these attributes. If one highly esteem and delight in the virtues of a friend, as wisdom, justice, etc., that have relation to action, this will make him delight in the exercise and genuine effects of these virtues: so if God both esteem and delight in his own perfections and virtues, he can't but value and delight in the expressions and genuine effects of them. So that in delighting in the expressions of his perfections, he manifests a delight in his own perfections themselves: or in other words, he manifests a delight in himself; and in making these expressions of his own perfections his end, *he makes himself his end*. (*Works* 8, 437)

Edwards elaborated on this point, developing the idea that God's focal point in His existence was the enjoyment of His own glory:

> The moral rectitude of God's heart must consist in a proper and due respect of his heart to things that are objects of moral respect: that is, to intelligent beings capable of moral actions and relations. And therefore it must chiefly consist in giving due respect to that Being to whom most is due; yea, infinitely most, and in effect all. For God is infinitely and most worthy of regard. (*Works* 8, 421–22)

The essence of this section is that God's majestic nature not only enables but calls Him to glory in Himself. As a perfect being, a figure of absolute eternality, greatness, loveliness, power, wisdom, holiness, and goodness, God deserved to celebrate and glorify Himself. This assertion of Edwards intensifies one's understanding of the beauty and worth of God. Because of His excellent nature, God is wholly justified in seeking glory and honor and praise and worship for Himself. This is the foundation for Edwards's entire theological system, and it shapes his view of creation, Christ, the church, and heaven, as subsequent chapters will show.

Edwards's treatment of the traits of God offers a framework by which to comprehend and approach the Lord. God alone is self-sufficient and worthy of worship. Writing three hundred years ago, Edwards illuminated this fundamental reality of Scripture and showed that God, possessing beauty beyond human comprehension, is the only being deserving of worship. We began our study in the dust, like the prophet Ezekiel, and we end like another Old Testament figure, Moses, coming down from the mountain with faces shining from the glory of God we have just glimpsed.

Pursuing Beauty

The Necessity of Humility

In the current day, we are taught by many writers and preachers, religious or otherwise, to begin our spiritual quests, our faith journeys, with ourselves. We are encouraged to seek God because He can meet our needs and satisfy our deepest desires. There is some truth to this claim, but the fundamental duty of every person before the holy God is to humble themselves (Eccl. 12:13). Unlike what certain leaders tell us, we do not come to God and begin articulating a list of deep-seated desires and needs. If we have biblical faith, we must fall before our majestic God, trembling to be in His presence, rejoicing that because of the blood of Christ we have access to Him and will not be crushed by the weight of His glory. If we have been taught that religion is all about us, if we find ourselves breathing the "me-centered" air of our day, then we must cleanse ourselves, reorient our minds, and approach God in a new way.

Because God is God, He must first be honored and treasured and reverenced. In our hearts, we must follow Edwards as he follows various biblical figures, and humble ourselves before the Lord (2 Chron. 7:14, for example). In doing so, we will truly care for ourselves. In dying to ourselves, we will live to Christ (Phil. 1:20). We need not reject concern for our souls and our eternal good, but we do need to rightly focus that concern upon a righteous, holy God.

Toward this end, the study of God's attributes provides nearly endless fuel for the daily life of the Christian. Contrary to what many think, these doctrines are not dry or lifeless, but packed with spiritual food by which to nourish our lives. Meditating on and applying each of the seven attributes covered above to real-life situations will transform our daily lives. We may not be able to change all of the circumstances that affect us, but we can make our lives beautiful as we study the beauty of the God we serve.

Chapter 10

THE BEAUTY OF CREATION

One day, while still a student, Edwards took a walk in his father's pasture, meandering around stalks of grass, gazing at the sky. He later said of that stroll,

> And as I was walking there, and looked up on the sky and clouds; there came into my mind, a sweet sense of the glorious majesty and grace of God, that I know not how to express. I seemed to see them both in a sweet conjunction: majesty and meekness joined together: it was a sweet and gentle, and holy majesty; and also a majestic meekness; an awful sweetness; a high, and great, and holy gentleness.
>
> After this my sense of divine things gradually increased, and became more and more lively, and had more of that inward sweetness. The appearance of everything was altered: there seemed to be, as it were, a calm, sweet cast, or appearance of divine glory, in almost everything. (*Works* 16, 793–4)

The walk was a special one, full of communion with the divine. It was by no means the only time in his life that Edwards tasted the beauty of God's created realm, however. A theologian with a deep love for nature, Edwards regularly meditated on the wisdom and beauty of God while walking, riding his horse, or working outside. So far from the stereotype of Edwards as a dry and dusty thinker, his love for nature reveals his deeply aesthetic side.

This chapter examines Edwards's understanding of nature as a testimony to the beauty of God and the communication in visible form of His excellence. It examines several facets of his love for nature—that it was wisely designed, that it played a unique role in the display and reflection of the beauty of the Lord, and that it pictured certain spiritual realities, a study known as typology. In sum, we will see that Edwards loved nature for deeply biblical reasons and saw it as a living exhibition of the wisdom and beauty of God.

THE WISE DESIGN OF CREATION

From an early age, when most children are content simply to trample plants and animals, birds and trees, young Jonathan applied his mind to the science of nature and the workings of the world. When he was twenty, he published a brief treatise on the habits of spiders that won him international acclaim. Called the "Spider Letter," the document demonstrates Jonathan's powers of observation and reveals his tendency, even early in his life, to trace the hand of God in the world of nature:

> In a very calm serene day in the forementioned time of year, standing at some distance between the end of an house or some other opaque body, so as just to hide the disk of the sun and keep off his dazzling rays, and looking along close by the side of it, I have seen vast multitudes of little shining webs and glistening strings, brightly reflecting the sunbeams, and some of them of a great length, and at such a height that one would think that they were tacked to the vault of the heavens, and would be burnt like tow in the sun, making a very pleasing as well as surprising appearance. . . . But that which is most astonishing is that very often there

appears at the end of these webs, spiders sailing in the air with
them, doubtless with abundance of pleasure, though not with
so much as I have beheld them and shewed them to others. And
since I have seen these things I have been very conversant with
spiders. (*Works* 16, 163–4)

Edwards showed an expert eye for the patterns and systems of the
spider world. Behind this research and the curiosity that drove it
was reverence for the natural order, a love nurtured by both the
preaching of his father and his own exploration of nature. From
his earliest days, Edwards saw what so many people miss in the
modern rush of life: the world contains great elegance and precise design. The young man saw these truths not simply in mead-
ows and trees, but also in spiders, creatures that most people
would rather run from than study. He knew, however, that God
had created all things and that one could discover His beauty in
even the strangest of places and the lowliest of creatures.

Finding God's imprint in the natural order was no theological
rabbit trail, but was one of the most natural endeavors of mankind. God, it turned out, had placed humanity in His personal
laboratory, with evidence of His presence flowing into all corners
of the earth. Man's duty was not to ponder whether the divine
scientist existed, but to study His creation in all of its intricate
beauty.

Edwards showed a similar capacity for observation in a work
entitled "Of the Rainbow." Where, he wondered, does the rainbow come from? He answered,

It cannot be the cloud from whence this [rainbow] reflection is
made, as was once thought, for we almost always see the ends
of rainbows come down, even in amongst the trees, below the
hills, and to the very ground, where we know there is no part of
the cloud there but what descends in drops of rain. And [I] can

convince any man by ocular demonstration in two minutes on a
fair day that the reflection is from drops, by only taking a little
water into my mouth, and standing between the sun and something that looks a little darkish, and spirting of it into the air so as
to disperse all into fine drops; and there will appear as complete
and plain a rainbow, with all the colors, as ever was seen in the
heavens. And there will appear the same, if the sun is near enough
to the horizon, upon fine drops of water dashed up by a stick from
a puddle. (*Works* 6, 298)

Edwards not only studied the spider in his backyard, but also an-
alyzed the strange and beautiful phenomena of the world around
him. Though he had an aesthetic appreciation for the rainbow,
Edwards's belief in a Creator-God also drove him to try to find
a rationale for the rainbow's magical appearance. His analysis
shows both a keen mind and a voracious curiosity, each of which
he used to trace the Lord's craftsmanship in the created realm.

THE NATURAL WORLD AS A REALM OF BEAUTY

On the same day that Edwards took his deeply moving walk in
his father's field, he found that

God's excellency, his wisdom, his purity and love, seemed to
appear in everything; in the sun, moon and stars; in the clouds, and
blue sky; in the grass, flowers, trees; in the water, and all nature;
which used greatly to fix my mind. I often used to sit and view the
moon, for a long time; and so in the daytime, spent much time in
viewing the clouds and sky, to behold the sweet glory of God in
these things: in the meantime, singing forth with a low voice, my
contemplations of the Creator and Redeemer. And scarce anything,
among all the works of nature, was so sweet to me as thunder and
lightning. Formerly, nothing had been so terrible to me. I used to

be a person uncommonly terrified with thunder: and it used to
strike me with terror, when I saw a thunderstorm rising. But now,
on the contrary, it rejoiced me. I felt God at the first appearance of
a thunderstorm. And used to take the opportunity at such times, to
fix myself to view the clouds, and see the lightnings play, and hear
the majestic and awful voice of God's thunder: which often times
was exceeding entertaining, leading me to sweet contemplations of
my great and glorious God. And while I viewed, used to spend my
time, as it always seemed natural to me, to sing or chant forth my
meditations; to speak my thoughts in soliloquies, and speak with a
singing voice. (*Works* 16, 794)

Earlier, we observed that Edwards found abundant evidence of
a wise design in creation. During his meaningful nature walk,
he focused on the created order as the physical display of the
personal beauty of God and His works. He contemplated his
physical surroundings "to behold the sweet glory of God in these
things." With his high view of the Lord and His beauty, Edwards
believed that it was only natural for the Lord to create a world
in which His "excellent perfections" could shine. Not content
with mere self-appreciation of His own beauty, He set in motion
a cycle of glory that began with Himself and continued to the
creation, a realm that reflected His character for all to see.

Edwards developed this doctrine in *The Dissertation Concerning the End for Which God Created the World*. There, he
argued that

there is an infinite fullness of all possible good in God, a fullness
of every perfection, of all excellency and beauty, and of infinite
happiness. And as this fullness is capable of communication or
emanation . . . so it seems a thing amiable and valuable in itself
that it should be communicated or flow forth, that this infinite
fountain of good should send forth abundant streams, that this

infinite fountain of light should, diffusing its excellent fullness,
pour forth light all around. . . . Thus it is fit, since there is an infinite fountain of light and knowledge, that this light should shine
forth in beams of communicated knowledge and understanding:
and as there is an infinite fountain of holiness, moral excellence
and beauty, so it should flow out in communicated holiness. And
that as there is an infinite fullness of joy and happiness, so these
should have an emanation, and become a fountain flowing out in
abundant streams, as beams from the sun. (*Works* 8, 432–33)

As Edwards conceived it, the world was no product of chance.
Every atom and molecule is created, on the contrary, to receive
and display the beauty and glory of God. The Lord is "an infinite
fountain of holiness, moral excellence, and beauty," and the earth
is the basin into which His beauty is poured. In Edwards's eyes,
the earth drinks richly from this fountain, for heaven "send[s]
forth abundant streams" with the same intensity and frequency
"as beams from the sun." Just as the sun continuously sends out
its rays, the rays of the Lord's splendor flow without interruption
into the earth, the catch-basin of God's glory.

God declared His absolute supremacy throughout Scripture,
Edwards noted, providing abundant testimony to the theologian's
argument that nature existed to display and reflect the beauty of
the Lord. "It is manifest," the pastor declared,

that the Scriptures speak, on all occasions, as though God made
himself his end in all his works: and as though the same Being,
who is the first cause of all things, were the supreme and last end
of all things. Thus in Isaiah 44:6, "Thus saith the Lord, the King of
Israel, and his redeemer the Lord of hosts, I am the first, I also am
the last, and besides me there is no God." Isaiah 48:12, "I am the
first, and I am the last." Revelation 1:8, "I am Alpha and Omega, the
beginning and the ending, saith the Lord, which is, and was, and

which is to come, the Almighty." Revelation 1:11, "I am Alpha and Omega, the first and the last." Revelation 1:17, "I am the first and the last." Revelation 21:6, "And he said unto me, it is done, I am Alpha and Omega, the beginning and the end." Revelation 22:13, "I am Alpha and Omega, the beginning and the end, the first and the last."

Edwards then interpreted these lofty statements:

And when God is so often spoken of as the last as well as the first, and the end as well as the beginning, what is meant (or at least implied) is, that as he is the first efficient cause and fountain from whence all things originate, so he is the last final cause for which they are made; the final term to which they all tend in their ultimate issue. This seems to be the most natural import of these expressions; and is confirmed by other parallel passages, as Romans 11:36, "For of him and through him and to him are all things." Colossians 1:16, "For by him were all things created, that are in heaven, and that are in earth, visible and invisible, whether they be thrones or dominions, principalities or powers, all things were created by him, and for him." Hebrews 2:10, "For it became him, by whom are all things, and for whom are all things." In Proverbs 16:4 'tis said expressly, "The Lord hath made all things for himself." (*Works* 8, 467)

These citations testify to the point Edwards made about the purpose of creation. In the biblical mind, creation is not an end in itself. It is a subordinate realm, a place made by the Lord for His purposes, chief of which is His self-glorification. When humanity praises nature for its beauty and fails to acknowledge God's authorship, it commits serious blasphemy. The world is beautiful in many respects, but in all of these the glory of God is displayed like a towering neon sign planted by the Almighty. In Edwards's theology, one cannot logically identify a scene of beauty and leave it disconnected from the character of its designer. Wherever one finds instances of beauty, one sees a picture and reflection of the "Alpha and Omega," the one who "made all things for himself."

It was from this foundation that the pastor understood all the sweet scenes the natural order provided. In "Beauty of the World," an early piece on nature by Edwards, he discussed various aspects of the creation with an eye to the design—and Designer—behind them:

> [T]here is a great suitableness between the objects of different senses, as between sounds, colors, and smells as between the colors of the woods and flowers, and the smell, and the singing of birds—which 'tis probable consist in a certain proportion of the vibrations that are made in the different organs. So there are innumerable other agreeablenesses of motions, figures, etc.: the gentle motions of trees, of lily, etc., as it is agreeable to other things that represent calmness, gentleness and benevolence, etc. The fields and woods seem to rejoice, and how joyful do the birds seem to be in it. How much a resemblance is there of every grace in the fields covered with plants and flowers, when the sun shines serenely and undisturbedly upon them. How a resemblance, I say, of every grace and beautiful disposition of mind; of an inferior towards a superior cause, preserver, benevolent benefactor, and a fountain of happiness.

The harmony and order of creation, reflected in things like "the number of vibrations that are caused in the optic nerve" and the "agreeablenesses of motions" of trees and plants, testified in the eyes of Edwards to "a superior cause" and a "benevolent benefactor." Such were easily observable glimpses of natural beauty. Another type existed as well, as Edwards saw it:

The latter sort are those beauties that delight us and we can't tell why. Thus we find ourselves pleased in beholding the color of the violets, but we know not what secret regularity or harmony it is that creates that pleasure in our minds. These hidden beauties are commonly by far the greatest, because the more complex a beauty is, the more hidden is it. In this latter sort consists principally the beauty of the world; and very much in light and colors. [The]. mixture of all sorts of rays, which we call white, is a proportionate mixture that is harmonious (as Sir Isaac Newton has shewn) to each particular simple color and contains in it some harmony or other that is delightful. And each sort of rays play a distinct tune to the soul, besides those lovely mixtures that are found in nature—those beauties, how lovely, in the green of the face of the earth, in all manner of colors in flowers, the color of the skies, and lovely tinctures of the morning and evening. (*Works* 6, 305–6)

The world was bursting with beauty, whether plainly seen or hidden from view. All of it called to humanity, playing "a distinct tune to the soul" as with the mixed light rays identified by Isaac Newton. Creation was not pragmatic in Edwards's view. It was a love song from the Creator to mankind. In a thousand fields of study, God had coded the music of His creation. One hears the music of God testifying to the beauty of God not only through musical notes, but through genes, and chemicals, and all the mysterious workings of nature.

THE EFFECTS OF THE FALL ON CREATION

The beauty of creation, however, was not pure. Unlike its Creator, creation was both subservient and fallen. In his unfinished *History of the Work of Redemption*, Edwards covered the fall of mankind and its effects on the creation:

This lower world before the fall enjoyed noonday light, the light of knowledge of God, the light of his glory and the light of his favor. But when man fell all this light was at once extinguished and the world reduced back again to total darkness, a worse darkness than that which was in the beginning of the world that we read of in the Genesis 1:2, "And the earth was without form and void [and darkness was upon the face of the deep]." This was a darkness a thousandfold worse or remediless as that neither man nor angels could find out any way whereby this darkness might be scattered. This darkness appeared in its blackness, then, when Adam and his wife first saw that they were naked and sewed fig leaves, and when they heard the voice of the Lord God walking in the midst [of the garden] and hid themselves among the trees of the garden. And then when God first called them to an account and said to Adam, "What is this that thou hast done, hast thou [eaten of the tree]?"—then we may suppose that their hearts were filled with shame and terror. (*Works* 9, 133)

When Adam and Eve sinned against God by listening to the serpent and eating the forbidden fruit from the Tree of Knowledge of Good and Evil, they brought devastation upon the creation (see Gen. 3). Edwards does not dwell for long on the physical effects of the fall, but he believed that sin had marred this "lower world." One could find great beauty on the earth but also great ugliness and corruption. This passage does not weaken the celebratory tone of earlier quotations, but it does show that the beauty of creation, unlike the beauty of the Creator, weakened as a result of the fall.

The fall disconnected man from His Creator. But this did not mean in Edwards's mind that God had left humanity without testimony to Himself and the truth of His Word. Edwards argued strongly throughout his career for the legitimacy of a field of study called *typology*. Typology is the study of biblical entities that foreshadow a larger reality. Many scholars believe that King David, for example, is a "type" of Christ, a shadow of the more majestic King to come, the Lord Jesus. Most interpreters confine their typology to the Bible, but Edwards, with his belief that all corners of the creation testify in some way to the Creator, unearthed countless "natural types" in the created realm.

Edwards laid out his view of typology in one selection of a notebook devoted to finding examples from the created order that pointed to spiritual truths. The pastor believed that lesser created things pointed to greater created things, as he recorded in his notebook:

> There are some types of divine things, both in Scripture and also in the works of nature and constitution of the world, that are much more lively than others. Everything seems to aim that way; and in some things the image is very lively, in others less lively, in others the image but faint and the resemblance in but few particulars with many things wherein there is a dissimilitude. God has ordered things in this respect much as he has in the natural world. He hath made man the head and end of this lower creation; and there are innumerable creatures that have some image of what is in men, but in an infinite variety of degrees. Animals have much more of a resemblance of what is in men than plants, plants much more than things inanimate.

Edwards justified this view by an appeal to numerous scriptural texts:

> That natural things were ordered for types of spiritual things seems evident by these texts: John 1:9, "This was the true Light, which lighteth every man that cometh into the world"; and John 15:1, "I am the true vine." Things are thus said to be true in Scripture, in contradistinction to what is typical. The type is only the

representation or shadow of the thing, but the antitype is the very substance, and is the true thing. Thus heaven is said to be the true holy of holies, in opposition to the holy of holies in the tabernacle and temple. Hebrews 9:24, "For Christ is not entered into the holy places made with hands, which are figures of the true; but into heaven itself, now to appear in the presence of God for us." So the spiritual gospel tabernacle is said to be the true tabernacle, in opposition to the legal typical tabernacle which was literally a tabernacle. Hebrews 8:2, "A minister of the sanctuary, and of the true tabernacle, which the Lord pitched, and not man."

Though few Christians today would approach biblical interpretation in this way, Edwards's arguments deserve consideration. Edwards was not like most of us, who tend to compartmentalize our lives and segment parts of it off from our relationship with God. Edwards's view of God was large and encompassed every aspect of creation. In His great design, God had given "natural things" as types of "spiritual things." "Everything," said Edwards, "seems to aim that way."

One need not agree with every nuance of his typology to learn an important lesson from Edwards, namely, that the human-centered view of the universe so common in our day prevents us from a richer, fuller vision of the world and natural order. Psalm 19:1 rings in our ears on this point: "The heavens declare the glory of God, and the sky above proclaims his handiwork." Edwards applied this verse by finding types of spiritual truths in creation. His notebook entries are creative and lively. Consider what he wrote about roses:

Roses grow upon briers, which is to signify that all temporal sweets are mixed with bitter. But what seems more especially to be meant by it, is that true happiness, the crown of glory, is to be come at in no other way than by bearing Christ's cross by a life of mortification, self-denial and labor, and bearing all things for Christ. The rose, the chief of all flowers, is the last thing that comes out. The briery prickly bush grows before, but the end and crown of all is the beautiful and fragrant rose. (*Works* 11, 52)

In the sea, Edwards discovered the wrath of God:

The waves and billows of the sea in a storm and the dire cataracts there are of rivers have a representation of the terrible wrath of God, and amazing misery of [them] that endure it. Misery is often compared to waters in the Scripture—a being overwhelmed in waters. God's wrath is compared to waves and billows (Psalms 88:7, Psalms 42:7). Job 27:20, "Terrors take hold as waters." Hosea 5:10, "I will pour out my wrath upon them like water." In Psalms 42:7, God's wrath is expressly compared to cataracts of water: "Deep calleth unto deep at the noise of thy waterspouts." And the same is represented in hail and stormy winds, black clouds and thunder, etc. (*Works* 11, 58)

In the silkworm, Edwards saw Christ:

The silkworm is a remarkable type of Christ, which, when it dies, yields us that of which we make such glorious clothing. Christ became a worm for our sakes, and by his death finished that righteousness with which believers are clothed, and thereby procured that we should be clothed with robes of glory. See 2 Samuel 5:23–24 and Psalms 84:6; the valley of mulberry trees. (*Works* 11, 59)

And in the serpent's cunning, Edwards glimpsed Satan's schemes:

> In the manner in which birds and squirrels that are charmed
> by serpents go into their mouths and are destroyed by them, is
> a lively representation of the manner in which sinners under
> the gospel are very often charmed and destroyed by the devil.
> The animal that is charmed by the serpent seems to be in great
> exercise and fear, screams and makes ado, but yet don't flee away.
> It comes nearer to the serpent, and then seems to have its distress
> increased and goes a little back again, but then comes still nearer
> than ever, and then appears as if greatly affrighted and runs or
> flies back again a little way, but yet don't flee quite away, and soon
> comes a little nearer and a little nearer with seeming fear and
> distress that drives 'em a little back between whiles, until at length
> they come so [near] that the serpent can lay hold of them: and so
> they become their prey. (*Works* 11, 71)

These lively explorations of the created order show how Edwards worked out his understanding of nature as a display of God's glory and wisdom. In Edwards's worldview, the Creator planted these figments of Himself and His truth in creation to stimulate the faith of mankind. Wherever one looked —roses, the sea, silkworms, or serpents—one found the hand and mind of God.

Edwards's God was simultaneously a designer, aesthete, and instructor. The natural order existed for the magnification, pleasure, and use of the One who created it. Even with the effects of the fall corrupting God's handiwork, the world still brimmed with beauty. Wherever one discovered intelligence, loveliness, or depictions of spiritual realities, one found prime evidence of God's design. Beauty was not a concept one could abstract from God, but was the very essence of God. Thus the realm God created displayed His beauty. Creation derived not from pragmatics, from a mere desire by the Creator to create. Creation existed because God desired to put His glory, His beauty, before a celestial audience.

In the pastor's eyes, creation sung the praises of God and exhibited the wisdom of God. One did not have to squint to see this truth; one had only to open one's eyes. If one stopped to look at the flight of spiders or the soft light of a rainbow, one saw a reflection of a figure still more beautiful than these. If one only stopped to listen, one could hear, however faintly, a distant song calling a fallen world to discover the beauty of the Lord.

Pursuing Beauty

Appreciating the Design of Creation

Christians need to take time to celebrate the intelligence of the creational order. Examples abound of God's wise design. In the natural workings of nature, we see God's wisdom (see Job 40:20–24, for example). In the subtleties of the human body, we see God's handiwork (Ps. 139:14). In the makeup of the cell, we see God's impossibly complex mind. We should follow the lead of Edwards when we make these discoveries and direct lavish praise to the Creator. His example reminds us that these findings are not coincidental—that an infinitely wise God dedicates His ingenuity to our natural world. We must overcome the influence of secularistic science and philosophy and free our hearts and voices to celebrate the intelligence of God. We need to clear space in our technologically saturated lives to recognize the wisdom of the Lord in the natural realm. Instead of lavishing praise on humanity, we should acknowledge with Edwards and the biblical authors that this place is filled with the beauty of God's wisdom (Ps. 136).

Caring for Creation

Certain sectors of evangelicalism have maligned Christians who express a desire to care for the world. Environmental concerns can surely get out of hand, but it seems logical when holding a God-centered view of creation to take action to preserve and care for it (see Lev. 25:1–12 and Ps. 104). Christians who have such a view possess a unique opportunity for witness when they meet people who love the earth but have no faith in its Creator. Our care for the world, sensibly handled, can be both an act of worship and a means of evangelism.

Chapter 11

THE BEAUTY OF CHRIST

The beauty of Christ often grips young believers. After years of sorrow and sin, the new believer finds hope and forgiveness through His atoning death and resurrection. Where things of the world once promised fulfillment, now the Christian finds satisfaction in spiritual pursuits. Over time, however, this delight can wane. Faith can grow dull. Christ can fade into the background. Where the believer once lived passionately for God, he now takes Him for granted. The difficulties of life seem huge, and Christ seems small, a figure far off in the distance.

Jonathan Edwards knew this tendency of the human condition, this propensity of the heart to lose its passion for Christ. He frequently preached sermons that exalted the Savior and that gave his church a breathtaking view of the second person of the Trinity. It is the purpose of this chapter to present several of Edwards's descriptions of the Savior's excellence. Here the reader will find some of the richest material Edwards ever produced. The pastor emphasized the beauty of Christ in a multitude of sermons throughout his career. Though all are worthy of study, a few stand out: "Christ the Light of the World," "Honey from the Rock," "Seeking after Christ," and the capstone of the genre, "The Excellency of Christ."

THE SWEETNESS OF JESUS CHRIST

We begin with "Christ the Light of the World," a sermon in which a young Edwards identified the special loveliness of the Lord:

> There is scarcely anything that is excellent, beautiful, pleasant, or profitable but what is used in the Scripture as an emblem of Christ. He is called a lion for his great power, victory, and glorious conquests; he is called a lamb for his great love, pity, and compassion: for that merciful, compassionate, condescending, lamblike disposition of his; for his humility, meekness, and great patience, and because he was slain like a lamb. He was brought as a lamb to the slaughter, so he opened not his mouth. He is called the bread of life and water of life, for the spiritual refreshment and nourishment he gives to the soul; he is called the true vine, because he communicates life to his members, and yields that comfort to the soul that refreshes it as the fruit of the vine doth the body; he is called life, for he is the life of the soul. He is called a rose and lily, and other such similitudes, because of his transcendent beauty and fragrancy. He is called the bright and morning star, and the sun of righteousness; and in our text, the light of the world, of which it is our business at present to speak. (*Works* 10, 535)

This section is noteworthy for the plethora of images Edwards uses to describe the unique beauty of the Son of God—"lion," "lamb," "bread and water of life," "true vine," "life," "rose and lily," "bright and morning star," "sun of righteousness," and "light of the world." This collection of images speaks to the young preacher's impressive grasp of biblical theology. Unlike some preachers today, who pay little attention to the development of a given idea in Scripture, Edwards frequently searched the whole canon to enrich his exegesis.

Creation revealed the beauty of God, as depicted in the

last chapter, but Jesus Christ displayed the loveliness of the Godhead in an even more direct way. He was, after all, God in human flesh, and as such shone with a special light. As Edwards explains,

> God the Father is an infinite fountain of light, but Jesus Christ is the communication of this light. Some compare God the Father to the sun and Jesus Christ to the light that streams forth from him by which the world is enlightened. God the Father, in himself, was never seen: 'tis God the Son that has been the light that hath revealed him. God is an infinitely bright and glorious being, but Jesus Christ is that brightness of his glory by which he is revealed to us: "No man hath seen God at any time, but the only begotten Son, which is in the bosom of the Father, he hath declared him" (John 1:18). (*Works* 10, 535–36)

In light Edwards found an excellent analogy for Christ, for the mind could easily conceive of light as simultaneously pure, beautiful, and glorious. When the sun shone, it powerfully affected that which received its rays, warming cold bodies, banishing darkness. So it was with Christ, "that brightness" of the Father's glory.

Edwards described in vivid detail the ways in which Christ's light manifested glory in the hearts of sinners:

> Before he shines into men's souls, they are dead and dull in a deep sleep, are not diligent at their work, but lie still and sleep and do nothing respecting their souls. All their affections are dead, dull and lifeless; their understandings are darkened with the dark shades of spiritual night, and there is nothing but spiritual sleep and death in their souls.
>
> But when Christ arises upon them, then all things begin to revive, the will and affections begin to move, and they set about the work they have to do. They are now awakened out of their

sleep: whereas they were still before, now they begin to be diligent and industrious; whereas they were silent before, now they begin to sing forth God's praises. Their graces now begin to be put into exercise, as flowers send forth a fragrancy when the sun shines upon them. (*Works* 10, 540)

Converting to Christ was no mere transaction in Edwards's mind. It signaled the awakening of one's "will and affections" for the Savior. Faith, as Edwards conceived it, involved a full-hearted embrace of Christ. The converted believer experienced a transformation of heart and mind, rising to spiritual life out of "spiritual sleep and death." As they learned to live for Christ, they sent "forth a fragrancy" that smelled of the Son. When Christ claimed a person, He made them anew and made them to smell and look like Him.

THE SATISFIER OF THE SOUL

In "Honey from the Rock," Edwards switched the metaphor from light to a rock, but continued the theme of Christ's all-sufficient and soul-satisfying work in the hearts of believers. As described in the book of Deuteronomy, Christ's "meanness," His lowliness, concealed a river of delights, just as the rock Moses struck burst with water in the parched desert (Ex. 17:6):

It was a wonderful work of God in the wilderness when he caused water to gush out of the rock, upon Moses' smiting of it with his rod, in such abundance as to supply all the congregation, and is spoken of as such; Deuteronomy 8:15, "Who led thee through that great and terrible wilderness, wherein were fiery serpents, and scorpions, and drought, where there was no water; who brought thee forth water out of the rock of flint." But this was but a little thing to this glorious work that is typified by it. It was a glorious

work of God's power, as well as mercy, to provide such blessings
for a lost world by Jesus Christ. It was wonderful that such blessings should be made to flow from this rock, whether we consider
this similitude of a rock as denoting his outward meanness or his
divine greatness. (*Works* 10, 137)

Edwards concluded the section with a summation of the qualities of Christ's beauty:

> And 'tis wonderful also if we consider Christ's divine greatness, for
> this is also signified by this metaphor of a rock. As we have shown,
> it signifies his divine perfection and holiness, his omnipotence, his
> eternity, his immutability. Now, 'tis a wonderful work of God that
> such a glorious person should be made the head of influence and
> fountain of spiritual nourishment to lost mankind: that so great,
> so glorious a person should be given to us, to be to us a fountain
> of blessings to be enjoyed by us who are so mean and unworthy.
> (*Works* 10, 137–38)

In this discussion, Edwards interpreted the rock Moses struck
in a Christological way, arguing that beneath Christ's exterior
flowed an unending channel of God's love and beauty. The interpretation is imaginative and moving. Few of us, after all, have too
large a view of God. Most of us have far too small a view of God
and His goodness. Edwards shows us that Christ is nothing less
than "a fountain of blessings" for His people. Moses had only a
single chance to strike the rock; we have constant access to the
stream of the blessings of Christ's person. Every Christian, whatever their circumstances, has equal and absolute access to Christ
and all His glorious perfections.

ACCESS TO DIVINE LOVELINESS

Edwards continued this awesome theme in "Seeking After Christ." When a person seeks after the Son of God, he declared,

> the person that they find is exceeding excellent and lovely. Before Christ is found, there is nothing that is truly lovely that is ever found or seen. Those things that they had been conversant with before and had set their hearts upon, had no true excellency. They only deceived 'em with a false, empty show. But now they have found Christ, they have found one that is excellent indeed. They see in him a real and substantial excellency.

It was not always so. Before the sinner comes to Christ, they find Him a subject of "fear and terror":

> Before that, while they were under trouble, they had before them only those things that were objects of fear and terror, such as their own guilt, the wickedness of their hearts, and the wrath of God, and death and hell, but nothing pleasant or lovely. But [when] they came to find Christ, what was terrible in those objects disappears, and they found a glorious object and far surpassing all things that ever they saw, one of excellent majesty and of perfect purity and brightness, purer than the light of the sun, infinitely farther from all deformity or defilement than the highest heavens themselves; and this conjoined with the sweetest grace, one that clothes himself with mildness and meekness and love. How refreshing and rejoicing must this be after they have nothing before their eyes but their sins staring them in the face, appearing with a frightful countenance, and God's terrible anger, and frightful devils, and death's pale and ghastly countenance, and the devouring flames of hell. How exceeding refreshing must it be to find so lovely an object after they have so long had nothing but such objects before 'em. (*Works* 22, 289)

This section offers a simple but striking summation of the differences between the hope of the unbeliever and the believer. Try as they might, the unbeliever cannot access any lasting, meaningful kind of hope. All that appears hopeful is in the end unfulfilling. "Fear and terror," "guilt," "the wrath of God," and "death and hell" plague them all their days. Those who appear happiest often end up being the least happy and most fearful people we know. Those who appear most confident and precise in their thinking often live with ethical turmoil and intellectual confusion. The absence of Christ leaves a hole that nothing can fill.

When Christ claims a person, however, everything changes. The lost soul, tormented with terrible thoughts and a guilty conscience, discovers "a glorious object," a being "of excellent majesty and of perfect purity and brightness," whose love brings "the sweetest grace." There is an element in these words of *eros*, romantic attraction, that few today would understand but was a staple of Edwards's descriptions of the love between God and His people. In his view, it was entirely proper that the church, gazing on the beatific Son of God, feel the deepest passion for Him, a deep affection that transcended physicality and represented the purest form of covenantal love.

THE COMFORT OF THE SAVIOR

Edwards developed a different image of the Savior in "Christ the Spiritual Sun." He discussed first how the Son comforted believers with His presence:

> The hearts of true believers are greatly comforted and refreshed with the beams of this. The day that this Sun brings on, when it arises, is a pleasant day to them. As the light of the sun is sweet to the bodily eye, so, and much more, is the light of the spiritual Sun sweet to the spiritual eye of the believer. It is a pleasant thing for

the eye to behold the sun, but much more pleasant to a believer to behold Jesus Christ that is fairer than the sons of men [Psalms 45:2]. It is refreshing to see the light of the sun down in the east to a man that has been lost and long wandering in the night, in a wilderness, groping in darkness, not knowing whither he went; but much more refreshing and sweet to behold the dawning light of the Sun of righteousness.

Edwards's love for nature is evident in his celebration of Christ:

How does the face of the Earth seem to rejoice when the sun comes to shine pleasantly upon it in the spring. The pastures are clothed with green grass and many pleasant flowers that open their bosom to receive the sunbeams. How are the trees as it were clothed with garments of rejoicing, with green leaves and beautiful and fragrant blossoms, as though they sang and shouted for joy at the influences of the sun. Psalms 65:13, "The pastures are clothed with flocks; the valleys also."

This is a lively image of that sweet spiritual comfort, joy and excellent refreshment that the souls of believers have under the beams of the Sun of righteousness. (*Works* 22, 55–56)

Christ not only nourished believers, but restored their soul in the midst of pain and suffering brought on by sin and a fallen world:

The beams of this spiritual Sun don't only refresh but restore the souls of believers. Thus it is said that the Sun of righteousness [shall arise] with healing [in his wings]. These beams heal the souls of believers. As we often see that when the trees or plants of the earth are wounded, the beams of the sun will heal the wound and by degrees restore the plant, so the sweet beams of the Sun of righteousness heal the wounds of believers' souls. When they have been wounded by sin and have labored under the pain of wounds of conscience, the rays of this Sun heal the wounds of conscience. When they have been wounded by temptation and made to fall to their hurt, those benign beams, when they come to shine on the wounded soul, restore and heal the hurt that has been received.

The pastor powerfully described the tender ministry of Christ to His people:

The sick soul by these beams is restored, as plants that have grown in shady and cold places appear sickly and languishing, if the shade be removed and the sunbeams come to shine down upon them, will revive and flourish; or as the clear shining of the sun after the rain.

The beams of this Sun heal of the mortal poison of the fiery serpent, as the children of Israel were healed by looking on the brazen serpent in the wilderness. Yea, these beams don't only restore from wounds but from death; they don't only give light but life. The soul of a convert is raised from the dead by the shining of the beams of this Sun, as we see the rays of the sun in the spring revives the grass and herbs as it were from the dead and causes a resurrection of them from the dust, making 'em to spring out of the ground with new life. The beams of the Sun of righteousness, when it rises in the morning of the last day, will revive not only the souls but the bodies of the saints, will cause at once an universal resurrection of them; as we see in the morning when the sun returns, it causes all animals to rise out of a state of darkness and sleep, which is the image of darkness. (*Works* 22, 56–7)

Edwards's depiction of Christ as a sun made clear that His emanations warmed the soul just as the physical sun warmed the body. The believer, beset by personal sin, would find it constantly "refreshing and sweet to behold the dawning light of the Sun of righteousness." Christ infused the heart of the Christian with radiant warmth, a sense of absolute love that brought fresh hope to the heart and fresh confidence to the mind.

Christ also took on the work of restoring the heart. Edwards preached that as "the beams of the sun will heal the wound and by degrees restore the plant, so the sweet beams of the Sun of righteousness heal the wounds of believers' souls." The shining beauty of the Son gives life to hurting believers. Constantly wounded, either by oneself or by others, the Christian finds restoration and hope in their personal connection to the "Sun of righteousness." When believers trap themselves in a pattern of sin, Christ imparts fresh forgiveness to them; when sinned against, Christ reassures the believer, reminding them of their acceptance in the beloved.

THE MAJESTY OF THE SON

Edwards's preaching on Christ reached its apex in the classic sermon "The Excellency of Christ." Based on Revelation 5:5–6, the passage in which Christ is depicted as both a lion and a lamb, the sermon presented Edwards's insights on the "admirable conjunction of diverse excellencies in Jesus Christ." The first of these conjunctions was the simultaneous condescension and highness of Jesus Christ, the one both "infinitely great" and "low and mean," as Edwards put it. First, the pastor covered His "infinite highness":

> There do meet in Jesus Christ, infinite highness, and infinite condescension. Christ, as he is God, is infinitely great and high above all. He is higher than the kings of the earth; for he is King of Kings, and Lord of Lords. He is higher than the heavens, and higher than the highest angels of heaven. So great is he, that all men, all kings and princes, are as worms of the dust before him, all nations are as the drop of the bucket, and the light dust of the

balance; yea, and angels themselves are as nothing before him.
He is so high, that he is infinitely above any need of us; above
our reach, that we cannot be profitable to him, and above our
conceptions, that we cannot comprehend him. Proverbs 30:4,
"What is his name, and what is his Son's name, if thou canst tell?"
Our understandings, if we stretch them never so far, can't reach
up to his divine glory. Job 11:8, "It is high as heaven, what canst
thou do?" Christ is the Creator, and great possessor of heaven and
earth: he is sovereign lord of all: he rules over the whole universe,
and doth whatsoever pleaseth him: his knowledge is without
bound: his wisdom is perfect, and what none can circumvent: his
power is infinite, and none can resist him: his riches are immense
and inexhaustible: his majesty is infinitely awful.

He then discussed the "infinite condescension" of the Savior:

And yet he is one of infinite condescension. None are so low, or
inferior, but Christ's condescension is sufficient to take a gracious
notice of them. He condescends not only to the angels, humbling
himself to behold the things that are done in heaven, but he also
condescends to such poor creatures as men; and that not only so
as to take notice of princes and great men, but of those that are
of meanest rank and degree, "the poor of the world" (James 2:5).
Such as are commonly despised by their fellow creatures, Christ
don't despise. 1 Corinthians 1:28, "Base things of the world, and
things that are despised, hath God chosen." Christ condescends
to take notice of beggars (Luke 16:22) and of servants, and people
of the most despised nations: in Christ Jesus is neither "Barbarian,
Scythian, bond, nor free" (Colossians 3:11). He that is thus high,
condescends to take a gracious notice of little children. Matthew
19:14, "Suffer little children to come unto me." Yea, which is
much more, his condescension is sufficient to take a gracious
notice of the most unworthy, sinful creatures, those that have no

good deservings, and those that have infinite ill deservings. (*Works* 19, 565–66)

Next Edwards considered the "infinite justice" and "infinite grace" of Christ:

There meet in Jesus Christ, infinite justice, and infinite grace. As Christ is a divine person he is infinitely holy and just, infinitely hating sin, and disposed to execute condign punishment for sin. He is the Judge of the world, and the infinitely just judge of it, and will not at all acquit the wicked, or by any means clear the guilty.

And yet he is one that is infinitely gracious and merciful. Though his justice be so strict with respect to all sin, and every breach of the law, yet he has grace sufficient for every sinner, and even the chief of sinners. And it is not only sufficient for the most unworthy to show them mercy, and bestow some good upon them, but to bestow the greatest good; yea, 'tis sufficient to bestow all good upon them, and to do all things for them. There is no benefit or blessing that they can receive so great, but the grace of Christ is sufficient to bestow it on the greatest sinner that ever lived. And not only so, but so great is his grace, that nothing is too much as the means of this good: 'tis sufficient not only to do great things, but also to suffer in order to it; and not only to suffer, but to suffer most extremely, even unto death, the most terrible of natural evils; and not only death, but the most ignominious and tormenting, and every way the most terrible death that men could inflict; yea, and greater sufferings than men could inflict, who could only torment the body, but also those sufferings in his soul, that were the more immediate fruits of the wrath of God against the sins of those he undertakes for. (*Works* 19, 567)

Few written documents so capture the beauty of Christ and His work as "The Excellency of Christ." The sermon in its entirety deserves careful reading and meditation by every Christian. It is a masterpiece. Here, Edwards offered his people a picture of Jesus Christ that elegantly balanced the traits of majesty and humility, grace and justice. Never before had such a figure existed. Never had one person sustained such paradox, such tension in their inner being, and carried both the majesty of heaven and the meekness of earth in their flesh. As majestic and "terrible" as one could be, Jesus was and is; as humble and kind as one could be, Jesus was and is.

These traits were not merely admirable. They were foundational for the crucifixion Christ faced for the salvation of the lost. Edwards next discussed the beauty Christ displayed in His atoning death, focusing first on how He showed His love for His Father:

> He never in any act gave so great a manifestation of love to God, and yet never so manifested his love to those that were enemies to God, as in that act. Christ never did anything whereby his love to the Father was so eminently manifested, as in his laying down his life, under such inexpressible sufferings, in obedience to his command, and for the vindication of the honor of his authority and majesty; nor did ever any mere creature give such a testimony of love to God as that was: and yet this was the greatest expression of all, of his love to sinful men, that were enemies to God. Romans 5:10, "While we were enemies, we were reconciled to God, by the death of his Son." The greatness of Christ's love to such, appears in nothing so much, as in its being dying love. That blood of Christ that was sweat out, and fell in great drops to the ground, in his agony, was shed from love to God's enemies, and his own. That shame and spitting, that torment of body, and that exceeding sorrow, even unto death, that he endured in his soul, was what he underwent from love to rebels against God, to save them from hell, and to purchase for them eternal glory. Never did Christ so eminently show his regard to

God's honor, as in offering up himself a victim to revenging justice, to vindicate God's honor: and yet in this above all, he manifested his love to them that dishonored God, so as to bring such guilt on themselves, that nothing less than his blood could atone for it.

Next Edwards considered how Christ's atonement satisfied divine justice:

Christ never so eminently appeared for divine justice, and yet never suffered so much from divine justice, as when he offered up himself a sacrifice for our sins. In Christ's great sufferings, did his infinite regard to the honor of God's justice distinguishingly appear; for it was from regard to that, that he thus humbled himself: and yet in these sufferings, Christ was the mark of the vindictive expressions of that very justice of God. Revenging justice then spent all its force upon him, on account of our guilt that was laid upon him; he was not spared at all; but God spent the arrows of his vengeance upon him, which made him sweat blood, and cry out upon the cross, and probably rent his vitals, broke his heart, the fountain of blood, or some other internal blood vessels, and by the violent fermentation turned his blood to water: for the blood and water that issued out of his side, when pierced by the spear, seems to have been extravasated blood; and so there might be a kind of literal fulfillment of that, in Psalms 22:14, "I am poured out like water, and all my bones are out of joint: my heart is like wax, it is melted in the midst of my bowels." And this was the way and means by which Christ stood up for the honor of God's justice, viz. by thus suffering its terrible executions. For when he had undertaken for sinners, and had substituted himself in their room, divine justice could have its due honor, no other way than by his suffering its revenges. (*Works* 19, 577–78)

The One who bore "the arrows" of God's justice was Himself shot into the world by God to pierce the heart of sin and death.

Each fiber of His being was perfectly tuned for the cross so that the "enemies of God" might taste life and the "justice of God" find its eternal vindication. This latter burden formed Christ's ultimate concern. Christ gave His life for "rebels," but He cared above all for "God's honor" and reputation. For Edwards, the cross, as with all things, found its highest significance in relation to its glorification of God. Jesus loved the lost, and suffered "terrible executions" of wrath to save them from hell. But the character and reputation of God was Christ's highest concern in bearing the Father's "vengeance" for sin. In the world made to display the beauty of God, the Son's obedience to the Father elevated Him above all, rendering Him worthy of eternal adoration and praise.

PROCLAIMING CHRIST'S BEAUTY

Jonathan Edwards devoted a large part of his pastoral career to expounding the magnificent beauty of God the Son. He used every fitting analogy he could find to unfurl the glory of Christ, referencing light, rocks, the sun, lions and lambs, and more. He strove to bring his congregation and all who would read his works into the realm where the clouds of this world lift and the glory of the risen Lord is all that is visible. The colonial theologian showed Christ to be a Savior who takes our breath away at the sight of His beauty.

Pursuing Beauty

Thinking Less About Ourselves

The world encourages us to focus an inordinate amount of attention on ourselves and our concerns. We are coaxed by countless voices to "stay true to ourselves," to "focus on me for a while," to "not let anyone tell me what to do." The study of Edwards's material on Christ hits the mute button on the world and allows us to break free from our self-interests and revel in the glory of Christ. It shows us that our central need is not to become psychologically satisfied, but to treasure Jesus Christ above all things by bowing in repentance and worship before Him (Heb. 3:1–6). Each day that we live is an opportunity not to glorify our sinful selves, but to glorify the one who bled and died for our salvation, our liberation from Satan's shackles. Let us clear space in our hearts for adoration not of ourselves, but of Christ. Life is not about us. It is about Jesus Christ and a fixed, unrelenting, soul-satisfying pursuit of Him.

Stoking Our Love for Christ

If we would follow Christ and honor Him by obedient lives, we must learn to love Him. We must cultivate affection for Christ through study of the Bible and prayer that celebrates Christ's person and work. We need to see the Bible as a book that testifies to Christ in both direct and indirect ways (Matt. 5:17–20; Luke 24:27, 44). We need to bring before our ears and eyes teaching that exalts Christ, turning off and tuning out chatterbox media that do nothing to energize our love for Him. We need to praise the Father in our prayers for Jesus Christ and all His perfections. We can use material like that left for us by Edwards, working our way through a sermon like "The Excellency of Christ" on our lunch break or our evening downtime. The challenge is simply this: to think much about Christ. We need to stoke our hearts to think about Him not just on Sunday morning, but all throughout the week, such that we are Christ-saturated, brimming with affection and love for Him (see Col. 3:1–10).

Chapter 12

THE BEAUTY
OF THE CHURCH

For many Christians, the church would not normally be considered an object of beauty. In common evangelical parlance, the church is a building, a collection of bricks and mortar that houses the activity of Christians. Little wonder that so many people profess so little love for the church. When coupled with a bad experience or two, the church can feel impersonal, cold, and lifeless.

It shouldn't be this way. In one section of his "Notes on Scripture," Jonathan Edwards sketched a simple portrait of the *ecclesia* that drives to the heart of the church's identity. Edwards suggested:

> That God's church, that in Scripture is represented as Christ's house or temple, and as his raiment and ornament, and as a golden candlestick, etc., is wholly constituted of those saints that are his jewels, that are the spoils of his enemies, that were once his enemies' possession, but that he has redeemed out of their hands. (*Works* 15, 337)

The church, Edwards noted, is the people of God, "those saints that are his jewels," the diverse collection of believers whom

Christ rescued from "his enemies' possession." The "ornament" of the Savior, His prized belonging, the church is an entity unlike any other on the earth. Transcending organization or institution, the church is the "mystical body" of Jesus Christ, according to other writings of Edwards, the living manifestation of the Lord in this realm that provides a picture of the Savior for a world that has lost sight of Him.

In this chapter, we look at Edwards's understanding of the role humanity plays in the scheme of God's cosmic plan. We then examine two sources of Edwards's doctrine of the church: first, his "Notes on Scripture," and second, "The History of the Work of Redemption." The first text reveals Edwards's understanding of the nature of the church, while the second shows how he saw the church fitting into the great story of the ages. Taken together, these texts reveal the beautiful character and purpose of the people of God, those whom Christ died to make His own for the glory of the Father.

THE CHURCH AS A "GLORIOUS SOCIETY"

As discussed earlier, Edwards believed that God was the preeminent one, the being for whom all things existed and in whom true beauty was found. Living in a realm that teemed with God's glory, mankind found its calling in joining with God in the work of His self-glorification. Edwards dictated this vision for human life in his *Dissertation Concerning the End for Which God Created the World*. In the section below, Edwards discusses how God created a "glorious society" to consciously display His own perfections:

> It seems to be a thing in itself fit and desirable, that the glorious perfections of God should be known, and the operations and expressions of them seen by other beings besides himself. If it be fit that God's power and wisdom, etc., should be exercised and

expressed in some effects, and not lie eternally dormant, then it seems proper that these exercises should appear, and not be totally hidden and unknown. . . . As God's perfections are things in themselves excellent, so the expression of them in their proper acts and fruits is excellent, and the knowledge of these excellent perfections, and of these glorious expressions of them, is an excellent thing, the existence of which is in itself valuable and desirable. 'Tis a thing infinitely good in itself that God's glory should be known by a glorious society of created beings. (*Works* 8, 430–2)

As Edwards makes clear, God desired that His beauty transcend passive representation, as rocks, trees, and oceans allow. He wanted His perfections to "be known" and considered according to self-conscious "knowledge." Here humanity found its reason for existence. The purpose of human life in Edwardsean thought is to know with the fullness of one's mind and senses the "excellent perfections" of God.

Thus, the race of mankind was created for this lofty end. As noted in chapter 2, Edwards also asserted that God designed the world to satisfy the desires of the human beings He had formed for communion and love. The fall of Adam and Eve, however, resulted in the loss of this bounty. Though everyone in some sense would taste the goodness of God through life on earth, only those whom God called to be His children would join the "glorious society" dedicated to the adoration of the Almighty. Edwards identified this society as the church, which included the children of God of every age. In every generation, it was the church's privilege to taste the Lord's goodness and love; in all seasons, it was the church's mission to celebrate and magnify this goodness in a foreign and hostile world.

THE CHURCH AS AN "IMPERFECT EMBRYO"

As mentioned at the beginning of the chapter, Edwards defined the church as the people of God in his "Notes on Scripture," an unpublished collection of reflections written over the course of the expositor's life. A different type of source than Edwards's polished sermons or refined theological treatises, the notes allow us to peer over Edwards's shoulder as he recorded insights in his study. Early in the notes Edwards mused:

> 47. John 2:21. "But he spake of the temple of his body." And it seems to me likely that he should speak of his body in two senses: in one sense of the church, which is called his body, and is also called the temple of God, of which the temple of Jerusalem was a type. The temple of Jerusalem may signify the Jewish church, which Christ put an end to by his coming, and in three ages after erected his spiritual temple, the Christian church. (*Works* 15, 63)

Using the Old Testament, Edwards described how the Lord shaped His church into His temple:

> 1 Kings 6:7. "And the house, when it was in building, was built of stone made ready before it was brought thither; so that there was neither hammer, nor ax, nor any tool of iron heard in the house, while it was in building." This temple represents the church of God, who are called God's temple, a spiritual house, Jesus Christ being chief cornerstone, and all the saints as so many stones. Particularly by Solomon's temple is meant the church triumphant, as by the tabernacle the church militant; by the exact fitting, squaring, and smoothing of those stones before they were brought thither, represents the perfection of the saints in glory. Heaven is not a place to prepare them; they are all prepared before they come there. They come perfectly sinless and holy into heaven.

The world is the place where God hews them, and squares them by his prophets and ministers (1 Kings 5:6), by the reproofs and warnings of his word, which God compares to a hammer, by persecutions and afflictions. There shall be no noise of these tools heard in heaven, but all these lively stones of this spiritual and glorious building are exactly fitted, framed, and polished before they come there. (*Works* 15, 64)

Because Edwards so closely connected the Old and New Testaments, he was able to draw stunning comparisons between scriptural institutions and ideas. In this section, Edwards argued that the Lord fitted His church for heaven with the same care and precision that the Israelite craftsmen used to construct the great temple of the Lord. Here Edwards noted that God "hews" and "squares" His people, rendering them beautiful and holy in His sight. The divine craftsman employs biblical "reproofs and warnings" and temporal "persecutions and afflictions" to accomplish this end. Though Christians may at times feel downcast and beaten by their sufferings, Edwards's words remind the church that the sovereign Lord sends trials to beautify His people and leave them "fitted, framed, and polished" for the life to come where "no noise of these tools" will sound.

The Lord's blueprint for the church was Christ. As He fitted the church for heaven, the Lord conformed His people to the express image of the Son. Edwards explored this matter in a note on conformity:

Ephesians 4:13. "Till we all come in the unity of the faith, and of the knowledge of the Son of God, to the measure of the stature of the fullness of Christ." That is, till we all come to agree in the same faith, which is fully conformed to Christ, and therein are come to his rule and measure; and in faith, and perhaps in other graces, the body of Christ becomes complete, being completely conformed to Christ. The church [is] the completeness of Christ, "the fullness of him that filleth all in all" [Ephesians 1:23]. But this body is not complete, and but an imperfect embryo, till it is perfectly conformed to his mind in faith and to his image in other graces. Christ and his church, as here, so elsewhere, being as body and soul, are called one man. 'Tis as if he had said, "Till Christ's body is complete in stature." The church, the body of Christ, is called a man (Ephesians 2:15). (*Works* 15, 65)

Though an "imperfect embryo" and an inconsistent student in the school of conformity, the church as Edwards conceived it enjoyed a relationship with Christ so close that the two "are called one man." The church was not simply an organization, a likeminded group with leaders and helpers. The church was the very body of Christ, the enfleshment of His being on the earth. It enjoyed communion with Christ, its "soul," and underwent spiritual transformation as the soul melded with the body.

THE CHURCH AS "CHRIST'S MOTHER"

Edwards dwelt further on the spiritual union shared between Christ and the church in his notes, describing in intense, biblically saturated language the marriage between them:

The Old Testament church was as Christ's mother, but the New Testament church is his wife, whom he is joined to, and whom he treats with far greater endearment and intimacy. He forsook his mother also in this respect, viz. as he made a sacrifice of that flesh and blood, and laid down that mortal life which he had from his mother, the Virgin Mary. "That which [is] born of the flesh is flesh," though he did not derive flesh from his mother in the sense in which it is spoken of, John 3:6, viz. corrupt sinful nature, and therefore did not forsake his mother for the church in the same

sense wherein the church is advised to forsake her father's house
for Christ's sake, viz. to forsake sin and lusts derived from parents,
by crucifying the flesh with the affections and lusts. Yet Christ
derived flesh from his mother, viz. the animal nature and human
nature, with that corruption that is the fruit of sin, viz. with frailty
and mortality. This Christ forsook, and yielded to be crucified for
the sake of the church. (*Works* 15, 182)

The doctrine of the church developed here is quite unique. Old
Testament followers of God represent "Christ's mother," while
New Testament believers are "his wife." The passage emphasizes
the "far greater endearment and intimacy" Christ held for His
wife. Christ "derived flesh" from the "human nature" He as-
sumed in His incarnation, which made possible His "sacrifice"
of "flesh and blood" given "for the sake of the church" of all eras.
Edwards shows a creative streak even as he articulates a commonly held understanding of the atonement. Christ could not
take an impure "wife"; He had to have a pure bride, spotless
and holy, and yet only He could provide this purity for a sinful
people. At the heart of the spiritual unity between Christ and the
church, then, is the cross, which made possible this unity and
which cleansed the bride of every spot and blemish she bore.

Christ's gift to His bride extended beyond His sacrificial
cleansing. In another note, Edwards discussed how, after saving
His people, Christ "filled" them and satisfied their souls with His
love, and was in turn satisfied by them. Referring to Ephesians
1:22–23, he wrote,

[H]ere the Apostle teaches that Christ, who fills all things,
all elect creatures in heaven and earth, himself is filled by the
church. He, who supplies angels and men with all that good in
which they are perfect and happy, receives the church as that
in which he himself is happy. He, from whom and in whom all

angels and saints are adorned and made perfect in beauty, himself receives the church as his glorious and beautiful ornament, as the virtuous wife is a crown to her husband. The church is the garment of Christ, and was typified by that coat of his that was without seam [John 19:23], [which] signified the union of the various members of the church, and was typified by those garments of the high priest that were made "for glory and for beauty" (Exodus 28:2), as seems evident by the Psalms 133:2, and by the precious stones of his breastplate in a particular manner, on which were engraven the names of the children of Israel.

Edwards proved his point by referencing several Scriptures:

Isaiah 62:3, "Thou shalt also be a crown of glory in the hand of the Lord, and a royal diadem in the hand of thy God," i.e. in the possession of God. So Zechariah 9:16–17, "And the Lord their God shall save them in that day as the flock of his people, for they shall be as the stones of a crown, lifted up as an ensign upon his land." As 'tis from and in Christ that all are supplied with joy and happiness, so Christ receives the church as that in which he has exceeding and satisfying delight and joy. Isaiah 62:5, "As the bridegroom rejoiceth over the bride, so shall thy God rejoice over thee." This seems to be the good that Christ sought in the creation of the world, who is the beginning of the creation of God, when all things were created by him and for him, viz. that he might obtain a spouse that he might give himself to and give himself for, on whom he might pour forth his love, and in whom his soul might eternally be delighted. Till he had attained this, he was pleased not to look on himself as complete, but as wanting something, as Adam was not complete till he had obtained his Eve (Genesis 2:20). (*Works* 15, 185–86)

The passage covers several themes, not least among them the matter of Christ's filling His bride. To be filled means that "ye might have your souls satisfied with a participation of God's own good, his beauty and joy." The satisfaction of the Christian involved a constant sampling of God's goodness, a "participation" in the glory of His being. The Christian finds "fullness" of happiness and joy not from the world or anything in the world, but only in God. As believers seek the Lord, He fills them not simply with what is good but with His goodness, His beauty, His joy. The church, constantly "supplied with joy and happiness," is called to drink deeply of God and His goodness.

THE CHURCH AS A "MULTITUDE OF DROPS"

In turn, Edwards noted that "Christ, who fills all things, all elect creatures in heaven and earth, himself is filled by the church." Having made the church beautiful by His love, Jesus finds satisfaction in its beauty. Edwards did not believe that Christ needed the church to be happy, but instead thought that the church magnified Christ's existing happiness and self-satisfaction. The relationship of Christ and the church is a reciprocal one, then, with each party receiving joy in an unending cycle.

Having traced the way in which Christ nurtures and satisfies His people, Edwards went on to explore the beauty of both the individual believer and the church. Using the metaphor of a rainbow, Edwards discussed the role of each in the economy of divine beauty:

> The multitude of drops, from which the light of the sun is so beautifully reflected, signify the same with the multitude of the drops of dew, that reflect the light of the sun in a morning, spoken of, Psalms 110:3. . . . They are all God's jewels; and as they are all in heaven, each one by its reflection is a little star, and so do more

fitly represent the saints than the drops of dew. These drops are all from heaven, as the saints are born from above; they are all from the dissolving cloud. So the saints are the children of Christ; they receive their new nature from him, and by his death they are from the womb of the cloud, the church. So Jerusalem, which is above, is "the mother of us all" [Galatians 4:26]. The saints are born of the church that is in travail with them, enduring great labors, and sufferings, and cruel persecutions; so these jewels of God are out of the dissolving cloud. These drops receive and reflect the light of the sun just breaking forth, and shining out of the cloud that had been till now darkened, and hid, and covered with thick clouds. (*Works* 15, 330–31)

The illustration is striking for the manner in which it captures both the greatness of Christ and the small though significant beauty of every member of the church. Christ is the sun in Edwards's mind, the light that beams over all the creation. The saints are the tiny "drops" of moisture. Just as the sun's rays catch each drop, however small or insignificant, so does the love of Christ extend to each of His children. This light beautifies each person, each "drop," allowing each the opportunity to participate in the reflection of the Lord's loveliness. The combined beauty of all the raindrops is greater still, for "the whole as united [is] together much more beautiful," just as the church possesses a special beauty as it shines in collective witness across all lands. The church in gathered form, then, is an aesthetic exhibit of beauty that receives and reflects light from heaven.

THE CHURCH AS "MILITANT" BUT UNDEFEATED

Edwards gave his doctrine of the church historical weight and depth in his unfinished masterpiece "History of the Work of Redemption." There he disclosed that the church was not only linked to Christ, but satisfied by Him, and a unified display of His glory. While in the world, the church was "militant." Attacked by Satan and his minions, the church faced great trial. Believers lived no easy existence, but often had to endure terrible opposition and difficulty. However, this reality did not dim the beauty of the church, but only intensified it. The militant church consistently overcame the persecution it faced, giving great glory to God and rendering it more beautiful than before. In one section of the work, Edwards wrote that the church's preservation

> is still the more exceeding wonderful if we consider how often the church has been approaching to the brink of ruin, and the case seemed to [be] lost, and all hope gone; they seemed to be swallowed up. In the time of the old world when wickedness so prevailed, as that but one family was left, and yet God wonderfully appeared and overthrew the wicked world with a flood and preserved his church. And so at the Red Sea, when Pharaoh and his host thought they were quite sure of their prey, yet God appeared and destroyed them, and delivered his church. And so it was from time to time in the church of Israel, as has been shown. So under the heathen persecution [of the Christian church]. . . . after the darkest times of the church God has made his church most gloriously to flourish.

He closed the section by celebrating the sovereignty of God in the trials of the church:

> If such a preservation of the church of God from the beginning of the world, hitherto attended with such circumstances, is not sufficient to show a divine hand in favor of it, what can be devised that would? But if this be from the divine hand, then God owns the church, and owns her religion, and owns that revelation and those Scriptures on which she is built; and so it will follow that

> their religion is the true religion or God's religion, and the Scrip-
> tures that they make their rule his Word. (*Works* 9, 449)

Though Edwards did not include the word *beauty* in this passage, it is clear that he viewed the persecuted but persevering church as an emblem of God's glory and beauty. Throughout the ages, in "the darkest times," the Lord allowed the people of God "most gloriously to flourish." History was full of instances in which an antichrist sought to destroy the people of God, who became living screens on which the faithfulness of God, the "divine hand" of the Lord, most clearly appeared. For Edwards, the perseverance and victory of the saints in all ages, empowered by God, revealed beyond a shadow of a doubt the church's otherworldly orienta-tion. As with all the created order, the life of the church proved a medium in which the Lord could further showcase His majesty and exalt the Son who secured His people in the palm of His hand (John 10:28).

Because God authored it, the story of the church was not, in Edwards's mind, a weak or precarious one. Considerable forces and foes rose up throughout history to stamp out the light of Christ as carried by His people, but they never succeeded, and never would. The "divine hand" made the history of the people of God a strong and resilient one. The unflagging perseverance of God's people testified to the strength and beauty of the one who empowered them. The church was militant and besieged, but it was also strong and highly favored—the possession of God who by their courage in all eras displayed "most gloriously" the beauty of the sovereign.

THE MANY-SPLENDORED CHURCH

As we have seen, the church is not a building. It is not a structure that one must heat, an edifice that one must repair. The church of God is part of the "mystical body" of Christ. The people of God who form the church in all its rich diversity share the highest privilege known to mankind, that of participating in the beauty, joy, and goodness of the Lord, of being satisfied in Christ and giving Him satisfaction. So, far from being a building or a religiously minded organization, the church embodies the Savior. Through the Spirit, Christ is present in His church as it marches on, militant in this world, triumphant in the next.

Pursuing Beauty

Realize Church Is Not a Building but a Living Fellowship

The body of Christ is a spiritual entity made physical. The church is an incarnate, embodied manifestation of God's glory, love, and mercy in the world (Rom. 12:4–5). It is not only a spiritual institution but a physical presence, a tangible testimony to the existence and majesty of God. Where believers are gathered, they form the church. This is true whether one's local church (gathering of believers) is great or small. Wherever Christians worship together, they form a living picture of God's character, a visible demonstration of divine glory. Perhaps remembering this will help us to transcend boredom and discouragement in our times of meeting. In the kingdom of God, every community of believers has great significance and purpose.

Furthermore, it is essential that Christians remember that they have a very specific identity. We are not another religious group, a mere gathering of people with a shared background and ideology. We are the called-out children of God who have the mission of loving and proclaiming Jesus Christ together (Matt. 18; 1 Cor. 11; Heb. 13). Membership with a local church is thus very important. Nowhere does the Bible commend "lone ranger"

Christianity in which we act and live alone. We are called to fellowship together (Heb. 10:25) and to bear one another's burdens and sorrows (Gal. 6:2). When one of our number sins grievously against the Lord, and refuses to repent, we must remove them from our community in order that the Lord's name not be tarnished (Matt. 18). Within this body, we need to submit to our deacons and elders and work with them for the furtherance of the gospel (1 Tim. 5).

Let us not forget this, either: because the church is empowered by the "divine hand," Christians are not weak people, and the church is not a weak institution. Against all odds and appearances, the church of God can and will prevail over its persecutors, foes, and obstacles (Matt. 16:18). Every believer should live by such a view and every local church should operate according to this reality. Though outnumbered and outgunned, the church belongs to Christ and He sustains it with His own presence and power through union with believers in the Holy Spirit (Acts 1:8). This divine orientation renders us incredibly strong, despite appearances, and necessitates that we live and practice our faith with boldness and confidence in our sovereign God.

Chapter 13

THE BEAUTY OF THE TRINITARIAN AFTERLIFE

As noted earlier, the study of God begins in the dust. To think and speak of God requires a posture of humility, the recognition of one's finitude. As one lies in the dust, and the words of God roll over one's back, filling the air with the weight of holiness, one learns the truths of God and experiences the beauty of His presence. Such encounters transform us and leave us humbled and awestruck at what we have seen and heard. In certain instances, however, the believer is not laid low by God but lifted up. Like the old apostle John, who sat quietly in a prison cell in first-century Greece, the believer who searches the Scripture may suddenly catch a glimpse of another realm (Rev. 1 and following). In John's revelation and other places in Scripture, the believer sees a place where sickness and pain cannot invade, where streams of living water flow, and where the Lord reigns over all. The vision is brief and breathtaking, and it leaves the believer, like John, both stunned at the sight and stirred to press on until this new day dawns.

Throughout his life, Jonathan Edwards caught scripturally inspired glimpses of heaven. As he studied the Scripture and meditated on the age to come, he discovered "a world of love" where God, the fountain of beauty, lived with His beautified church in a cycle of mutual delight that filled all the heavens. It is the purpose of this chapter to illuminate the nature of Trinitarian beauty as exchanged by the members of the Godhead in heaven and experienced by believers in that "world of love." Through studying his capstone Trinitarian sermon, "Discourse on the Trinity," this chapter will bring to light Edwards's unique understanding of the identities of the Trinitarian persons. The text will then cover the sermon "Heaven Is a World of Love," where Edwards developed the ways in which believers will share communion with the Godhead and participate in its exchange of love. In all, the believer will catch a vision of heaven and discover fresh desire for uninhibited communion with God in the life to come.

THE RELATIONSHIP BETWEEN THE MEMBERS OF THE TRINITY

Edwards began the "Discourse on the Trinity" by outlining the fundamental set of relationships between the persons of the Trinity. He wrote of the foundation of the Godhead that

> The Godhead being thus begotten by God's having an idea of himself and standing forth in a distinct subsistence or person in that idea, there proceeds a most pure act, and an infinitely holy and sweet energy arises between the Father and Son: for their love and joy is mutual, in mutually loving and delighting in each other. Proverbs 8:30, "I was daily his delight, rejoicing always before [him]." This is the eternal and most perfect and essential act of the divine nature, wherein the Godhead acts to an infinite degree and in the most perfect manner possible. The Deity becomes all act; the divine essence itself flows out and is as it were breathed forth in love and joy. So that the Godhead therein stands forth in yet another manner of subsistence, and there proceeds the third person in the Trinity, the Holy Spirit, viz. the Deity in act: for there is no other act but the act of the will. (*Works* 6, 121)

The Trinity takes its existence in Edwards's mind from "God's having an idea of himself." This idea, as Edwards conceives it, is the Son, the second person of the Trinity who personifies God's perfect conception of Himself. The Father thinks about Himself, imagining Himself as a person, and the Son is the personification of this thought. The Spirit, the third person of the Trinity, flows forth from both Father and Son "in another manner of subsistence," proceeding from the first and second persons as their "will." As Edwards understood them, the persons of the Trinity shared life together in an unending mutual exchange of love. The pastor outlined this idea in the following passage:

> We may learn by the Word of God that the Godhead or the divine nature and essence does subsist in love. 1 John 4:8, "He that loveth not knoweth not God; for God is love." In the context of which place I think it is plainly intimated to us that the Holy Spirit is that love, as in the 1 John 4:12–13: "If we love one another, God dwelleth in us, and his love is perfected in us. Hereby know we that we dwell in him, because he hath given us of his Spirit." 'Tis the same argument in both verses: in the 1 John 4:12 the Apostle argues that if we have love dwelling in [us], we have God dwelling in us; and in the 1 John 4:13 he clears the force of the argument by this, that love is God's Spirit. Seeing we have of God's Spirit dwelling [in us], we have God dwelling in [us]: supposing it as a thing granted and allowed, that God's Spirit is God. 'Tis evident also by this verse that God's dwelling in us, and his love—or the love that he hath or exerciseth—being in us, are the same thing. The same is intimated in the same manner in the last verses of the foregoing chapter. The Apostle was in the foregoing verses speaking of love as a sure sign of sincerity and our acceptance with God, beginning with the 1 John 4:18, and he sums up the argument thus in the last verse: "And hereby do we know that he abideth in us by the Spirit that [he] hath given us." (*Works* 6, 121–22)

According to Edwards, the "essence" of the Trinity was love. The ground and substance of interaction between the persons of the Godhead was transcendent affection and delight in one another. This bond of love proceeded from the inherent holiness of each of the Trinitarian persons and enabled them to enjoy one another without interruption or compromise. The Trinitarian love was of such strength that Edwards equated "God's dwelling in us" with "his love." To know God is to know His love, to drink from its constant flow, to experience the sweetness of life in the Spirit.

A "SOCIETY" OR "FAMILY"

Having sketched the essence of Trinitarian life, Edwards carefully defined the identities of the persons of the Godhead. All three members shared the majesty of divine being and each possessed the same traits, living together in a "society or family" characterized by perfect harmony. Each member, however, expressed these traits in different ways and with different functions:

> Hereby we see how the Father is the fountain of the Godhead, and why when he is spoken of in Scripture he is so often, without any addition or distinction, called God; which has led some to think that he only was truly and properly God. Hereby we may see why, in the economy of the persons of the Trinity, the Father should sustain the dignity of the Deity; that the Father should have it as his office to uphold and maintain the rights of the Godhead, and should be God, not only by essence, but as it were by his economical office. Hereby is illustrated the doctrine of the Holy Ghost preceding both the Father and the Son. Hereby we see how that it is possible for the Son to be begotten by the Father, and the Holy Ghost to proceed from the Father and Son, and yet that all the persons should be co-eternal. Hereby we

may more clearly understand the equality of the persons among themselves, and that they are every way equal in the society or family of the three. They are equal in honor besides the honor which is common to 'em all, viz. that they are all God; each has his peculiar honor in the society or family. They are equal not only in essence. The Father's honor is that he is as it were the author of perfect and infinite wisdom. The Son's honor is that he is that perfect and divine wisdom itself, the excellency of which is that from whence arises the honor of being the author or generator of it. The honor of the Father and the Son is that they are infinitely excellent, or that from them infinite excellency proceeds. But the honor of the Holy Ghost is equal, for he is that divine excellency and beauty itself. (*Works* 6, 135)

The concepts of *unity* and *diversity* are essential to understanding this passage. The Trinity is unified in that all its members share the essence of divinity. The Father, Son, and Spirit are all God, in other words, and each possesses all the entailments of being God. The members share a perfect harmony of soul that results from their divine unity. Though this may sound confusing, Edwards in fact gives us a very helpful metaphor by which to understand the Trinity, that of a family or society. The "family members" are united by sharing the essence of divinity.

At the same time, there is diversity within the Godhead, just as there is diversity within a family. As Edwards conceived of the family's roles, the Father issues a trait, like holiness; the Son, the exact image and idea of the Father, personifies this trait, being perfectly holy; the Spirit represents the expression of this trait from the Father and Son that emanates from the Godhead into the lives of believers, thus making them holy. In the Edwardsean view, each member of the Trinity has a distinct role to play in glorifying the Godhead and displaying this glory in the world. The diversity of the Godhead enhances the harmony of the family just as the different members of a family play different roles, or as the members of a symphony play different instruments in creating a harmonious and beautifully blended sound.

The love this family shares is so intense, so rich, that it spills out from heaven into the world. In the era of the church, when Christ has accomplished His redemptive mission, the Father and the Son send the Holy Spirit into the world to bring mankind into communion with them. The Holy Spirit brings the collective love and beauty of the Trinity to the hearts of sinners through the gospel. Where the gospel is received by faith, the Holy Spirit comes to dwell. In the following section, Edwards discusses how the Spirit unites the believer to the love of the Holy Trinity:

> It is a confirmation that the Holy Ghost is God's love and delight, because the saints' communion with God consists in their partaking of the Holy Ghost. The communion of saints is twofold: 'tis their communion with God, and communion with one another. 1 John 1:3, "That ye also may have fellowship with us: and truly our fellowship is with the Father, and with his Son Jesus Christ." Communion is a common partaking of goods, either of excellency or happiness. So that when it is said the saints have communion or fellowship with the Father and with the Son, the meaning of it is that they partake with the Father and the Son of their good, which is either their excellency and glory—2 Peter 1:4, "Ye are made partakers of the divine nature"; Hebrews 12:10, "That we might be partakers of his holiness"; John 17:22–23, "And the glory which thou hast given me I have given them; that may be one, even as we are one: I in them, and thou in me"— or of their joy and happiness, John 17:13, "That they may have my joy fulfilled in themselves." But the Holy Ghost, being the love and joy of God, is his beauty and happiness; and it is in our partaking of the same Holy Spirit that our communion with God consists. . . . In this also eminently consists our communion with the saints, that we drink into the same Spirit: this is the common

excellency and joy and happiness in which they all are united; 'tis the
bond of perfectness by which they are one in the Father and the Son,
as the Father is in the Son, and [he in him]. (*Works* 6, 129–30)

The section is noteworthy for its helpful definition of a key term
in this discussion, "communion," which Edwards defines as "a
common partaking of goods, either of excellency or happiness."
Christians who share communion with the Godhead "partake
with the Father and the Son of their good, which is either their
excellency and glory, or their "joy and happiness."

The Holy Spirit's indwelling presence, then, allows the believer to know in a personal way the "excellency or happiness" of
the Trinity and to taste, accordingly, "the love and joy of God" and
the "beauty and happiness" of the divine. Salvation, then, means
that the believer enters a stream of divine love and beauty that
sweeps them into the boundless pool of Trinitarian happiness. In
a way that is difficult to comprehend but refreshing to contemplate, believers will in heaven drink unendingly from Trinitarian
goodness and experience eternal delight in their communion, or
fellowship, with the Godhead. Much more than earthly fellowship, heavenly communion will allow the believer to "partake,"
or experience in the most intimate and involved way, the beauty
of God.

THE "WORLD OF LOVE"

Armed with a basic grasp of the workings of the Trinity and the
believer's participation in its relationship of love, we look now
at Edwards's meditation on heaven in his unforgettable sermon
"Heaven Is a World of Love." While Edwards covers the identities and roles of the Godhead in heaven, he devotes special attention to the nature of heaven itself. Early in the sermon he lays
out his basic conception of heaven as the dwelling place of God:

Heaven is a part of the creation which God has built for this end, to be the place of his glorious presence. And it is his abode forever. Here he will dwell and gloriously manifest himself to eternity. And this renders heaven a world of love; for God is the fountain of love, as the sun is the fountain of light. And therefore the glorious presence of God in heaven fills heaven with love, as the sun placed in the midst of the hemisphere in a clear day fills the world with light. The Apostle tells us that God is love, 1 John 4:8. And therefore seeing he is an infinite Being, it follows that he is an infinite fountain of love. Seeing he is an all-sufficient Being, it follows that he is a full and overflowing and an inexhaustible fountain of love. Seeing he is an unchangeable and eternal Being, he is an unchangeable and eternal source of love. There even in heaven dwells that God from whom every stream of holy love, yea, every drop that is or ever was proceeds.

Edwards sketched out the interplay of love between Father, Son, and Spirit in heaven, showing how the Godhead's "infinite fountain" poured out its love in the world above:

There dwells God the Father, and so the Son, who are united in infinitely dear and incomprehensible mutual love. There dwells God the Father, who is the Father of mercies, and so the Father of love, who so loved the world that he gave his only begotten Son, that whosoever believeth in him should not perish, but have everlasting life [John 3:16]. There dwells Jesus Christ, the Lamb of God, the Prince of peace and love, who so loved the world that he shed his blood, and poured out his soul unto death for it. There dwells the Mediator, by whom all God's love is expressed to the saints, by whom the fruits of it have been purchased, and through whom they are communicated, and through whom love is imparted to the hearts of all the church. There Christ dwells in both his natures, his human and divine, sitting with the Father in the same throne. There is the

Holy Spirit, the spirit of divine love, in whom the very essence of God, as it were, all flows out or is breathed forth in love, and by whose immediate influence all holy love is shed abroad in the hearts of all the church [cf. Romans 5:5]. There in heaven this fountain of love, this eternal three in one, is set open without any obstacle to hinder access to it. There this glorious God is manifested and shines forth in full glory, in beams of love; there the fountain overflows in streams and rivers of love and delight, enough for all to drink at, and to swim in, yea, so as to overflow the world as it were with a deluge of love. (*Works* 8, 369–70)

Heaven, in Edwards's mind, is most fundamentally a realm of love. The Father, Son, and Spirit reign in heaven, loving one another and sharing their love "without any obstacle to hinder access to it." The human heart, created to thirst after love, finds its ultimate satisfaction in heaven. On earth, the Christian tastes love for a time, but the delight is quickly interrupted by one's sins and troubles. In addition, Satan is a powerful force in this realm, and he carries out a campaign of terror that desperately tries to undermine the communication of God's love to His people (see Job 1, for example). In heaven, however, neither sin nor Satan has a place. Only the Trinity lives and acts there. The happy "streams" and "rivers" of love "overflow" that world and overwhelm the senses. The moments of happiness that sprinkle us on this earth will one day give way to an eternal "deluge of love" that flows from the Godhead to our souls without end or interruption.

This love had a definite object, an end, which is God, in Edwards's mind. For him, heaven was a world of love, and the center of this world was God. Though some define heaven in terms of experiences and pleasures, Edwards characterized the realm as most fundamentally the place where God reigns bright as a sun, drawing all eyes to gaze upon Him:

The love of God flows out towards Christ the Head, and through him to all his members, in whom they were beloved before the foundation of the world, and in whom his love was expressed towards them in time by his death and sufferings, and in their conversion and the great things God has done for them in this world, and is now fully manifested to them in heaven. And the saints and angels are secondarily the subjects of holy love, not as in whom love is as in an original seat, as light is in the sun which shines by its own light, but as it is in the planets which shine by reflecting the light of the sun. And this light is reflected in the first place and chiefly back to the sun itself.

The pastor detailed how God's people participated in this happy world:

As God has given the saints and angels love, so their love is chiefly exercised towards God, the fountain of it, as is most reasonable. They all love God with a supreme love. There is no enemy of God in heaven, but all love him as his children. They all are united with one mind to breathe forth their whole souls in love to their eternal Father, and to Jesus Christ, their common Head. Christ loves all his saints in heaven. His love flows out to his whole church there, and to every individual member of it; and they all with one heart and one soul, without any schism in the body, love their common Redeemer. Every heart is wedded to this spiritual husband. All rejoice in him, the angels concurring. And the angels and saints all love one another. All that glorious society are sincerely united. There is no secret or open enemy among them; not one heart but is full of love, nor one person who is not beloved. As they are all lovely, so all see each other's loveliness with answerable delight and complacence. Everyone there loves every other inhabitant of heaven whom he sees, and so he is mutually beloved by everyone. (*Works* 8, 373–74)

Against views of heaven that paint mainly sentimental scenes, Edwards declared that believers "all are united with one mind to breathe forth their whole souls in love to their eternal Father, and to Jesus Christ, their common Head." There, believers will not struggle to focus on God and devote themselves to Him as we do on earth. All the sin and strife that clouds our love for God here will melt away in heaven, and we will see God in His glory. Our hearts that we must continually stoke now will soar with delight. Just as the sight of an adorable baby or a beautiful vista causes our jaw to drop, the vision of God that we see in the next life will impel us to adore God and celebrate His beauty. Though we sometimes wrestle with our hopes for heaven—Will beloved pets be there? Will we grow bored in worship?—Edwards's biblically infused words focus us on the essential reality of heaven, the goodness and beauty of God, and remind us that we will be so enraptured by Him that everything else will pale in significance.

After sketching the identity and roles of the Trinity and covering the way in which the Trinity shared its communion with the church, Edwards offered his audience a powerful oration on the heavenly blessing that awaited the church. Sojourning now through a "great and terrible wilderness," we so often observe the "fading of the beauty" of everything that we love. The shadows of divine beauty on this earth must all give way to the forces of time. Only the people of God possess a beauty that does not fade. Only the church will enter a resting place where God will give to us unending "milk and honey":

> And all this in a garden of love, the Paradise of God, where every-
> thing has a cast of holy love, and everything conspires to promote
> and stir up love, and nothing to interrupt its exercises; where
> everything is fitted by an all-wise God for the enjoyment of love
> under the greatest advantages. And all this shall be without any
> fading of the beauty of the objects beloved, or any decaying of love

in the lover, and any satiety in the faculty which enjoys love. O! what tranquility may we conclude there is in such a world as this! Who can express the sweetness of this peace? What a calm is this, what a heaven of rest is here to arrive at after persons have gone through a world of storms and tempests, a world of pride, and selfishness, and envy, and malice, and scorn, and contempt, and contention and war? What a Canaan of rest, a land flowing with milk and honey to come to after one has gone through a great and terrible wilderness, full of spiteful and poisonous serpents, where no rest could be found? What joy may we conclude springs up in the hearts of the saints after they have passed their wearisome pilgrimage to be brought to such a paradise? Here is joy unspeakable indeed; here is humble, holy, divine joy in its perfection. Love is a sweet principle, especially divine love. It is a spring of sweetness.

Love could not flow as a "spring" only, however. It would grow and grow:

But here the spring shall become a river, and an ocean. All shall stand about the God of glory, the fountain of love, as it were opening their bosoms to be filled with those effusions of love which are poured forth from thence, as the flowers on the earth in a pleasant spring day open their bosoms to the sun to be filled with his warmth and light, and to flourish in beauty and fragrancy by his rays. Every saint is as a flower in the garden of God, and holy love is the fragrancy and sweet odor which they all send forth, and with which they fill that paradise. Every saint there is as a note in a concert of music which sweetly harmonizes with every other note, and all together employed wholly in praising God and the Lamb; and so all helping one another to their utmost to express their love of the whole society to the glorious Father and Head of it, and to pour back love into the fountain of love, whence they are supplied and filled with love and with glory. And thus they will

live and thus they will reign in love, and in that godlike joy which
is the blessed fruit of it, such as eye hath not seen, nor ear heard, nor
hath ever entered into the heart of any in this world to conceive [cf.
1 Corinthians 2:9]. And thus they will live and reign forever and ever.
(*Works* 8, 385–86)

Emanating from heaven, beauty spans the created realm and
returns to heaven. The cycle that began with God returns to
Him as the church, the possession of the Son, joins the angels
to express "to their utmost" their love "to the glorious Father and
Head of it." Though divided on earth, where unity is precarious,
the church gathers for eternity in heaven to commune with God
and experience the fullness of His beauty. No discordance or dis-
harmony can be heard there; all is a "concert of music" that plays
a symphony of adoration. No darkness will fall there; only the
"warmth and light" of almighty God will exist in heaven. Every
sense, every second of thought, every intention of the heart, will
focus on God and His beauty. "The fountain of love" from God
will overflow, and the saints will always drink of that love, even as
they pour out their own love to God.

HEAVEN'S TRIUNE BEAUTY

So closes our study of the Trinitarian afterlife, the future dwelling place of the church. We end much like the apostle John after
he received his revelation of heaven—awestruck at what we have
seen, captivated by the hope of that realm, yearning for beauty
and love that does not fade or wane. We are comforted by the
knowledge that we will soon be there. In the blink of an eye, we
will see the Lord. We will join with our guides and teachers, with
holy saints of old, with fellow servants like Jonathan Edwards,
and we will worship the God of glory, tasting His love, savoring
His goodness, and participating for eternity in the cycle of beauty.

Pursuing Beauty

Study and Worship the Trinity

The first order of application for most of us is this—to make contemplation of the Trinity a part of our spiritual lives. Many of us affirm the existence of the Trinity but go for years without studying it. Many of our churches, unfortunately, do little to help us in this area. We will never fully understand it, of course, but merely beginning to study it will greatly help us to comprehend the magnificence and multifaceted beauty of the Godhead. Many of us are captivated instead by paltry, shallow things because we have been fed a diet of fluffy media and airy preaching and spend very little time and energy looking into transcendent realities. Yet if we will allow it to do so, the Trinity as laid out in Scripture will blow our socks off. We can never exhaust the beauty of divine oneness; neither should we cease to explore the wonders of eternal threeness.

Books like Bruce Ware's *Father, Son, and Holy Spirit* (Crossway, 2005) and Robert Letham's *The Holy Trinity* (P&R, 2004) will help us to worship the Trinity with knowledge and insight.

Seek Trinitarian Love Above All

The fact that heaven is a "world of love" as Edwards put it must inspire us to love God on earth in order that we might love God in heaven. We should use Edwards's spellbinding picture of heaven as a motivation for holy living (see Col. 3:1–10). Our reward awaits us. Though our journey to the other side involves sacrifice and hardship, all our effort to honor the Lord through the power of the Spirit will prove worthwhile in heaven. Knowing that we will live in a sea of love in heaven should inspire us to avoid the cesspools of sin that tempt us here. On this earth and in this day, love is often equated with extramarital sexual gratification and the sudden rush of emotion it brings. If we do not cultivate our love for the Trinitarian God, we will find ourselves weak when tempted by this momentarily satisfying vision of "love." But if we constantly remember the great flood of love that we taste now and will experience for all eternity, we will find ourselves able to regularly evade the fleeting pleasures of this world.

Part 3

The Good Life

Chapter 14

THE NEARNESS
OF THE GOOD LIFE

The gaze is direct. The posture is straight. The face is serious, even stern. In his portraits, Jonathan Edwards stares back at the viewer. To a person unfamiliar with the theologian, he looks like any other stereotypical colonial parson, severe and austere, brooking no foolishness, itching to declaim the evils of everyday life. Wearing a powdered wig of tight white curls, staring alertly back at the observer, Edwards as portrayed on canvas seems to substantiate the image of Edwards cultivated for generations in high-school classrooms. Here is the man who unleashed the thunder of "Sinners in the Hands of an Angry God." Small wonder that such a gloomy person would bore into us from his portrait.

But appearances are often deceiving. In reality, Edwards was not an angry man. He was one of the happiest men around. He loved to play and talk with his children, and he enjoyed much cheer and laughter with Sarah. He cherished his time in his study. Jonathan's happiness, however, transcended the joys of home and work, significant as they are. Unlike many people, Edwards knew happiness at the very core of his being. In a way that many of us don't even think about, Edwards possessed a holistic intellectual and spiritual happiness. He strove to know God with his mind, to experience the goodness of God with his heart, and to lead others to do the same. Though his temperament was calm, he lived with zest and vigor, modeling the happy way of life he taught his people.

Many people today do not know such peace and happiness. They live with constant tension, often acting contrary to what their mind and their conscience tell them is right. They rebel against their Creator and His design for their life. Though they may know satisfaction for a brief period, lasting happiness evades them. This results in a broken, frustrating, and ultimately pointless life.

Though his era differed from ours, Jonathan identified the same problem in his day. Gifted from his youth with great passion for God and His Word, Jonathan discovered early on in his life that true and lasting happiness in this life was attainable. All that the human heart desired it could have, and far more besides. The riches of God's Word could satisfy the intellectual hunger of the human mind for a balanced, cohesive, meaningful worldview and the spiritual hunger of the human heart for a joyful, hopeful, transformative existence.

In sum, Jonathan discovered a simple but vitalizing truth: God had not made mankind to be miserable. Being a Christian did not mean the absence of pleasure. Much to the contrary, God had made mankind to experience unending delight and joy in Him, to be happier and happier as knowledge of God increased, and to constantly soak up the sweetest pleasure the world affords in the life of faith—all of which flow together to constitute "the good life." In a world filled with people who lived in the gloom of darkness, Jonathan Edwards preached to set his hearers' hearts on fire, to alter forever the way they understood themselves and their lives. He knew that any life created by the majestic, undomesticated, loving God of the Bible could not be mundane or boring. He preached in such a way as to altogether change the way we think about our faith and the way we practice it.

In this chapter, we will explore the initial, pre-fall design of God for human life through interaction with a number of noteworthy Edwardsean texts: *A Dissertation Concerning the End for Which God Created the World*, *A Dissertation Concerning the Nature of True Virtue*, the sermon "Charity Contrary to a Selfish Spirit," and the homily "The Pleasantness of Religion." By studying carefully these sources, we will develop an understanding of the original intention of the Creator for mankind and clear our minds of false and unbiblical conceptions of the good, Christian life. God, we shall see in this chapter, has not made people to be grimly obedient. Rather, He desires that we find transcendent, unassailable, undimmed satisfaction in Him.

GOD THE FOUNDATION

The foundation of the good life is God. In Edwards's world, God reigned over all as the emblem of majesty, authority, and goodness. The sum of His perfections rendered God beautiful, or more accurately, Beauty itself. As covered in part 2, God created the world to display and reflect His glory. All that the eye can see exists to "remanate," or send back, God's original glory to Himself. God alone is worthy of such a system, for He alone is God. All of creation participates in this "cycle of beauty" that begins with God and returns to God.

But while all things in some way display and reflect the beauty of God, only humans may do so with awareness. Only mankind can participate consciously in the cycle of beauty. It was for this very purpose that God created the race. He desired a special sort of being to commune with Him and to joyfully image His goodness in the world. Edwards discussed this in his foundational text *The End for Which God Created the World*:

It seems to be a thing in itself fit and desirable, that the glorious
perfections of God should be known, and the operations and
expressions of them seen by other beings besides himself. . . .
As God's perfections are things in themselves excellent, so the
expression of them in their proper acts and fruits is excellent, and
the knowledge of these excellent perfections, and of these glorious
expressions of them, is an excellent thing, the existence of which is in
itself valuable and desirable.

Because God was so excellent, it was only right that His excellence be enjoyed by others:

'Tis a thing infinitely good in itself that God's glory should be
known by a glorious society of created beings. And that there
should be in them an increasing knowledge of God to all eternity
is an existence, a reality infinitely worthy to be, and worthy to be
valued and regarded by him, to whom it belongs in order that it
be, which, of all things possible, is fittest and best. If existence
is more worthy than defect and nonentity, and if any created
existence is in itself worthy to be, then knowledge or understanding is a thing worthy to be; and if any knowledge, then the most
excellent sort of knowledge, viz. that of God and his glory. The
existence of the created universe consists as much in it as in
anything: yea, this knowledge is one of the highest, most real
and substantial parts, of all created existence most remote from
nonentity and defect. (*Works* 8, 430–32)

The passage touches on numerous ideas, but the key sentence for
our purposes is this: "'Tis a thing infinitely good in itself that God's
glory should be known by a glorious society of created beings." Edwards believed that mankind was made for an "increasing knowledge of God," a knowledge of "the most excellent sort" that would
satisfy and fill the mind and heart as nothing else can. Adam and

Eve, and the race they produced, were not mere chess pawns in the hands of the Grandmaster, but possessed a supremely noble purpose that would make for a life of the most exhilarating kind.

THE GOOD LIFE DOES NOT SQUASH HAPPINESS

In giving his picture of the good life, Edwards had to overcome two specific objections. First, he had to show how a universe that existed to glorify God did not squash or prohibit the happiness of mankind. Central to the following passage is the idea that God "emanates" or sends His beauty (or glory) out, and the creature receives and delights in it. Edwards teaches us here that the happiness of God and the happiness of humanity are not, as some have suggested, at odds. Instead, God and man ideally work in harmony, with God "emanating" glory that is received and reflected by mankind, who grows happy in performing this divine duty:

> God in seeking his glory, therein seeks the good of his creatures: because the emanation of his glory (which he seeks and delights in, as he delights in himself and his own eternal glory) implies the communicated excellency and happiness of his creature. And that in communicating his fullness for them, he does it for himself: because their good, which he seeks, is so much in union and communion with himself. God is their good. Their excellency and happiness is nothing but the emanation and expression of God's glory: God in seeking their glory and happiness, seeks himself: and in seeking himself, i.e. himself diffused and expressed (which he delights in, as he delights in his own beauty and fullness), he seeks their glory and happiness.

Edwards continued the argument by putting it in grander terms:

> In this view it appears that God's respect to the creature, in the whole, unites with his respect to himself. Both regards are like two

lines which seem at the beginning to be separate, but aim finally to meet in one, both being directed to the same center. And as to the good of the creature itself, if viewed in its whole duration, and infinite progression, it must be viewed as infinite; and so not only being some communication of God's glory, but as coming nearer and nearer to the same thing in its infinite fullness. The nearer anything comes to infinite, the nearer it comes to an identity with God. And if any good, as viewed by God, is beheld as infinite, it can't be viewed as a distinct thing from God's own infinite glory. (*Works* 8, 459)

In this passage, Edwards refutes the charge that God's glory and man's happiness are mutually exclusive. His central point is that "God in seeking his glory, therein seeks the good of his creatures." As some mistakenly believed, if God is going to be happy, then He will create a world that pleases only Himself and that yields little or no happiness to the people placed in the world to do His bidding. Humanity functions as little more than a race of slaves forced to execute the tyrannical will of a cruel king. Edwards, however, shows that this line of thought fails miserably. God, if He is God, is not a tyrant. As God, He is the embodiment of goodness. "[T]he emanation of his glory (which he seeks and delights in, as he delights in himself and his own eternal glory)," then, "implies the communicated excellency and happiness of his creature." Life as this kind and awesome God created it to be cannot be slavish or sad; it is filled with "excellency and happiness" that flows from the divine fountain.

All of the God-centered life is calibrated to bless the people of God as they glorify the Lord in all they do (1 Cor. 10:31). Those who seek the Lord and live to magnify Him will know His "communicated excellency and happiness" even as they participate in the great work of glorifying Him. God's glory and man's happiness are not at odds with one another—far from it. The two ideally work hand in hand.

Thus, we see Edwards's brilliant and transformative doctrine of the good life. At its deepest, most profound level, the good life is the life lived for the glory of God. Those who live to display and image the beauty of God will, in whatever circumstance they find themselves, experience happiness that comes directly from God Himself. Happiness, then, is not a state outside of ourselves that we must strive for. It does not ebb and flow with our life situation. Happiness *is* doing the will of God, for the will of God always yields the glory of God. What is the will of God? It is God's revealed purposes and desires in the Bible. In short, the good life is the existence that takes shape according to the teachings and commands of Scripture. When one obeys God by loving His Son and following His Word, one glorifies the Lord and tastes the sweetest, richest happiness known to man. This and no other substitute is the good life. It is what God has always intended for mankind.

THE GOOD LIFE DOES NOT DESTROY SELF-LOVE

In unfurling his vision of the good life, Edwards had to overcome a second objection. He had to show how the God-centered life corresponded with the natural human instinct to love and preserve oneself, which he defined as follows: "Self-love, I think, is generally defined: a man's love of his own happiness" (*Works* 8, 575). Did living for God, in other words, mean that one had to sacrifice concern for oneself and adopt a pattern of living that impeded happiness for the sake of obeying God?

Edwards had a ready answer to this question. He refused, at the start, to separate love for God and love for oneself. One best loved oneself by loving God. Loving oneself without God meant that one strayed from the source of all wisdom and truth, and thus consigned oneself to destruction. On the contrary, loving oneself through loving God meant that one experienced the joys of the virtuous life. Instead of living selfishly, mankind could live for God and experience His boundless goodness. In doing so, they would actually care for themselves far better than if they ignored the Lord and went their own way.

Edwards, we see, also refused to separate happiness from obedience. He argued that exercising virtue in service to God actually enabled a person to love themselves best. "True virtue," he argued in *Dissertation Concerning the Nature of True Virtue*, "most essentially consists in benevolence to Being in general. Or perhaps to speak more accurately, it is that consent, propensity and union of heart to Being in general, that is immediately exercised in a general good will" (*Works* 8, 540). The "Being" of which Edwards spoke was God and the system of creaturely being He had created. Living a life of "benevolence" (or loving goodwill) toward God and His creatures meant that one possessed "true virtue." Virtue and happiness actually went hand in hand. When one acted virtuously to others out of a desire to love God and preserve his soul, he found true happiness. Happiness did not come from gratification of one's selfish instincts, but rather from one's desire to bless others and please the Lord.

In the final analysis, Edwards revealed that virtue and self-preservation did not naturally conflict. God designed man to be good. When a person acts on these instincts and lives a life of "benevolence" to God and, accordingly, to his fellow man, he preserves his soul and, as a result, loves himself more than the person who lives without virtue and who operates out of selfishness. Christianity, the life of Spirit-empowered virtue, does not require that one sacrifice happiness. As a believer in Christ lives the good life of obedience to the Lord, he tastes true and lasting happiness, blesses God and mankind, and ultimately preserves his soul. Edwards's doctrine expresses on a theological level the simple truth taught by Christ centuries before in Matthew 16:25:

"Whoever would save his life will lose it, but whoever loses his life for my sake will find it."

A DEEPLY IRONIC DOCTRINE

The Edwardsean doctrine of happiness is rich with irony. To save one's soul and experience deepest delight, one must abandon the instinct to selfishly pursue one's well-being. True self-interest involves turning one's life over to God and accepting His plan for life over against anything the human mind can conceive. One cannot win salvation and happiness for oneself by selfish cunning or slick plans. If one desires to know happiness in this life and the next, one must hand one's life over to the Lord. A Christian is a person who hands the keys over to Jesus. The believer trusts Him to lead and guide, knowing that whatever way He directs will be best.

It may not always appear this way, of course. One may trust Christ and find that the going soon gets rough. This is no indication that Christ has failed and that happiness is lost. While God often allows His children to feel happy because of favorable circumstances, His fundamental gift to believers is not the promise of a life without challenges, but a state of deep happiness rooted in Himself that transcends all situations, good or ill. This is the kind of happiness that lasts beyond a mood or an emotional high. It is a persevering, bold happiness that is rooted in faith in God and love for Him.

Some people who know this Edwardsean kind of happiness, this rich brand of spiritual joy, express it with great emotion. Edwards himself regularly experienced a sort of rapturous communion with God. Others, however, express their joy in quieter form, their deep satisfaction in Him manifesting itself in a quiet, contented way of life. Neither mode is best; both are valid and good. The challenge for most of us is to find the happiness common to both groups of happy believers. Too many Christians fail to taste the profound satisfaction offered them in the gospel. They have a sense of their salvation, but they have little awareness of the greatness of the gospel and its ability to altogether transform their existence. They know that God wants them to be happy, but they have not realized that joy comes not primarily from having one's desires met by God, but by serving God and doing what He desires.

LIFE IN UNCOMFORTABLE TENSION

Too many of us live in a strenuous push-and-pull relationship with the Lord. We obey Him, to some extent, but we also push for the accomplishment of our plans, the fulfillment of our desires, not realizing that He has a better plan and better desires for us. The happiest Christians are not those who manage to accomplish all of their personal goals. Rather, the happiest Christians are those who embrace what God wants for their lives. Thus, the irony of faith reveals itself once again. One does not become happy by liberating oneself from duty; one becomes happy by obeying and following the plans of the Lord, who in turn provides the happiness one naturally desires. In duty, in serving the Lord, we find true happiness.

In his sermon "Charity Contrary to a Selfish Spirit," Edwards highlighted this theme as he exhorted his Northampton congregation to live charitably, or lovingly, with their fellow men. He taught them that their performance of charity would not diminish their own happiness, but would increase it to a depth that they had never thought possible. Fundamentally, said the pastor,

> A Christian spirit seeks to please and glorify God. The things
> which are well pleasing to God and Christ, and tend to the glory
> of Christ, are called the things of Jesus Christ in opposition to

our own things. Philippians 2:21, "For all seek their own, not the things which are Jesus Christ's." Christianity requires that we should make God and Christ our main end. Christians, so far as they live like Christians, live so that for them to live is Christ [Philippians 1:21]. Christians are required to live so as to please God. Romans 12:2, "That ye may prove what is that good, and acceptable, and perfect will of God." We should be such servants of Christ as do in all things seek to please our Master. Ephesians 6:6, "Not with eye-service as men-pleasers: but as the servants of Christ, doing the will of God from the heart." So we are required to seek the glory of God. 1 Corinthians 10:31, "Whether therefore ye eat, or drink, or whatsoever ye do, do all to the glory of God." And this is the Christian spirit. (*Works* 8, 259)

Having defined "the Christian spirit" as that which "seeks to please and glorify God," Edwards discussed how divine love far exceeds natural "self-love":

But divine love or that Christian charity which is spoken of in the text is something above self-love, as it is supernatural or above and beyond all that is natural. It is no branch which springs out of that root of self-love as natural affection and civil friendship, and the love which wicked men may have one to another. It is something of a higher and more noble kind. Self-love is the sum of natural principles, as divine love is of supernatural principles. This divine love is no plant which grows naturally in such a soil as the heart of man. But it is a plant transplanted into the soul out of heaven; it is something divine, something from the holy and blessed Spirit of God, and so has its foundation in God, and not in self. (*Works* 8, 263–4)

Edwards provides a memorable image to describe the source of charity. The love in a Christian's heart "is a plant transplanted into the soul out of heaven." This plant, a gift from "the holy and blessed Spirit of God," causes the believer to live for God with God squarely in one's line of sight. As one matures, one's love for God and His creation spills over into the lives of others, just as a maturing plant or tree stretches across an ever-widening distance and shelters it. The believer who seeks to live for God ultimately cannot avoid blessing others.

Edwards then sketched how believers could embody this spirit:

> A Christian spirit disposes them in many cases to forego and part with their own things for the sake of the things of others. It disposes them to part with their own private temporal interest, and totally and finally to renounce it, for the sake of the honor of God and the advancement of the kingdom of Christ. Such was the spirit of the Apostle. Acts 21:13, "I am ready not only to be bound, but also to die for the name of the Lord Jesus." And they have a spirit to forego and part with their own private interest for the good of their neighbors in many instances; ready to help bear others' burdens, to part with a less good of their own for the sake of a greater of their neighbors'; and as the case may be, to lay down their lives for the brethren [1 John 3:16]. (*Works* 8, 259)

The pastor closed with a stirring summation of the nature and power of Christian charity:

> And therefore divine and Christian love, above all love in the world, is contrary to a selfish spirit. Though other-love, a moral love, may in some respects be contrary to selfishness, as it may move men to a moral liberality and generosity, yet in other respects it agrees with a selfish spirit; because if we follow it up to its original, it arises from the same root, viz. a principle of self-love. But divine love has its spring elsewhere; its root is in Christ Jesus, and so is heavenly.

It is not anything of this world, and it tends thither whence it comes. As it does not spring out of self, so neither does it tend to self. It delights in the honor and glory of God for his own sake, and not merely for their sakes. And it seeks and delights in the good of men for their sakes, and for God's sake. How Christian love is in a peculiar manner above and contrary to a selfish spirit appears by this, viz. it goes out even to enemies. There is that in the nature and tendency of it to go out to the unthankful and evil, and to those that injure and hate us, which is directly contrary to the tendency of a selfish principle, and quite above nature. (*Works* 8, 264)

In these sections, Edwards captured the special nature of Christian happiness. Rooted in "divine love," Christians act out of an "other-love" that simultaneously blesses their fellow man and cares for their own soul. In doing so, they find true and lasting happiness. This brand of existence counters sharply the thinking of sinful natural man, which is driven by a selfish and deeply proud mindset. The Christian life, the good life, is driven by a selfless and humble mindset. Though it might seem natural to devote all kinds of attention to one's own needs, the Christian goes the opposite way and humbly seeks to serve even his enemies. Here is love that turns the thinking of the natural mind on its head. Love of this kind is both deeply ironic and unquestionably divine.

THE HAPPIEST PERSON WHO EVER LIVED

Edwards's doctrine of happiness and the good life helps us to see how Jesus Christ, despite all the injustices thrust upon Him, was the happiest person who ever lived. Christ devoted every second of His life to serving God and blessing His people. Though He often faced great trials, Jesus knew a satisfaction that no human hand could diminish. Even in His agonizing crucifixion, Jesus rested firmly in the will of God, and endured the agonies of Calvary "for the joy that was set before him" (Heb. 12:2). Though the cross itself produced no happiness in Jesus, submission to God's will did. Christ's example brings home how important it is to understand that happiness is not simply an emotional state. It is both emotion and commitment, both outward exultation and inner satisfaction. As we follow Jesus and obey the Father, serving our fellow man with love in our hearts, we make ourselves happy in the most profound sense, just like Jesus Himself.

We should emphasize that we are not constructing a merely intellectual argument here. There is delight of the most intense and lasting kind in vibrant Christian faith. At one point in his sermon corpus, Edwards went so far as to say that the goodness of Christianity is such that even if Christianity were not true, it still provides the best way to live. It is such a pleasant way to live that it would be the best lifestyle even if the Bible were not true. "Seeing it is so," the pastor concluded in his sermon entitled "The Pleasantness of Religion," "that 'tis worth the while to be religious if it were only for the delight and pleasantness of it, then hence we may learn that sinners are left without any manner of objection against religion" (Kimnach, 23). Edwards believed firmly that Christianity offered humanity the deepest pleasure possible. Even the most apparently happy worldly life could not compare to biblical faith:

> [H]ow exceeding great is the reward of the godly. What a reward have they in the world to come; what joys [in another life]. But yet this is not all; no, they have a reward in this life. In the very keeping of God's commands, there is great reward (Ps. 19:11). The reward they have in hand, besides that which is promised, is well worth all the pains they take, all the troubles they endure. God has not only promised them a great reward, and exceeding great beyond conception; but he has given them a foretaste in this world.

And this taste is better than all the pleasure and riches of the wicked. (Kimnach, 24)

The Christian faith was true, according to Edwards. He made this very clear in countless sermons and writings. It yielded both a joyful earthly life and an endlessly happy existence in heaven. In comparison to the richest sinner, even the poorest Christian possessed wealth beyond belief. While the "wicked" courted temporal pleasure, the Christian experienced in the good life a "foretaste" of heaven that nothing could ruin or spoil.

The Northampton pastor's preaching illuminated the divine nature of earthly Christian life. All who would follow Christ would find that it not only satisfied the soul on earth, but also placed them on the trajectory of heaven. Though this world dealt "pains" and "troubles" to the people of God, Edwards knew that these things would soon pass and that the church would reach its destination, tasting sumptuous delights not even the richest pleasure-seeker could imagine.

THE HAPPINESS OF THE GOOD LIFE

All of the preceding material shapes and perhaps alters our understanding of Jonathan Edwards. The man who wears the slightest of smiles in his portrait may not be the vindictive, pleasure-squashing parson some imagine him to be. Edwards's conception of the good life suggests that Edwards was much happier than we might initially think. Certainly, life as he pictured it in its ideal form reflected an existence of the most satisfied kind. This life, as we have seen, was no exercise in sinful hedonism, but was instead a lifelong walk of faith on the biblical path. This life glorified God and made men happy. It did not conflict with self-interest, it included continual service to God and man, and it required humility and sacrifice. The good life included noteworthy irony that turned conventional human wisdom on its head. It was demanding, challenging, and deeply involved, yet it offered humanity the opportunity to taste the very goodness, love, and peace of God.

Such was life as God created it to be.

Living the Good Life

We Are Made to Be Happy

It is imperative that we realize that God has not designed us for a somber, miserable subsistence of a life. He has made us to be unshakably happy. Our first order of business in processing Edwards's illumination of this biblical teaching is to enter the thought stream of our minds, so to speak, and to banish any thinking that undermines the idea that God wants us to be happy in Him. He does not want to squelch our pleasure, and He does not parse out a crumb of blessing at a time for us to sample. God intends to pour a flood of happiness into our lives, and He will do so if we only recognize that this is so (Ps. 128; Jer. 32:36–41).

This means on a practical level that we must reorient our thoughts, our words, and our actions. We must not doubt our Lord and His good plan for our lives. We should not speak against the Lord and complain to other people about our circumstances. Romans 8:31–39 teaches us that every single thing that occurs in our lives is placed before us to sanctify us and to glorify God. How, then, can we doubt the Lord? We must accept whatever comes from His hand and remember that He has our happiness in mind, not our misery. This reorientation of thinking and acting will help us to switch from a glum, self-defeated way of life into a courageous, defiantly joyful existence that smacks of another world.

Obedience Is Joy

Edwards shows us that the happiest people on earth are not those who do whatever they naturally, sinfully want to do, but those who do what God desires. God, being all-wise and all-good, has designed the ideal way of life. This way of life involves obedience, or submission, to the divine will (Eccl. 12:13). Obedience, then, is joy; following God is happiness (see 1 John 3 for a similar theme). Knowing and applying this truth to our lives will free us from thinking that, though saved, we're missing out on the really good stuff of life that the unredeemed around us get to enjoy every day. If we understand that we're heaven bound, and that all our obedience brings both blessing on earth and an eternal reward in the afterlife, we'll avoid much of the doleful thinking of misled Christians. The good stuff, and the good life, is not to be had in the world of sin, but in the world of faith.

Chapter 15

THE DISTANCE
OF THE GOOD LIFE

The scenario is all too familiar. We have all seen it play out. A person with great potential rises to the surface, promising great things by their gifting and background: a flash of genius, a stunning performance, a thrilling creation. Whether working in the field of art, music, literature, sports, politics, or other areas, this person creates a buzz and draws a crowd. Suddenly, everyone is talking about "the next big thing." This pattern characterizes a world that often cares more for that which dazzles—personality, wit, looks—than substantive things like character.

How disappointing it is when the rising star falls, as so many do. No matter how much attention they initially receive, few people in this world seem able to live up to the standards set before them. As Edwards knew, this theme is as old as the world itself. In his writing and preaching, Edwards explored the ongoing tragedy of ruined humanity. He looked into the fall's beginnings and its implications and he offered an explanation for the original sin of Adam and Eve, showing how they, not God, were to blame for it. In doing so, Edwards showed how, in losing fellowship with God, mankind had lost contact with true happiness, the good life intended for God's creation. He revealed that God did not oppose

pleasure and joy, but rather disordered, misdirected "happiness."
Mankind, Edwards argued, possessed a vast capacity for pleasure,
a capacity given to it by the Lord. In the wake of the fall, however,
only the Holy Spirit's work in the human heart could direct it to
the rightful fulfillment of this capacity.

In this chapter, we explore Edwards's conception of the fall,
its effects on the human race, and the state of sin-clouded affections. We will examine Edwards's treatment of these subjects
in his classic works *Original Sin* and *Religious Affections*. In the
process, we will see how humanity has lost the good life, and
what must happen before we can experience it again and find
true happiness in this broken place.

EDWARDS'S DOCTRINE OF SIN

To comprehend the sad condition of the human race and its vast
natural distance from the life of happiness God intended for it,
it is first necessary to review Edwards's basic understanding of
sin. In studying it, we find the reason for the unhappiness of
this world. The pastor worked through his doctrine of sin most
substantively in the book *Original Sin*, where he offered his
basic definition of the title subject: "By original sin, as the phrase
has been most commonly used by divines, is meant the *innate
sinful depravity of the heart*" (*Works* 3, 107). For Edwards, original sin was most fundamentally a disposition of the heart that
manifested itself in wicked acts. As he countered the arguments
of some who denied the existence of original sin, he pointed
out that Scripture overwhelmingly substantiated the idea. One
simply could not profess to follow the Bible and deny the innate
sinfulness and guilt of all people, said Edwards:

> That every one of mankind, at least of them that are capable of
> acting as moral agents, are guilty of sin (not now taking it for

granted that they come guilty into the world) is a thing most
clearly and abundantly evident from the holy Scriptures. (1 Kings
8:46), "If any man sin against thee, for there is no man that sinneth not." (Ecclesiastes 7:20), "There is not a just man upon earth
that doeth good, and sinneth not." (Job 9:2–3), "I know it is so of
a truth" (i.e. as Bildad had just before said, that God would not cast
away a perfect man, etc.), "but how should man be just with God? If
he will contend with him, he cannot answer him one of a thousand."
To the like purpose (Psalms 143:2), "Enter not into judgment with thy
servant; for in thy sight shall no man living be justified." So the words
of the Apostle (in which he has apparent reference to those words of
the Psalmist, Romans 3:19–20), "That every mouth may be stopped,
and all the world become guilty before God. Therefore by the deeds
of the law there shall no flesh be justified in his sight: for by the law
is the knowledge of sin." . . . All are represented, not only as being
sinful, but as having great and manifold iniquity (Job 9:2, Job 9:3;
James 3:1, James 3:2). (*Works* 3, 114–15)

To summarize the point and make it even clearer, Edwards reiter-
ated that sin proceeded from *every* human heart:

In God's sight no man living can be justified; but all are sinners,
and exposed to condemnation. This is true of persons of all constitutions, capacities, conditions, manners, opinions and educations;
in all countries, climates, nations and ages; and through all the
mighty changes and revolutions, which have come to pass in the
habitable world. (*Works* 3, 124)

With his methodical mind, Edwards first established that sin existed and that it came directly from the hearts of people. Against
some who contended that sin was more an external matter than
an internal one, the Northampton theologian asserted that the
Bible abounded with condemnation of all people. His treatment

makes clear that the Bible deals constantly with sin. From one angle or another, the authors of Scripture return over and again to the concept. Prophets denounce kings for adultery, kings denounce prophets for laxity, priests make sacrifices for the nation, the nation suffers from wicked priests. In these and a thousand other ways, the Bible addresses sin. It is not too much to say, presumably with Edwards, that it is in one sense a book about sin.

No person, furthermore, can escape the presence of sin. Every person nurses it in their heart, regardless of their "constitutions, capacities, conditions, manners, opinions and educations." Those of "all countries, climates, nations and ages" carry sin in their core. With a flurry of terms, Edwards reinforced his point, leaving none outside of the sphere of sin, implicating all as guilty. His words, unpopular in his day, are no more popular in ours, however staunchly supported they were and are by even a brief glance at world affairs and personal circumstances.

THE GOD-DEFYING NATURE OF SIN

Having established the reality of sin and its widespread nature, Edwards ramped up his discussion, showing that sin is so heinous because it offends God and refuses Him the respect and obedience He deserves:

> The heinousness of this must rise in some proportion to the
> obligation we are under to regard the Divine Being; and that must
> be in some proportion to his worthiness of regard; which doubtless
> is infinitely beyond the worthiness of any of our fellow creatures.
> But the merit of our respect or obedience to God is not infinite.
> The merit of respect to any being don't increase, but is rather
> diminished in proportion to the obligations we are under in strict
> justice to pay him that respect. There is no great merit in paying
> a debt we owe, and by the highest possible obligations in strict

justice are obliged to pay; but there is great demerit in refusing to pay it. (*Works* 3, 130)

The argument corrects the mistaken claim that human goodness can counterbalance human sin and overcome it in the eyes of God. God, Edwards pointed out, deserves not finite respect, but "infinite." The best we humans can offer, however, is "respect or obedience to God [that] is not infinite." This difficulty is compounded by the fact that we not only fall short of paying our debt of righteousness to God, but also often "refus[e] to pay" that which in "highest possible obligations in strict justice" we "are obliged to pay." We do God no favor in seeking to honor Him; He deserves our honor. But without the righteousness of Christ, even our best efforts to honor Him fall utterly short of the mark.

Edwards advanced the discussion further, insisting that we are not merely obligated to honor God, but to go beyond mere performance of duty and love Him with our hearts. This duty is not arbitrarily imposed; that is, it does not flow out of some artificial, purposeless law. We are called to love God because of who God is in Himself. Edwards writes,

How far the generality of mankind are from their duty with respect to love to God, will further appear, if we consider, that we are obliged not only to love him with a love of gratitude for benefits received; but true love to God primarily consists in a supreme regard to him for what he is in himself. . . . If God be infinitely excellent in himself, then he is infinitely lovely on that account; or in other words, infinitely worthy to be loved. And doubtless, if he be worthy to be loved for this, then he ought to be loved for this. And 'tis manifest, there can be no true love to him, if he be not loved for what he is in himself. For if we love him not for his own sake, but for something else, then our love is not terminated on him, but on something else, as its ultimate object. . . . If we love

not God because he is what he is, but only because he is profitable
to us, in truth we love him not at all. If we seem to love him, our
love is not to him, but to something else. (*Works* 3, 144)

Here, Edwards lays bare the depravity of humanity. Humanity
transgressed against God by not doing what He desires—true; by
not respecting as He deserves—yes; but most damningly, by not
obeying Him out of a heart justifiably filled with love and adoration for who He is. Here is wickedness at its core and rebellion
at its worst. Though mankind had every reason to trust and love
God, he chose not to in the wake of Adam's fall. Choosing to love
lesser things and live a lesser life, he resigned himself to sadness
and death.

THE INFERIOR AND SUPERIOR PRINCIPLES

But why did man choose such a path, and hurtle himself toward
hell in the process? Why did Adam and Eve choose to sin against
God despite having every reason to follow Him and shun the
serpent? To this question, Edwards's creative mind produced a
compelling answer that forms the crux of this chapter and reveals
the ultimate source of earthly unhappiness. In the following quotation, the theologian suggests that God created Adam with two
different "principles," as he calls them. The first was the "inferior"—spiritually neutral principles that included man's "natural
appetites and passions." The second was the "superior"—those
that "were spiritual, holy and divine." Edwards discussed each
kind in *Original Sin*:

> The case with man was plainly this: when God made man at first,
> he implanted in him two kinds of principles. There was an *inferior*
> kind, which may be called *natural*, being the principles of mere
> human nature; such as self-love, with those natural appetites and

passions, which belong to the nature of man, in which his love to his own liberty, honor and pleasure, were exercised: these when alone, and left to themselves, are what the Scriptures sometimes call flesh. Besides these, there were superior principles, that were spiritual, holy and divine, summarily comprehended in divine love; wherein consisted the spiritual image of God, and man's righteousness and true holiness; which are called in Scripture the divine nature. (*Works* 3, 381)

God had created man with "mere human nature," which consisted of the natural principles, the natural instincts, and dispositions of man—his drive to eat, reproduce, work, and so on all fell in this category. Though these instincts certainly could involve spiritual evil or good, they were at base neutral, infused with neither sin nor grace. Man in his natural state, in his "flesh," was thus subject neither to condemnation nor blessed immortality. The supernatural principles residing in him—characteristics of a "spiritual, holy, and divine" orientation—came from God Himself.

THE CONSEQUENCES OF THE FALL

The fall occurred when the inferior principles, the flesh, overtook the superior or supernatural principles, the spirit, as Edwards spelled out:

These superior principles were given to possess the throne, and maintain an absolute dominion in the heart: the other, to be wholly subordinate and subservient. And while things continued thus, all things were in excellent order, peace and beautiful harmony, and in their proper and perfect state. These divine principles thus reigning, were the dignity, life, happiness, and glory of man's nature. When man sinned, and broke God's Covenant, and fell under his curse, these superior principles left his heart: for indeed God then left him; that communion with God, on which these principles depended, entirely ceased; the Holy Spirit, that divine inhabitant, forsook the house. Because it would have been utterly improper in itself, and inconsistent with the covenant and constitution God had established, that God should still maintain communion with man, and continue, by his friendly, gracious vital influences, to dwell with him and in him, after he was become a rebel, and had incurred God's wrath and curse. Therefore immediately the superior divine principles wholly ceased; so light ceases in a room, when the candle is withdrawn: and thus man was left in a state of darkness, woeful corruption and ruin; nothing but flesh, without spirit.

Edwards explained the effects of this disastrous shift:

> The inferior principles of self-love and natural appetite, which were given only to serve, being alone, and left to themselves, of course became reigning principles; having no superior principles to regulate or control them, they became absolute masters of the heart. The immediate consequence of which was a fatal catastrophe, a turning of all things upside down, and the succession of a state of the most odious and dreadful confusion. Man did immediately set up himself, and the objects of his private affections and appetites, as supreme; and so they took the place of God. (*Works* 3, 382)

Edwards's language captures the chilling instance when, for the first time in creation, the inferior principles, "given" to man "only to serve" him (by providing for his natural, neutral appetites) overthrew the superior principles and "became absolute masters of the heart." In that moment, "man did immediately set up himself . . . as supreme" and sought "the place of God." Thousands of years after the event, one's blood still grows cold while meditating on it. Seeking to become all-wise, humanity in fact became stupid; chasing immortal life, mankind seized hold of eternal death.

WHERE WAS GOD IN THE FALL?

Anticipating questions that would naturally flow from this argument, the pastor next considered God's role in those events. If God was sovereign, as Edwards so strenuously insisted, why did man fall? For this, Edwards had a ready answer. It was not God's direct action but His permission that was operative:

> The first existence of an evil disposition of heart, amounting to a full consent to Adam's sin, no more infers God's being the author of that evil disposition in the child, than in the father. The first arising or existing of that evil disposition in the heart of Adam, was by God's *permission*; who could have prevented it, if he had pleased, by giving such influences of his spirit, as would have been absolutely effectual to hinder it; which, it is plain in fact, he did withhold: and whatever mystery may be supposed in the affair, yet no Christian will presume to say, it was not in perfect consistence with God's holiness and righteousness, notwithstanding Adam had been guilty of no offense before. So root and branches being one, according to God's wise constitution, the case in fact is, that by virtue of this oneness answerable changes of effects through all the branches coexist with the changes in the root: consequently an evil disposition exists in the hearts of Adam's posterity, equivalent to that which was exerted in his own heart, when he eat the forbidden fruit. Which God has no hand in, any otherwise, than in not exerting such an influence, as might be effectual to prevent it. (*Works* 3, 394)

The "permission" of God, not the active decree of His will, enabled the fall of mankind. The theologian acknowledged that the

Lord "could have prevented it, if he had pleased," but did not. "God ha[d] no hand" in this matter, according to Edwards, other than to "not exert an influence" that would have prevented it. His conclusion, therefore, was that (a) man caused the fall, (b) God could have prevented it but did not, and (c) that the workings of this difficult situation were a mystery best left to the mind of God and not the speculation of man. Edwards held the fall of man and the sovereignty of God in tension, emphasizing each in turn as directed by Scripture, but allowing for mystery due to the finitude of human understanding.

INHERITING THE FALL

The tragic effects of the fall extended not only to Adam and Eve but to all their "posterity," every person who would ever live. On the question of why God allowed the fall, the council of the divine mind hid itself; on the matter of humanity's wickedness, the depravity of the human race showed itself plainly. Because they ate the forbidden fruit, "consequently an evil disposition exists in the hearts" of all mankind. "[T]he depravity of nature," Edwards said elsewhere, "remaining an *established principle* in the heart of a child of Adam, and as exhibited in after-operations, is a consequence and punishment of the first apostacy thus participated, and brings new guilt" (*Works* 3, 391). Every person stands guilty before God as a result of the representative role Adam occupied before the Lord. Yet he did not merely represent humanity in the presence of God; when he sinned, he actually passed on his "apostasy" and "guilt" to all people in an organic, holistic way. All people inherited a sin nature at birth, and could do nothing to overturn the curse and its effects.

WHY SATISFACTION ESCAPES US

All of this leaves us with an answer to the enigma of man's unhappiness and inability to find satisfaction. When our first parents sinned by eating the forbidden fruit, they ensured that for all of time, the inferior principles, not the superior principles, would govern the human heart. The flesh, in short, would forever rule the spirit. Man did not lose his conscience in this instance. But he did lose his ability to obey his conscience consistently. In this awful condition, he could glimpse that a higher, better, way of life existed than that which he chose, but he could never lay hold of it, and he often did not want to, preferring the filth of his natural, sin-driven lifestyle. He could see, fleetingly, that true happiness existed, but could not capture it. Instead of loving what was good and true and beautiful, he ran wherever his sinful, selfish appetites drove him. Because of the first sin, and the transmission of a sinful nature to all people, our natural principles rule us and subject us to unhappiness, despair, death, and ultimately, eternal death.

THE DIFFERENCE BETWEEN "TRUE" AND "FALSE" AFFECTIONS

What, then, does all of the preceding show? We were not created for this. God did not intend our lives to take this shape, to play this tragic tune. He gave us natural desires and instincts that He intended to be vessels of pleasure and satisfaction for us. He gave us what Edwards called "affections," natural passions that He desired we direct toward Him in joyful worship. With the fall, we did not lose our desires and affections. Instead, the sin of Adam and Eve disordered our affections, confused them, and caused us to love sin and hate God. In essence, where once the spiritual, or superior, principles ruled the affections, now the inferior, fleshly, principles directed them. In a section in his treatise *Religious Affections*, the pastor discussed this situation. He showed that there are two types of affections, "false" and "true":

> There are false affections, and there are true. A man's having much affection, don't prove that he has any true religion: but if he has no affection, it proves that he has no true religion. The right way, is not to reject all affections, nor to approve all; but to distinguish between affections, approving some, and rejecting others; separating between the wheat and the chaff, the gold and the dross, the precious and the vile.

Edwards believed some in his day were trying to remove all sense of emotion and pleasure from religion—a shift he denounced:

> This manner of slighting all religious affections, is the way exceedingly to harden the hearts of men, and to encourage 'em in their stupidity and senselessness, and to keep 'em in a state of spiritual death as long as they live, and bring 'em at last to death eternal. The prevailing prejudice against religious affections at this day, in the land, is apparently of awful effect, to harden the hearts of sinners, and damp the graces of many of the saints, and stunt the life and power of religion, and preclude the effect of ordinances, and hold us down in a state of dullness and apathy, and undoubtedly causes many persons greatly to offend God, in entertaining mean and low thoughts of the extraordinary work he has lately wrought in this land. (*Works* 2, 121)

He then restated the effect of such a deplorable approach to the affections: "for persons to despise and cry down all religious affections, is the way to shut all religion out of their own hearts, and to make thorough work in ruining their souls" (*Works* 2, 121). To summarize these quotations, Edwards believed that

God had given mankind feelings and emotions. These natural passions were not sinful, wrong, or destined to be destroyed by conversion. God, in Edwards's thinking, did not wish to remove feeling—and feeling of the deepest, strongest sort—from the redeemed life. Those who argued that line, contended the pastor, would "harden the hearts of sinners, and damp the graces of many of the saints, and stunt the life and power of religion." As one can see, Edwards held nothing back in his denunciation of a passionless Christianity. His life shows that he made it a key part of his pastoral and theological work to exalt the goodness of feeling and true passion for God. Edwards had his qualifiers and exceptions, to be sure, but he believed ardently that God had given the human race feelings and passion to experience the full range of joy and delight in Him. In Edwards's day, as in other times, God had done "extraordinary work," which deserved not lightly murmured thanks but an explosion of gratitude and praise.

Unlike what some urged in Edwards's day (and ours), the secret of vibrant and effective Christianity centered on the *sanctification* of our natural appetites and passions, not the *squandering* of the same. It was not emotion and passion that needed correcting, but *sinful* emotion and *transgressive* passion. Godly emotion and Christ-centered passion went up as a sweet savor to the Lord.

All this clarifies the Christian's duty and approach to the non-Christian. The Lord calls us, in a sense, to be emissaries of true passion, ambassadors of lasting delight to unconverted people. We do not approach unbelievers with the mindset that they need to repent of their emotions. Rather, we share with the lost that they need to repent of their *sin*, and that they need to redirect their joy, delight, affection, happiness, and satisfaction toward God and the things of God. The lost, in sum, need to leave "false" affections, passions rooted in sin, and take up "true" affections, passions rooted in God and everlasting delight.

A RECONCEPTUALIZATION OF
EVANGELISM AND CHRISTIAN LIFE

Edwards's material clarifies the nature of Christian evangelism and, even more, the Christian life. God does not redeem us to save us from pleasure. He is not seeking to scrub happiness from the earth. God redeems us to *give* us pleasure and to make us happy. He wishes to satisfy us at the core of our being, to bring peace to our mind and happiness to our souls through His Spirit. He wants to give not a trickle of blessing mixed with tons of rules, but a flood of happiness that pours into our hearts and minds and that bursts out of us through our affections and our joyful stewardship of our appetites. God, in sum, has made us to be happy above all. He will do so if we allow Him the opportunity.

This carries tremendous implications for our evangelism. Edwards teaches us that we do not contact the lost to tell them *only* that they are sinning and live in danger of the mighty wrath of God, though this is certainly an essential part of Christian witness. Instead, we must give attention in our evangelism to informing unsaved people that they need not lose many of their passions and appetites (though some must go), but that such passions need to be redirected according to the righteous and beneficial plan of Scripture.

At this point in their lives, the lost act according to the inferior principles. They are ruled by them. They have lost the superior principles and, accordingly, possess misdirected affections and appetites. They must now embrace the Holy Spirit and His regenerating work and watch as the spiritual principles, the superior graces given by God, take root in their hearts. Much more will be said on this in the following chapters; here, we simply state the reality and the need every heart has for this transformation. Without the Spirit's restoration of the reign of the superior principles, we cannot know true happiness, and we cannot please God, but only bring great suffering to ourselves and great dishonor to the Lord.

ATTAINING THE GOOD LIFE

In conclusion, we see what great potential every person has. We are not referring here to athletic or intellectual ability, or artistic or political capacity. We signify the deepest potential, the spiritual, which pervades every aspect of a person's being. Human beings have the ability, if they follow the Word of God according to the Spirit of God, to transcend this world, to triumph over their sin, and to enter the presence of God. We alone among all the creation may live forever. We alone may taste the very goodness and happiness of God. We were, after all, created to do so. Yet at present, our sin has confused us, impeded our happiness, disordered our experience. We live in unhappiness, gratifying our appetites and pleasing our passions in ungodly ways. None of us can escape this fate; all of us receive it from our parents and pass it on to our children.

But we may yet fulfill our potential, our purpose, for life. We may find the satisfaction we have always sought. We can conquer disappointment, doubt, and the last enemy, death. If we will follow the Lord and His Word, our highest virtue and greatest happiness will come together in the Spirit-filled life God intends us to experience.

Living the Good Life

Realize the Nature and Effect of Sin

Edwards's understanding of the fall, consonant with traditional understandings but more fully explored than some, shows us the depth of our depravity. Sin, fundamentally, is not loving God. In all of our offenses, we in some way fail to love and treasure God. We break God's rules, yes; we fail to live up to His standards. But why do we do so? Because we do not love God enough. We hate Him by nature (see Ps. 51:5; Jer. 17:9; Rom. 3).

This has strong implications for our everyday lives. Why do we live selfishly with our spouse? Because we don't love God and His gift of a spouse enough. Why do we turn in a substandard performance day after day at work or school? Because we don't love God and His blessing of provision or education enough. Why do we fight with our friends, disobey our parents, squander our talents? Because we don't love God and His tangible expressions of kindness. Sure, there are psychological and other factors that play into our patterns of sin—some of them significant—but we need to know that our fundamental problem is not psychological or external, but spiritual (see Ps. 14:1).

Know the Goodness of Your Passions and Appetites

When the Spirit regenerates us, He enables us to use our natural passions and appetites according to the superior, not the inferior, principles. As Christians, we must recognize this and avoid misrepresenting God and the good life. The ideal Christian life is not a prim, stifling affair in which we moralistically perform righteousness for the Lord as joylessly as possible. The ideal Christian life, the good life God intends for us, is a joyful, pleasurable, happy affair in which we shun sin and seek holiness because we treasure God and desire to taste His goodness in all facets of our lives. We pursue holiness with abandon, but we do so in full view of the expressed mercy of the cross. We live sacrificially and in moderation, but also treasure our bodies and the good gifts available to us on this earth. Swept up in happiness, we exude not a self-righteous, judgmental spirit but a deep joy rooted in conviction and love for God and man.

Chapter 16

THE TASTE FOR THE GOOD LIFE

What is the deepest difference between the unbelieving life and the Christian life?

For Jonathan Edwards, the answer came down to the affections, the emotions of the heart that fundamentally drive a person's actions. The difference between heaven and hell, then, is a matter of heart-disposition. Edwards described this newfound appetite in a variety of ways—as a "sense," a "taste," and similar metaphors. With each of them, he sought to capture the essence of conversion. The fundamental mark of the Christian, Edwards argued, was this elevated taste for the things of God. Given by the Holy Spirit through the preaching of the gospel, the taste for divine things redirected one's natural passions and appetites to the spiritual riches of the good life.

In this chapter, we examine Edwards's understanding of this taste and its role in conversion, revealing it to be the fundamental mark of regeneration. This chapter surveys a number of important sermons, including "A Divine and Supernatural Light," "The Reality of Conversion," and "The Importance and Advantage of a Thorough Knowledge of Divine Truth." Through engagement with these sermons, we will discover what the taste is, describe how it comes to the sinner, and explore the kind of life it creates. In sum, we find that the Edwardsean material offers a powerful explanation of Christian identity and an invigorating exploration of the blessings of the good life.

THE REORIENTATION OF CONVERSION

As noted above, Edwards discussed in a number of places the way conversion produces reorientation of the affections, the natural appetites, and passions. He presented these ideas with clarity and beauty in the sermon "A Divine and Supernatural Light," where he discussed the "light" imparted to the soul at conversion. First, Edwards discussed the way in which a mere conviction of sin and guilt in the sinner's heart did not equate with repentance:

> Those convictions that natural men may have of their sin and misery is not this spiritual and divine light. Men in a natural condition may have convictions of the guilt that lies upon them, and of the anger of God, and their danger of divine vengeance. Such convictions are from light or sensibleness of truth: that some sinners have a greater conviction of their guilt and misery than others, is because some have more light, or more of an apprehension of truth, than others. And this light and conviction may be from the Spirit of God; the Spirit convinces men of sin: but yet nature is much more concerned in it than in the communication of that spiritual and divine light, that is spoken of in the doctrine; 'tis from the Spirit of God only as assisting natural principles, and not as infusing any new principles.

Edwards's argument was that the Holy Spirit could convict a sinner's conscience, but that this conviction did not regenerate the sinful heart until He wrought a fresh work of grace. He went on to describe this work as follows:

> But in the renewing and sanctifying work of the Holy Ghost, those
> things are wrought in the soul that are above nature, and of which
> there is nothing of the like kind in the soul by nature; and they
> are caused to exist in the soul habitually, and according to such a
> stated constitution or law, that lays such a foundation for exercises
> in a continued course, as is called a principle of nature. Not only
> are remaining principles assisted to do their work more freely and
> fully, but those principles are restored that were utterly destroyed by
> the fall; and the mind thenceforward habitually exerts those acts that
> the dominion of sin had made it as wholly destitute of, as a dead body
> is of vital acts. (Works 17, 410–11)

This section provides an exquisite description of the effects of
conversion on a person's mind and soul. When the Holy Spirit
moves in a heart to cause it to love Jesus Christ and to believe in
His atoning death and life-giving resurrection, "principles" that
are "above nature" take root. In addition, "remaining principles"
are freed "to do their work more freely and fully," by which Edwards meant that conversion enhanced the natural appetites
and enabled them to function properly. Accordingly, principles
"destroyed by the fall" were "restored" such that the mind "exerts
those acts" of a spiritual, not natural or lowly, nature.

THE ROOT OF TRUE CONVERSION

Edwards did not spell out *all* of the implications of these new
and revived principles, but he did describe in vivid language the
reality of the transformation wrought in conversion. The Holy
Spirit shone a "spiritual light" in the human heart in conversion,
which Edwards defined as "a true sense of the divine excellency
of the things revealed in the Word of God, and a conviction of
the truth and reality of them, thence arising." He elaborated on
this definition, noting that in the "spiritual light" there is

a true sense of the divine and superlative excellency of the things
of religion; a real sense of the excellency of God, and Jesus Christ,
and of the work of redemption, and the ways and works of God
revealed in the gospel. There is a divine and superlative glory in
these things; an excellency that is of a vastly higher kind, and more
sublime nature, than in other things; a glory greatly distinguishing
them from all that is earthly and temporal. He that is spiritually
enlightened truly apprehends and sees it, or has a sense of it. He
don't merely rationally believe that God is glorious, but he has a
sense of the gloriousness of God in his heart. There is not only a
rational belief that God is holy, and that holiness is a good thing;
but there is a sense of the loveliness of God's holiness. There is
not only a speculatively judging that God is gracious, but a sense
how amiable God is upon that account; or a sense of the beauty of
this divine attribute. (*Works* 17, 413)

The key distinction in this passage is that of "rational belief" and
being "spiritually enlightened." The person who has a rational
belief in God rightly comprehends the fundamental facts of God
as revealed in the Bible and agrees with them. Many people,
as Edwards notes, may believe that "God is holy," but there is a
chasm between this type of belief and "a sense of the loveliness
of God's holiness." Further in the sermon, the pastor expounded,

Thus there is a difference between having an opinion that God is
holy and gracious, and having a sense of the loveliness and beauty
of that holiness and grace. There is a difference between having
a rational judgment that honey is sweet, and having a sense of its
sweetness. A man may have the former, that knows not how honey
tastes; but a man can't have the latter, unless he has an idea of
the taste of honey in his mind. So there is a difference between
believing that a person is beautiful, and having a sense of his
beauty. The former may be obtained by hearsay, but the latter only

by seeing the countenance. There is a wide difference between mere speculative, rational judging anything to be excellent, and having a sense of its sweetness, and beauty. The former rests only in the head, speculation only is concerned in it; but the heart is concerned in the latter. When the heart is sensible of the beauty and amiableness of a thing, it necessarily feels pleasure in the apprehension. It is implied in a person's being heartily sensible of the loveliness of a thing, that the idea of it is sweet and pleasant to his soul; which is a far different thing from having a rational opinion that it is excellent. (*Works* 17, 414)

The passage makes an impression through its use of metaphor. In a now famous connection, Edwards likened a saving love of God to a "sense" of the "sweetness" of "honey," by which he meant a delightful partaking of the sweetness of honey. In the same way that one tasted the sweetness of honey for oneself, spooning it out and savoring it on the tongue, believers savor and delight in the sweet "excellency of Christ," finding it the best of all pleasures.

This helps clarify the distinction between rational judgment and affectional tasting. Those who taste the goodness of God as revealed in the gospel of His Son take *pleasure* in Him. They enjoy Him. They delight in Him. Edwards spoke of Christ as "beautiful," intending his hearers to connect God's beauty to the experience of romantic love. His words above remind us quite naturally of a marital relationship in which a husband, for example, gazes on his wife's beauty. In fixing his eyes on her, he does not merely acquire the rational idea that his wife is beautiful. He treasures her; he drinks her in; his rational awareness of her beauty intoxicates him. It is this kind of knowledge that Edwards identifies as the "light," the "sense," the "taste" that the Holy Spirit creates for God in the believing heart. As one can tell, this is no ordinary love. Conversion produces a holy passion for the Lord so strong that one of history's most articulate theologians struggled to describe it.

EDWARDS'S HUNGER FOR HIS CHURCH'S LASTING SATISFACTION

Because of his close spiritual communion with the Lord, Edwards experienced this delight firsthand. He yearned for Christians to leave the junk of this world and to taste the sweet excellency of the divine. His concern for such discovery was intense not only because of his devotion to the Lord but on account of the state of the Christian church in New England in his day. Colonial New England did not lack for people who held rational belief in the Bible and its truths. Most people attended church and believed what they heard. But few exhibited a real fire for God. There were many who knew the nature of honey, but few who had tasted its sweetness.

Edwards devoted himself to these people. Over and again in his pastoral career, he laid out the beauty of conversion and the goodness of the Christian life, displaying with intricate reasoning, eloquent speech, and personal ardor the glories of biblical faith. He was not unlike the two Israelite spies who first glimpsed the Promised Land and rushed back to tell the people of their findings. After they told the Israelites of the earthly paradise that awaited them, the people rejected their counsel, stunning the spies, who knew that no good reason existed to avoid entering the land prepared for them by God (Josh. 1–6). In his day, many centuries later, Edwards strove to do the same by educating his people about the good life and its ultimate end, heaven. Lackluster effort on the part of his hearers frustrated his good purposes, but he never stopped sharing the good news of the land to come.

THE FREE OFFER OF THE GOOD LIFE

A key part of Edwards's doctrine of the good life was its accessibility. The "saving evidence of the truth of the gospel," proclaimed the preacher in "A Divine and Supernatural Light":

> is attainable by persons of mean capacities, and advantages, as well as those that are of the greatest parts and learning. If the evidence of the gospel depended only on history, and such reasonings as learned men only are capable of, it would be above the reach of far the greatest part of mankind. But persons, with but an ordinary degree of knowledge, are capable, without a long and subtile train of reasoning, to see the divine excellency of the things of religion: they are capable of being taught by the Spirit of God, as well as learned men. The evidence that is this way obtained, is vastly better and more satisfying, than all that can be obtained by the arguings of those that are most learned, and greatest masters of reason. And babes are as capable of knowing these things, as the wise and prudent; and they are often hid from these, when they are revealed to those; 1 Corinthians 1:26–27, "For ye see your calling, brethren, how that not many wise men, after the flesh, not many mighty, not many noble, are called. But God hath chosen the foolish things of the world . . ." (*Works* 17, 423)

One did not taste the goodness of God only when possessing extreme intelligence or seasoned maturity. Any person at any time in any situation could "see the divine excellency of the things of religion." Children, mere "babes," Edwards noted, "are as capable of knowing these things, as the wise and prudent." Edwards assured his people that the good life was free to all and immensely beneficial. The unhappy had only to act in their best interests to experience the joy of Christianity. The hungry had only to direct their appetites to the sweetest delights on earth to taste the goodness of God. The good life's excellency is matched only by its sensible nature. It is not only the best way of life, it is the most sensible, fitting perfectly with common sense and self-preservation.

HOW THE BIBLE DISCLOSES THE GOOD LIFE

The Lord had not made the good life hard to find, but had disclosed its character in the Bible. Edwards sought to illuminate what the Scripture set forth on this important subject and to avoid moralistic views of the divine text. In a sermon entitled "The Importance and Advantage of a Thorough Knowledge of Divine Truth," Edwards suggested that the Bible gives us the only sure means to happiness in this world:

> But we who enjoy the light of the gospel are more happy; we are not left, as to this particular, in the dark. God hath told us about what things we should chiefly employ our understandings, having given us a book full of divine instructions, holding forth many glorious objects about which all rational creatures should chiefly employ their understandings. These instructions are accommodated to persons of all capacities and conditions, and proper to be studied, not only by men of learning, but by persons of all capacities and conditions, and proper to be studied, not only by men of learning, but by persons of every character, learned and unlearned, young and old, men and women. Therefore the acquisition of knowledge in these things should be a main business of all those who have the advantage of enjoying the holy Scriptures. (*Works* 22, 35)

The Bible was no mere collection of heady maxims to Edwards. It was "full of divine instructions" and "glorious objects" that "persons of all capacities and conditions" needed to make their "main business." The truth, argued the theologian, enlightened the mind and brought it out of "the dark," leaving Christians "more happy" than anyone else. Though Edwards gave considerable priority to the emotions, he believed that joy sprung from knowledge of the truth. Such thinking defies much popular thought of our modern age, in which many people place emotion or the pursuit of sensory pleasure before truth. For this reason many people live in a kind of dissonance, experiencing a lifestyle of constant tension and frustration, their actions never agreeing with their minds, their desires constantly pushing them to ignore their consciences and the innate knowledge of what is right. Edwards shows us that in order to live joyfully, we must first let truth grip and renew us. Only then will we apprehend the true nature of the text and find faith to defeat our doubts about the Word.

Edwards believed that the Bible both creates the good life and sustains it. In his view, expressed in "The Importance and Advantage of a Thorough Knowledge of Divine Truth," God had spring-loaded the content of the Bible with power to transform lives and fill them with fresh delight:

> The things of divinity are things of superlative excellency, and are worthy that all should make a business of endeavoring to grow in the knowledge of them. There are no things so worthy to be known as these things. They are as much above those things which are treated of in other sciences, as heaven is above the earth. God himself, the eternal Three in One, is the chief object of this science, in the next place, Jesus Christ, as God-man and Mediator, and the glorious work of redemption, the most glorious work that ever was wrought, then the great things of the heavenly world, the glorious and eternal inheritance purchased by Christ, and promised in the gospel; the work of the Holy Spirit of God on the hearts of men; our duty to God, and the way in which we ourselves may become like angels, and like God himself in our measure: all these are objects of this science. (*Works* 22, 35)

One's happiness in these things depended only on how much time and attention one gave to the Word, counseled the pastor:

> The more you have of a rational knowledge of the things of the gospel, the more opportunity will there be, when the Spirit shall be breathed into your heart, to see the excellency of these things, and to taste the sweetness of them. The heathens, who have no rational knowledge of the things of the gospel, have no opportunity to see the excellency of them; and therefore the more rational knowledge of these things you have, the more opportunity and advantage you have to see the divine excellency and glory of them. (*Works* 22, 100)

Time in the Word brought one to a "rational knowledge" of the gospel, which if converted to practice would furnish certain proof of the truth of Christianity, according to Edwards's sermon "A Divine and Supernatural Light":

> A true sense of the divine excellency of the things of God's Word doth more directly and immediately convince of the truth of them; and that because the excellency of these things is so superlative. There is a beauty in them that is so divine and godlike, that is greatly and evidently distinguishing of them from things merely human, or that men are the inventors and authors of; a glory that is so high and great, that when clearly seen, commands assent to their divinity, and reality. When there is an actual and lively discovery of this beauty and excellency, it won't allow of any such thought as that it is an human work, or the fruit of men's invention. This evidence, that they, that are spiritually enlightened, have of the truth of the things of religion, is a kind of intuitive and immediate evidence. They believe the doctrines of God's Word to be divine, because they see divinity in them, i.e. they see a divine, and transcendent, and most evidently

distinguishing glory in them; such a glory as, if clearly seen, don't leave room to doubt of their being of God, and not of men. (*Works* 17, 415)

Edwards's view of the Bible and its truths challenges superficial evangelical views of God's Word. So many of us struggle to even open the Bible, let alone allow it to transform our lives and shatter our nagging doubts. The Northampton theologian propels us out of a scriptural formalism, a mindset that perceives the Bible as dry and dusty, and into one that recognizes the "divine and godlike" beauty of the Bible and its "transcendent" glory. These attributes render the Word a text that "commands assent," that grips us with a sovereign force and lifts us up out of listlessness and boredom to contemplate the holy realities of God and His work.

WORD AND SPIRIT BIRTH POWERFUL FAITH

Edwards's electric view of conversion stemmed from a catalytic understanding of the Bible, as one can see. Little wonder that his own spiritual life and ministry generated so much heat and light. How one views the Word of God and interacts with it clearly plays a significant role in how one understands conversion and the life it creates. A big view of God, the Bible, and the Christian life brings deep faith and happiness; a shallow view of God, the Bible, and the Christian life creates shallow faith and malnourished happiness. The Bible creates faith through the work of the Spirit, and the Bible sustains and deepens faith as the Christian allows it to permeate his life.

While studying the natural world was engaging, believers found in the Bible a "knowledge" that "is above all others sweet and joyful." In "A Divine and Supernatural Light" he mused that

men have a great deal of pleasure in human knowledge, in studies of natural things; but this is nothing to that joy which arises from this divine light shining into the soul. This light gives a view of those things that are immensely the most exquisitely beautiful, and capable of delighting the eye of the understanding. This spiritual light is the dawning of the light of glory in the heart. There is nothing so powerful as this to support persons in affliction, and to give the mind peace and brightness, in this stormy and dark world. (*Works* 17, 424)

Many people, including some Christians, panic and lose hope when they encounter the afflictions and trials that come to us all. How tragic that this is so, for as Edwards pointed out, God has given all believers a "divine light shining into the soul" that will "support persons in affliction" and regularly "give the mind peace and brightness, in this stormy and dark world." To illustrate, Edwards pointed to the innumerable believers in history who had borne up under incredible hardship due to their intimate connection to the God of the Bible. He memorialized these people in his sermon "The Reality of Conversion," even as he urged his own flock to emulate their examples:

But many thousands—yea, and millions—of professing Christians that have had this trial have acquitted themselves so under it as to give the most remarkable evidences of a supernatural love to God and weanedness from the world, for they have been tried with the most extreme sufferings and cruel tortures that man could invent. And the sufferings of many of them have been lengthened out to a very great length. Their persecutors have kept 'em under trying torments that, if possible, they might conquer them by wearing out of their spirits. But they have rather chosen to undergo all and have held out in suffering unto the death rather than deny Christ. Such has been their faith and their love and their courage that their enemies could not by any means overcome it, though they had 'em in their hands to execute their will upon them. And very often have they suffered all with the greatest composedness of spirit, yea, and with cheerfulness. And many of them have appeared exceeding joyful under their torments and have glorified in tribulation.

The pastor continued his dramatic argument, seeking to inspire his congregation to stronger, deeper, thicker faith:

> And thus it has been not only with some few persons—or with here and there an exempt instance—that have braved it out through an extraordinary stoutness and ruggedness of spirit; but so it has been with multitudes of all sort: many that have been under the decays of old age, long after the strength of nature has begun to fail and they were in that state wherein are wont very much to lose their natural courage; and also in women and even children and persons of a delicate and weak constitution. Such as these have, by their faith and love to Christ and courage in his cause, conquered the greatest and cruelest monarchs of the earth. In all the most dreadful things that their power could inflict upon them, they have rather chosen to suffer affliction than in the least to depart from their dear Lord and Savior. (Kimnach, 87–88)

As one can see from this material, Edwards believed the "taste," the hunger for God given by the Spirit, changed the way a person understood themselves and their mission. The taste for the good life—the cruciform, Christ-centered, self-denying life—caused people to take on "an extraordinary stoutness and ruggedness of spirit," to power through a "delicate and weak constitution," and all manner of "dreadful things" in order to show "their faith and love to Christ." The pastor, as one can see, did not equate the good life with the easy life. Indeed, becoming a Christian often makes one's life harder, as Christ's own teachings show (see Matt. 5:2–12, for example). Yet even in the midst of bitter suffering brought on by Christian faith, believers tasted a spiritual sweetness that transcended all else. Clinging to Christ could have dramatic, even deadly, consequences, but even these did not deter many Christians from living boldly in the world, standing up for the Savior before "the greatest and cruelest monarchs of the earth."

As Edwards showed, the "taste" for spiritual things produced an unmistakably original way of life. The conversion of a sinner did not involve a subduing of the heart or a dulling of the mind. When a person came to living faith in the living Christ, they came alive. Others around them *seemed* alive, seemed to have it all as they pursued their natural appetites and gratified their inherent desires. But the Christian alone is truly happy, having discovered the taste, the undeniable passion, for the things of God, which alone can satisfy the heart of mankind forever. Only this fact explained the otherwise ordinary men and women throughout history who exchanged the temporal things of this life for the supernatural pleasures of overcoming, joyful, Spirit-filled faith.

TASTING THE GOOD LIFE

The world is complicated now. Thousands of paths present themselves to us, all offering a form of salvation or a type of promised transcendence. As we observe where these paths lead, however, we see that so many do not satisfy. The movie star with all the wealth and looks and attention overdoses on drugs. The politician with tremendous influence squanders it for a tryst. The spiritually enlightened seeker following mystic paths grows disillusioned when suffering punches a hole in her worldview. Over and again, these stories play out, all with the same ultimate ending: the natural affections, driven by sin, do not lead to lasting happiness, but to a wilderness of confusion and pain.

Only one path, one way, one life, offers us eternity and eternal happiness. "There is no kind of love in the world," wrote

Edwards, "that has had such great, visible effects in men as love to Christ has had, though he be an unseen object, which [is] an evidence of a divine work in the hearts of men, infusing that love into them" (Kimnach, 89). The "divine work," the taste for Christ, shows us the way to God. Scripture reminds us that "There is a way that seems right to a man, but its end is the way to death" (Prov. 14:12). This is the inevitable end of following our natural passions. But those who have been reborn by the Spirit will taste the good life given us by a great God.

Living the Good Life

Master Your Tastes

The Holy Spirit creates a taste in the Christian for God and the things of God (see Rom. 12). This renewing work, however, does not altogether eradicate our taste for the things of the world. Though saved, we must do battle on a daily basis with our natural predilection for sin.

We must do so in a personal way, based on our own specific struggles. If we have a weakness for pornography and lust, we must pray and work for mastery over this sin and seek to heal or change what is distorted. If we yearn for possessions, we must redirect our hunger toward the things of God, and push that same energy toward storing up treasures in heaven (Matt. 6:20). If we live selfishly, we must free ourselves from this trap by adopting a generous, others-centered way of life. In these and many other areas, we need to follow an Edwardsean way of life and rightly channel our passions and appetites. We do not need to eradicate or destroy them, but to direct them to holy things, to patterns of living that please the Lord.

Leave a Legacy of Faith

We are reminded as we read Edwards's testimony of past Christians that we ourselves will soon leave this world. We are faced now with the opportunity to leave a legacy of faith. It is not only pastoral leaders like Edwards who may author a story of faith, perseverance, and triumph. Every Christian—every single believer—may in their own way offer those who come behind a picture of faithful, vibrant Christianity.

The janitor who works with joy to the glory of God; the grandmother who prays constantly for her family from a nursing home bed; the professor who disciples his students and cares for them long after they leave school; the auto mechanic who regularly witnesses to his fellow workers in the garage; the athlete who gives glory to God in good seasons and bad—all of these people and many more may in their particular place and time leave a legacy. We should desire that our families, most of all, would testify to our faith and godliness and that our children, as with the Proverbs 31 woman, would rise up and call us blessed when we have left this earth. Each of us has the opportunity to be such a Christian, a salt-and-light Christian, who leaves his peers and friends with a "taste" of something divine, a living witness to a greater reality.

Chapter 17

THE PLEASURES OF THE GOOD LIFE

How do you like your religion? Light? Rules-based? Mystery-infused? Do you prefer it to be fun, or sober? Do you like structure, or do you prefer freedom? Perhaps we should narrow this line of questioning a bit. How do you like your gospel? Full and rich, pervading all areas of life? Or light and airy, salvific in the end, but requiring little commitment in the meantime?

Edwards bore into the Bible his entire life, spending countless hours plumbing its depths and offering his people the richest doctrine he could. In going directly to the text, Edwards found not a small gospel, but a large one. This large gospel promised not to chip away at the human heart, but to overhaul it, performing a kind of spiritual quadruple bypass so that sinners who once muddled along could experience the power and joy of the good life.

Though he spelled out the transforming effects of the biblical message in countless sermons, Edwards preached five in particular that extol the virtues of the Christian in particularly affective language: "The Spiritual Blessings of the Gospel Represented by a Feast," "Christ is to the Heart Like a Tree Planted by a River," "Love the Sum of All Virtue," "Divine Love Alone Lasts Eternally," and "The Peace Which Christ Gives His True

Followers." These sermons lay out sensory pleasures—feasting, drinking, peace—that in unique and moving ways show the depth of the *evangel* and the contours of the good life it creates. In these messages, we see that it is not a small-sized faith, neatly compartmentalized, that makes for the happiest existence, but a large, pervasive, scriptural gospel that conquers our sin, satisfies our hearts, and allows us to live the good life prepared for us by God Himself.

THE GOSPEL FEAST

In his sermon "The Spiritual Blessings of the Gospel Represented by a Feast," Edwards used the imagery of a harvest meal to illustrate the bounty of blessings that the gospel bestowed on the Christian. In our day, we are less acquainted with feasts, but in the eighteenth century, such a meal represented a grand occasion, a time of celebration, in which one forgot one's cares and shared food and happiness with friends and family. "In this feast," said the pastor,

> God is the host; 'tis he that makes the provision and invites the guests. And sinners are the invited guests. Believers are those that accept of the invitation. And Jesus Christ, with his benefits that he purchased by his obedience and death, and which he communicates by his Spirit, is the entertainment. This is the meat and drink. Christ gives himself for the life of the world. He is slain that we may as it were eat his flesh and drink his blood, as the sacrifices of old were slain and then that which was not burnt was eaten. Thus considered, God the Father is the host and Christ is the entertainment. Believers, as they live a life of faith, they do as it were feed upon Christ Jesus; they live upon him; he is their daily bread. (*Works* 14, 281–2)

God invites His guests, who have done nothing to deserve their place at the table. The "entertainment," or the center of the occasion, is "Jesus Christ, with his benefits that he purchased by his obedience and death." Edwards intended the picture this metaphor created to be a sensory one, reminding his hearers in a tangible way of the nearness and goodness of God.

Every feast comes at a cost, but no celebration came at a greater cost than did the gospel feast. God, Edwards noted, paid dearly for His people to dine with Him:

> As feasts are expensive and are provided at the expense of the host, so the provision which God has in the gospel made for our souls be exceeding expensive unto [him]. We have it for nothing. It costs us nothing, but it cost God a great deal. Fallen men can't be feasted but at vast expense. We are by sin sunk infinitely low, into the lowest depths of misery and want, and our famishing souls could not be provided for [but] under infinite expense. All that we have from God for the salvation and support and nourishment of our souls cost exceeding dear. Never were any that were feasted at so dear a rate as believers: what they eat and drink is a thousand times more costly than what they eat at the tables [of] princes, that is far-fetched and dear bought.

Edwards continued,

> Every crumb of bread that they eat and every drop of wine that they drink is more costly than so much gold or gems. God purchased it at no less a rate than with the blood of his only and infinitely dear Son. That holiness and that favor, and that peace and joy which they have, it was bought with the heart's blood of the Son of God, his precious life. He made his soul an offering. Christ Jesus obtained this provision by victory. He was obliged to fight for it as it were up to his knees in blood that he might

obtain it; yea, he waded through a sea of blood to get it for us.
(*Works* 14, 282–83)

Salvation did not come cheaply. Before he unfolded the glories
of the Christian life, Edwards took pains to show his people that
their salvation, their place at the table, cost the Father His Son
and the Son His life. Though so many of us covet the finer things
of life, which come at a great cost, the gospel feast that the saved
enjoy "is a thousand times more costly than what they eat at the
tables [of] princes," who spread the most lavish meals in all the
world. "Holiness," "favor," "peace and joy," all these Christ gave
His people in infinite amount. But He did not simply wave a
wand to make this happen; "he waded through a sea of blood"
to bless us. Contrary to the light and airy prosperity teachings of
some preachers today, which often touch briefly on the gospel
while majoring on the supposed wealth that it brings, Edwards
anchored His understanding of the blessings of the good life in
the atoning death of Christ, the price of salvation that only divinity could pay.

THE FOOD SPREAD BEFORE US IN THE FEAST

Having compared salvation to a great feast, Edwards considered
the character of its offerings. What, exactly, does the immense
gospel of the Bible do in the lives of those who believe it? Edwards answered,

> The grace of Christ Jesus, it nourishes the soul; it gives life and
> strength to it. Before the soul receives this grace, it is dead. In this
> it doth more than bread does to the body, that does but preserve the
> life of the body and revives it when weakened and languishing; but
> this heavenly food revives men when dead. And it also continues the
> life of the soul: the soul, after it is revived, would die again, were it

not for the continuance of supply of grace and spiritual nourishment. It strengthens the soul as food does the body. The soul in its natural condition is a poor, feeble, languishing thing, having no strength; but the grace of Christ makes it strong and vigorous. And this spiritual nourishment makes the soul to grow, as food doth the body. The supplies of the Spirit of God increase the life and vigor of the soul, increases the understanding, increases holy inclinations and affections; as bodily nourishment increases all the members of the body, makes a proportionable growth of every part. (*Works* 14, 284)

The gospel of Christ works in the heart to spiritually enrich it and saturate it with the sweet things of God. It is not a weak message, a pleasant but powerless story. It "revives men when dead," it "nourishes the soul," giving "life and strength to it," rendering it "strong and vigorous" in the things of the Lord. As we feed on divine grace, "this spiritual nourishment makes the soul to grow" just like food does "the body." "Every part" of our being, including our "understanding" and our "holy inclinations and affections," grows and flourishes and bursts with life due to the gospel. One cannot fully comprehend its effects. It is too great a message, too powerful a reality, to fully understand and appreciate. So said the pastor in another section of "The Spiritual Blessings":

There is every kind of thing dispensed in Christ that tends to make us excellent and amiable, and every kind of thing that tends to make us happy. There is that which shall fill every faculty of the soul and in a great variety. What a glorious variety is there for the entertainment of the understanding! How many glorious objects set forth, most worthy to be meditated upon and understood! There are all the glorious attributes of God and the beauties of Jesus Christ, and manifold wonders to be seen in the way of salvation, the glories of heaven and the excellency of Christian graces. And there is a glorious variety for the satisfying the will: there are pleasures, riches and honors; there are all things desirable or lovely. There is various entertainment for the affections, for love, for joy, for desire and hope. The blessings are innumerable. (*Works* 14, 285–86)

Edwards's God-soaked conception of the delights of Christianity soars past our reductionistic, narcissistic, Christianity-in-a-box kind of faith. As he saw things, life is not about us and the achievement of our own frequently shallow ideals and hopes. Those who possess faith in the gospel gain a connection to the Lord of the universe, who bursts with "glorious attributes." Like a feast that features every kind of food possible, Christians have "every kind of thing" through Christ "that tends to make us excellent and amiable" and "happy." Love, joy, peace, comfort, hope, grace, forgiveness, mercy, happiness, confidence—all these and a thousand other blessings are ours, flowing to us in "inexhaustible plenty" like "rivers of pleasure forevermore." This is what the good life looks like: more blessing than we can quantify in more areas than we can identify.

CHRISTIAN LIVING IS FUNDAMENTALLY JOYFUL LIVING

Because of the constant availability of all these good things, the Christian life was a joyful one. Edwards closed his sermon with words summarizing this point:

> Feasts are made upon joyful occasions and for the manifestations of joy. Ecclesiastes 10:19, "A feast is made for laughter." Christians, in the participation and communion of gospel benefits, have joy unspeakable and full of glory, a sweeter delight than any this world affords. We are invited in that forecited place, Isaiah 55:1–2, to come, that our souls may delight themselves in fatness. When the prodigal son returned, they killed the fatted calf

and made a feast, and sang and danced and made merry; which represents the joy there [is] in a sinner, and concerning him, when he comes to Christ. (*Works* 14, 287)

The fundamental reality of the Christian life was joy in the pastor's eyes. Not rigidity, not ecstasy, not sobriety, not gloominess, not emotional stasis. Because the Savior has substituted Himself for sinners, and has returned triumphant from the grave, so also may sinners return to life, and taste for all their lives "joy unspeakable and full of glory," that which is "a sweeter delight than any this world affords." This does not deny or trivialize real pain and suffering. But it reflects that the goodness of God so pervades the Christian life that nothing can rob a Christian of the delights of the gospel. For all our lives, we eat at a full table, and eat a rich feast, with Christ the head of all. The good life is a feast.

A VISION OF DIVINE LOVE

Though Edwards often elaborated on the fruits of the gospel, he rarely provided richer fare for his congregation than he did on the specific subjects of love and peace—spiritual principles given the children of God by the indwelling Spirit in the moment when the redeemed first tasted the sweetness of Christ. In his sermons "Love the Sum of All Virtue" and "Divine Love Alone Lasts Eternally," the Northampton theologian discussed the love given to believers by God. In the first sermon, he covered the flow of this love from the center of the Godhead to the heart of the Christian. In the gospel, he argued,

> there it is revealed how the Father and the Son are one in love, that we might be induced in like manner to be one with them, and with one another, agreeable to Christ's prayer, John 17:21–23, "That they all may be one; as thou Father art in me and I in thee, that they

also may be one in us; that the world may believe that thou hast
sent me. And the glory which thou gavest me I have given them;
that they may be one, even as we are one; I in them, and thou in
me, that they may be made perfect in one; and that the world may
know that thou hast sent me, and hast loved them, as thou hast loved
me." The gospel teaches us the doctrine of the eternal electing love of
God, and reveals how God loved those that are redeemed by Christ
before the foundation of the world; and how he then gave them to
the Son, and the Son loved them as his own. . . . The gospel reveals
such love as nothing else reveals. John 15:13, "Greater love hath no
man than this." Romans 5:7–8, "Scarcely for a righteous man will one
die; yet peradventure for a good man some would even dare to die.
But God commendeth his love towards us, in that while we were yet
sinners, Christ died for us." God and Christ in the gospel revelation
appear as clothed with love, as being as it were on a throne of mercy
and grace, a seat of love encompassed about with pleasant beams of
love. Love is the light and glory which are about the throne on which
God sits. (*Works* 8, 144–45)

The root of the love that Christians experience is the love shared
by the members of the Trinity. To rightly understand the biblical
notion of love according to Edwards, one had to first realize that
the object of God's love was the Godhead. The members of the
Trinity—the Father, Son, and Holy Spirit—exist in perfect harmony, constantly sharing delight in their relationships with one
another. From the overflow of this love came the offer of the
Father and Son "to be one with them, and with one another."
This association came through the "eternal electing love of God"
that commissioned the redeeming work of the Son.

   This section enriches our understanding of Christian love,
as it shows us the deeply God-centered nature of the love we
experience and reveals that we cannot claim pride of place in the
eyes of the Father. The Father has loved us, yes, but He has loved

us in the death of His Son. We see, then, that all of the blessings we experience in this life, including the love of God, come to us from the overflow of the love of the Trinity. The good life proceeds from the outflow of the love shared by the Father, Son, and Holy Spirit. Only then can we apprehend a right understanding of ourselves and a biblical definition of love. Only then will the gospel sparkle in our minds with an "exceeding sweet and pleasant light, pleasant like the beautiful colors of the rainbow," a message with greater depth than any mind could conceive.

THE ETERNAL NATURE OF DIVINE LOVE

The Northampton theologian concentrated on the effect of this love in the experience of the Christian in his sermon "Divine Love Alone Lasts Eternally." He connected this love with the work of the Holy Spirit, building on his belief that the character or identity of the Spirit is love:

> That divine love is that great fruit of the Spirit of Christ which never fails, and in which his continued and everlasting influence and indwelling in his church appears. You have heard that the Spirit of Christ is forever given to the church of Christ, or given that it may dwell in his church and people forever in influences which shall never fail. And therefore however many fruits of the Spirit may be but temporary, and have their periods in which they fail, yet it must be so that there must be some way of influence, and some kind of fruit of the Spirit, which is unfailing and everlasting. And this, even divine or Christian love, is that fruit in the communicating and maintaining and exercising of which his unfailing, eternal influences appear. This is a fruit of the Spirit which never fails or ceases in the church of Christ, whether we consider the church with respect to its particular members, or whether we consider it as a collective body. (*Works* 8, 356)

Edwards reminds the believer that the Spirit "never fails" and exercises a "continued and everlasting influence" on the children of God, bearing "fruit" in which "his unfailing, eternal influences appear." Love, in its fullest and most biblical sense, comes from God, emanating from heaven like a transmission from another world. The Spirit, our indwelling spiritual radar, allows us to receive this call, to see for the first time love in its truest form, and to receive it. Having picked up this signal, we send it back to God, and the cycle continues, love between God and Christian never ceasing.

As one can readily see, divine love is not weak. It is tough, and strong, and enables us to persevere. Once we have received the Spirit, the endowment of divine love, we find strength to transcend our difficulties and defeat our enemies:

> If we consider the church of Christ [individually], or with respect to the particular members of which it consists, divine love is an unfailing fruit of the Spirit. Every one of the true members of Christ's invisible church are possessed of this fruit of the Spirit in their hearts. Divine or Christian love is implanted there, and dwells there, and reigns there, and it is an everlasting fruit of the Spirit. It never fails; it never fails in this world, but remains through all trials and opposition. Romans 8:35–37, "Who shall separate us from the love of Christ? Shall tribulation, or distress, or persecution, or famine, or nakedness, or peril, or sword? As it is written, for thy sake we are killed all the day long; we are accounted as sheep for the slaughter. Nay, in all these things we are more than conquerors through him that loved us." (*Works* 8, 358)

Edwards believed that love, because of its triumphant nature, represents the greatest gift of any the Father could give. He elaborated,

This doctrine teaches us how greatly such influence and fruits of the Spirit working grace in the heart, summarily consisting in Christian and divine love, are to be valued. It is the design of the Apostle to teach us this by showing how charity never fails, though all other gifts and fruits of the Spirit fail. This is the most excellent fruit of the Spirit, without which the best extraordinary and miraculous gifts are nothing. This is the end of which they are the means, and which is more excellent than the means. Let us therefore earnestly seek this blessed fruit of the Spirit; and let us seek that it may abound in our hearts, that the love of God may more and more be shed abroad in our hearts, and that we may love the Lord Jesus Christ in sincerity, and love one another as Christ hath loved us. Hereby we shall possess that which never fails. We shall have that within us which will be of an immortal nature, and which will be a sure evidence of our own blessed immortality, and the beginning of eternal life in our souls. (*Works* 8, 365)

Edwards extolled all the gifts and fruits of the Spirit, but he made clear that love was "the most excellent." Without it, "the best extraordinary and miraculous gifts are nothing." Divine affection planted in the heart is nothing less than "the beginning of eternal life in our souls." The gospel as Edwards saw it was not small. It was great. It brought God's love to sinful, loveless, afflicted hearts, and gave them an "immortal nature." Love was the planted seed of God, given in this life, which would grow up to maturity and fullness in the next life. That which the human heart seeks in so many forms, whether romantic, parental, physical, affectional, or any other, that which it searches the world to find, is located in the gospel, the special communication of God's love to His creation. The good life is found in the gospel.

A VISION OF DIVINE PEACE

A second major effect of the gospel involved peace of a decidedly otherworldly kind. In his sermon "The Peace Which Christ Gives His True Followers," Edwards illuminated the nature of divine peace, identifying it as a product of faith in the gospel. He began by discussing Christ's personal gift of peace to His children:

> It was his peace that he gave them; as it was the same kind of peace which he himself enjoyed. The same excellent and divine peace which he ever had in God; and which he was about to receive in his exalted state in a vastly greater perfection and fullness: for the happiness Christ gives to his people, is a participation of his own happiness: agreeable to what Christ says in this same dying discourse of his, John 15:11, "These things have I said unto you, that my joy might remain in you." And in his prayer that he made with his disciples at the conclusion of this discourse; John 17:13, "And now come I unto thee, and these things I speak in the world, that they might have my joy fulfilled in themselves." And John 17:22, "And the glory which thou gavest me, I have given them." (*Works* 25, 539)

Along with providing His people security and hope, the peace He purchased through death brought reconciliation to all of man's relationships—to God, to others, and with himself:

> Our Lord Jesus Christ has bequeathed true peace and comfort to his followers. Christ is called the "prince of peace" (Isaiah 9:6). And when he was born into the world, the angels on that joyful and wonderful occasion sang "Glory to God in the highest, on earth peace"; because of that peace which he should procure for and bestow on the children of men; peace with God, and peace one with another, and tranquility and peace within themselves: which last is especially the benefit spoken of in the text. This

Christ has procured for his followers and laid a foundation for their enjoyment of, in that he has procured for them the other two, viz.: peace with God, and one with another. He has procured for them peace and reconciliation with God, and his favor and friendship, in that he satisfied for their sins, and laid a foundation for the perfect removal of the guilt of sin, and the forgiveness of all their trespasses, and wrought out for them a perfect and glorious righteousness, most acceptable to God and sufficient to recommend them to God's full acceptance and to the adoption of children, and to the eternal fruits of his fatherly kindness. (*Works* 25, 542)

Those who seek unbroken peace in the world outside of Christianity do not know that no other foundation for harmony and security exists. Lasting comfort is found not in a system, an ideology, or even a galvanizing figure, but only in the God-man, Jesus Christ. He *is* peace. Through His death and resurrection on behalf of His people, "He has procured for them peace and reconciliation with God," the ultimate need of all who live. While on earth, we seek and pray for peace, but we do so knowing that whatever treaty is agreed to, whatever truce is brokered, it is earthly and cannot ultimately last. With Edwards, we must affirm that only Christ and the "perfect and glorious righteousness" He gives can meet our needs and calm our hearts. The good life is a life of peace.

PEACE'S PRACTICAL EFFECTS

The peace offered mankind in the gospel did not simply meet a general need of humanity, but through grace had a transformational effect on the heart of a regenerated sinner. The theologian suggested in "The Peace Which Christ Gives His True Followers" that

grace tends to tranquility, as it mortifies tumultuous desires and
passions, subdues the eager and insatiable appetites of the sensual
nature and greediness after the vanities of the world. It mortifies
such principles as hatred, variance, emulation, wrath, envyings,
and the like, which are a continual source of inward uneasiness
and perturbation; and supplies those sweet, calming, and quieting
principles of humility, meekness, resignation, patience, gentle-
ness, forgiveness, and sweet reliance on God.

And it also tends to peace, as it fixes the aim of the soul to
a certain end; so that the soul is no longer distracted and drawn
contrary ways by opposite ends to be sought, and opposite portions to be obtained, and many masters of contrary wills and commands to be served; but the heart is fixed in the choice of one
certain, sufficient, and unfailing good: and the soul's aim at this,
and hope of it, is like an anchor to it that keeps it steadfast, that it
should no more be driven to and fro by every wind. (*Works* 25, 544)

Here, Edwards shows us how the grace of God given in the gospel
quiets the frenetic heart. Grace, said the pastor, "mortifies tumultuous desires and passions, subdues the eager and insatiable appetites of the sensual nature," kills "hatred, variance, emulation,
wrath, envyings," and "supplies those sweet, calming, and quieting principles" of a spiritual nature. The peace of the message
of faith addresses head-on the natural restlessness and senseless
destructiveness that characterize so many lost people. When the
Spirit converts a sinner, He brings the heart to rest. This rest,
Edwards contended, increases as one contemplates its presence:

But with respect to the peace which Christ gives, reason is its
great friend: the more that faculty is exercised, the more is it established; the more they consider and view things with truth and
exactness, the firmer is their comfort and the higher their joy. How
vast a difference is this, between [a Christian and a worldling]!

> How miserable are they who can't enjoy peace any otherwise than
> by hiding their eyes from the light and confining themselves to
> darkness, whose peace is properly stupidity: as the ease which a
> man has that has taken a dose of stupefying poison, and the ease
> and pleasure that a drunken man may have in an house on fire
> over his head, or the joy of a distracted man in thinking that he is
> a king, though a miserable wretch confined in Bedlam. Whereas,
> the peace that Christ gives to his true disciples is the light of life:
> something of the tranquility of heaven, the peace of the celestial
> paradise that has the glory of God to lighten it. (*Works* 25, 547–48)

The more one thinks of God's peace, and considers how much of
it one possesses, the more one will experience it, says Edwards.
Unlike the unbeliever, who hides from "consideration and reflection," the Christian counts "reason" his "great friend." This
is a perceptive point. When we are lost, we do not like to acknowledge it. Instead, we fill our days with distractions, avoiding
deep thought about our situations, choosing a constant stream of
action over quiet moments of thought. The Christian, however,
needs no such diversions. We are freed to evaluate our lives. We
have been freed from pride and pretending, and from the peace
that "is properly stupidity." As a result, we can live without fear.

Believers know that Christ has taken our burden from us,
has forgiven us for all eternity, and has given us every blessing.
We thus possess "something of the tranquility of heaven." In the
same way that one easily spots unrest and fear in the unbeliever,
one finds many Christians who radiate hope and calm trust in
the Lord in all kinds of circumstances. Despite the deterioration
of the body, the loss of a job, the death of a friend, Christians
rooted in the gospel display otherworldly peace and trust, showing that the good life always yields good fruit.

Edwards closed his sermon by reminding his hearers of the
eternal nature of the peace they possessed. His words nicely

close our study of the peace given to every follower of the Lord as he invites us to marvel at the hope that is ours in Christ:

> I invite you now to a better portion; there are better things provided for the sinful, miserable children of men. There is a surer comfort and more durable peace: comfort that you may enjoy in a state of safety, and on a sure foundation; a peace and rest that you may enjoy with reason and with your eyes open; having all your sins forgiven, your greatest and most aggravated transgressions blotted out as a cloud, and buried as in the depths [of] the sea, that they may be never found more: and being not only forgiven but accepted to favor, being the objects of God's complacence and delight, being taken into God's family and made his child; and having good evidence that your name was written on the heart of Christ before the world was made, and an interest in that covenant of God that is ordered in all things, and sure, wherein is promised no less than life and immortality, an inheritance incorruptible and undefiled, a crown of glory that fades not away: being in such circumstances that nothing shall be able to prevent your being happy to all eternity; having for the foundation of your hope that love of God which is from eternity to eternity; and his promise and oath, and his omnipotent power, things infinitely firmer than mountains of brass. The mountains shall depart and the hills be removed; yea, the heavens shall vanish away like smoke, and the earth shall wax old like a garment, yet these things will never be abolished. (*Works* 25, 551)

THE BOUNTIFUL BLESSINGS OF THE GOOD LIFE

The love and peace of God—along with a multitude of other blessings—are spread out before us like a feast. We have only to seek them and we will find them. The goodness of God is like the Lord Himself—vast and incomprehensible, stretching beyond all that we can think or imagine. It proceeds from the sweetest message this world knows, the gospel of Christ. As we have seen, the gospel is anything but small. It is massive. It looms before us, offering to catapult us into the realm of God where beauty and truth make their home. Far from a personal preference or an arbitrary indulgence, the gospel is the good news of God that claims our entire lives and then floods them with more blessing than any worldview, passion, or lifestyle we might consider. The gospel creates the good life.

In this modern, self-centered, consumerist age, we need to fasten ourselves to this biblical truth. We need to realize that the gospel is great, engulfing every inch of our lives. Viewed up close through the lens of Scripture, the good life in Christ yields not a trickle, but an ocean of love and peace; not a sampling of pleasures, but a feast of delights.

Living the Good Life

Understand True Love and Peace and Live Them Out

As mentioned earlier in the chapter, health-and-wealth preachers have made quite a name for themselves. Prosperity theology is hot, and probably always will be, because it taps into the natural desire of the human heart for riches and comfort. This theology suffers from a deficient reading of Scripture, primarily. But it also suffers from a weak product. Pastors of this stripe promise the nicest material goods this world affords, never knowing that the nicest car, the biggest house, the most exclusive address, the most stylish clothes, and the coolest technology all pale in comparison to the gifts the Lord waits to lavish upon His people. The Bible does not promise material wealth, it offers something far greater. It holds out the very riches of heaven, and invites all to come and enjoy them.

Know the Relationship Between Grace and Peace

We covered earlier Edwards's understanding of reconciliation between God and man, that is, how the Lord and His creation can find peace with one another. The doctrine of reconciliation through justification by faith illuminates how we conceive of our salvation and the very duties of our lives. As Edwards taught, we cannot obtain true and lasting peace by ourselves. This gift is given only by Christ, and it comes to us when the Spirit works in us to help us to understand how far away we are from God. Ironically, then, we can only be justified in God's sight and thereby reconciled to Him by realizing how bad we are and how great Christ's atonement is (Rom. 5). This flies in the face of our instincts. We naturally wish to justify ourselves in God's sight by demonstrating our fitness for heaven. But in the biblical scheme, only those who lay down their pride and self-justification can find reconciliation with God.

True grace creates true peace—and nothing else can.

Chapter 18

THE SHAPE
OF THE GOOD LIFE

A simple line divides the happy from the unhappy in this world. The happy obey God; the unhappy disregard Him. In a number of Edwards's writings, he taught this biblical doctrine, injecting great passion and intellectual energy into it, trying with all his strength to turn people away from worldly promises of happiness that he knew would prove deeply unsatisfying and joyless. In "The Importance and Advantage of a Thorough Knowledge of Divine Truth," a section from the *Religious Affections*, and "The True Christian's Life a Journey Towards Heaven," the pastor shows us that God has given us His Word and His law not to bind us or rob us of joy, but to show us the shape of the good life and lead us into fullness of happiness.

THE LONG PERSPECTIVE OF FAITH

In order to properly approach the Christian life, one had to view it from a long perspective. That is, Edwards believed that one needed to see one's existence in terms of eternity, and to factor one's daily choices into the life to come. In "The True Christian's Life a Journey Towards Heaven," Edwards challenged his congregation to motivate themselves to holy living by thinking ahead to the end of their earthly days. Life, he contended, is a journey toward heaven for the Christian, and so

> we ought not to be content with this world, or so to set our hearts on any enjoyments we have here as to rest in them. No, we ought to seek a better happiness. If we are surrounded with many outward enjoyments and things are comfortable to us; if we are settled in families and have those friends and relatives that are very desirable; if we have companions whose society is delightful to us; if we have children that are pleasant and likely, and in whom we see many promising qualifications, and live by good neighbors, and have much of the respect of others, have a good name and are generally beloved where we are known, and have comfortable and pleasant accommodations: yet we ought not to take up our rest in these things. We should not be willing to have these things for our portion, but should seek happiness in another world. . . . We should choose to leave 'em all in God's due time, that we might go to heaven, and there have the enjoyment of God. (*Works* 17, 430)

The pastor's main point was that Christians need always to be ready to "choose to leave" the things of this world. The believer, unlike the lost person caught up in worldly pleasure, chases "a better happiness" located "in another world." Edwards did not debase this world or the things of it, but rather exhorted his people to set their affection on heaven and God such that the things of this world would pale in comparison.

LIVING FOR THE FUTURE

Once the people of God freed themselves up to appreciate the things of God, they would have a greater desire to live holy lives. Without what is sometimes called an eschatological viewpoint—that is, a viewpoint that sees one's life in light of eternity—Christians would often struggle to live differently from the world. In "The True Christian's Life a Journey Towards Heaven," Edwards called his people to holiness, but he did so while reminding his people of the outcome of holiness:

> We ought to seek heaven by traveling in the way that leads thither. The way that leads to heaven is a way of holiness; we should choose and desire to travel thither in this way, and in no other. We should part with all those sins, those carnal appetites, that are as weights that will tend to hinder us in our traveling towards heaven; Hebrews 12:1, "let us lay aside every weight, and the sin that doth so easily beset us, and let us run with patience the race that is set before us." However pleasant any practice or the gratification of any appetite may be, we must lay it aside, cast it away, if it be any hindrance, any stumbling block, in the way to heaven.

All of the commands of God required the heaven-seeker's attention, according to the pastor:

> We should travel on as a way of obedience to all God's commands, even the difficult, as well as the easy, commands. We should travel on in a way of self-denial, denying all our sinful inclinations and interests. The way to heaven is ascending; we must be content to travel up hill, though it be hard, and tiresome, and contrary to the natural tendency and bias of our flesh, that tends downward to the earth. We should follow Christ in the path that he has gone; the way that he traveled in was the right way to heaven. We should take up our cross and follow him. We should travel along in the same way of meekness and lowliness of heart, in the same way of obedience, and charity, and diligence to do good, and patience under afflictions. (*Works* 17, 433)

The good life, as we have frequently noted, is the best life, but it is not always, or even often, easy. One has to fight against the flesh, one's sinful nature, to acquire holiness and taste the sweetness of Christ. Christian faith, contrary to what some may tell us, is "a way of obedience" plotted according to "all God's commands," both the "difficult" and the "easy." It is "a way of self-denial." It is "ascending" and can be "hard, and tiresome." If we would walk it, and follow the example of the Savior, we must "take up our cross and follow him." The good life, the existence full of joy, does not involve self-exaltation, pride, and boastful celebration of one's strengths and talents, but "meekness," "lowliness of heart," "charity" for all, and "patience under afflictions." But we need not adopt these attitudes grimly. As our lives take a cruciform shape, godliness brings us joy, far more joy than sin does. But we must recognize as Edwards wisely does that obedience often involves hard work and vigilant concentration. We don't placate or pacify our flesh to grow in holiness; we fight it and kill it, doing war with it as we journey to our home above (Col. 3:1–10).

KEEPING HEAVEN ALWAYS IN VIEW

The good life is lived with heaven firmly in view. It is far off, yes, and sometimes difficult to see. But it is always in view. When one loses sight of heaven, one's faith cannot help but slip, one's resolve naturally begins to weaken. For this reason, one must always evaluate one's days according to a heavenward perspective. Our business decisions, our parenting, our classwork, our entertainment—we must consider all these things and many more from an eternal perspective. If we do not, as the pastor noted in "Journey Towards Heaven,"

> all our labor will be lost. If we spend our lives in the pursuit of
> a temporal happiness; if we set our hearts on riches and seek

happiness in them; if we seek to be happy in sensual pleasures; if
we spend our lives to seek the credit and esteem of men, the good
will and respect of others; if we set our hearts on our children and
look to be happy in the enjoyment of them, in seeing them well
brought up, and well settled, etc., all these things will be of little
significancy to us. Death will blow up all our hopes and expectations, and will put an end to our enjoyment of these things. . . .
Where will be all our worldly employments and enjoyments when
we are laid in the silent grave? For "man lieth down, and riseth
not again: till the heavens be no more" (Job 14:12). (*Works* 17,
436–37)

Nothing temporal, however virtuous, would last in the end, not
the finest "sensual pleasures," not the tenderest care for our
children. "Death," the pastor boldly suggested, "will blow up all
our hopes and expectations." Edwards left no doubt about the
outcome of our worldly pursuits. The secular good life produces
nothing but dust in the wind, embers of a fire now gone out.
All one's "enjoyments" come to nothing. The wisdom of man, expressed in a thousand ways while living, crumbles "in the silent
grave." Having ignored the wisdom of God all his life, the natural
man follows his own wisdom to death.

THE BENEFITS OF DIVINE WISDOM

Edwards believed that God had designed His special creation,
the human race, to do more than die an insignificant death. He
had revealed Himself in the Bible so that sinners might abandon the broad way of destruction and find the narrow way of
resurrection. In "The Importance and Advantage of a Thorough
Knowledge of Divine Truth," Edwards discussed how the Bible
manifested the treasures of God to the human race:

These things are so excellent and worthy to be known, that the
knowledge of them will richly pay for all the pains and labor of
an earnest seeking of it. If there were a great treasure of gold
and pearls hid in the earth but should accidentally be found, and
should be opened among us with such circumstances that all
might have as much as they could gather of it; would not every one
think it worth his while to make a business of gathering it while
it should last? But that treasure of divine knowledge, which is
contained in the Scriptures, and is provided for everyone to gather
to himself as much of it as he can, is a far more rich treasure than
any one of gold and pearls. How busy are all sorts of men, all over
the world, in getting riches? But this knowledge is a far better kind
of riches, than that after which they so diligently and laboriously
pursue. (*Works* 22, 92)

Those who wanted to know true pleasure and lasting happiness,
Edwards argued, needed to mine the Scripture, for in it "is a far
more rich treasure than any one of gold and pearls." Everyone
could obtain this treasure, Edwards noted, and the delights of it
would "richly pay for all the pains and labor of an earnest seeking of it." Though some thought that following the Bible would
squelch happiness and rob people of pleasure, Edwards believed
that it offered mankind the only sure means to joy. God had made
it plain and understandable, the pastor contended, so that we
could receive the benefits of the good life. Therefore, we must
seek them with the same hunger a treasure-hunter has for gold,
or prospectors for oil:

When God hath opened a very large treasure before, for the supply
of our wants, and we thank him that he hath given us so much; if
at the same time we be willing to remain destitute of the greatest
part of it, because we are too lazy to gather it, this will not show
the sincerity of our thankfulness. We are now under much greater

advantages to acquire knowledge in divinity, than the people of God were of old; because since that time, the canon of Scripture is much increased. But if we be negligent of our advantages, we may be never the better for them, and may remain with as little knowledge as they. (*Works* 22, 95)

Edwards admonished his people to direct their natural appetites and energy to the Bible. He implored his fellow Christians to realize the powers of their mind and to harness these abilities to store up biblical knowledge that would fuel holy living:

> This knowledge is exceeding useful in Christian practice. Such as have much knowledge in divinity have great means and advantages for spiritual and saving knowledge; for no means of grace, as was said before, have their saving effect on the heart, otherwise than by the knowledge they impart. The more you have of a rational knowledge of the things of the gospel, the more opportunity will there be, when the Spirit shall be breathed into your heart, to see the excellency of these things, and to taste the sweetness of them. The heathens, who have no rational knowledge of the things of the gospel, have no opportunity to see the excellency of them; and therefore the more rational knowledge of these things you have, the more opportunity and advantage you have to see the divine excellence and glory of them. (*Works* 22, 99–100)

Without the hard work of Scripture reading, meditation, and memorization, one would never see the "divine excellence and glory" of the Bible. Many Christians, Edwards knew, wanted to grow spiritually. They wanted to know God and go to heaven. But far fewer believers worked hard to deepen their faith and, subsequently, their enjoyment of God. Too many presumed upon God and His grace, expecting Him to simply drop a bag of maturity and happiness out of the sky for quick and easy use. This was not how Christian growth and maturity worked, the pastor argued. One had to apply one's mind, one's "rational knowledge," to "the things of the gospel." Only then could one see their "excellency" and taste their "sweetness." Christians have incredible "opportunity and advantage" to do so, with guaranteed results, but have to hungrily pursue such a life to experience it (Matt. 5:6).

REFRAMING OUR UNDERSTANDING OF SCRIPTURE

Edwards's material reframes modern conceptions of the Scripture and its commands. As he understood it, the Bible is not a textbook or rulebook, but rather a living document that communicates the heart and mind of the Lord of the universe. It does not simply help us sharpen and hone our lives or merely teach us content about God. The Bible opens to us the character of God, presenting God and the things of God to us. From every corner of the Bible, we gain wisdom, instruction, encouragement, and an understanding of the magnificence and beauty of Christ. The stories of Israelite heroes propel us to take heart in God and attempt great things for Him. The Law teaches us the inherent holiness of God and the required holiness of mankind. The Prophets show us the need to put holiness into practice. The Wisdom writings offer us a model for godly living and sage counsel for all seasons of life. The Gospels bring us face to face with Christ the Redeemer. The Epistles deliver grace-saturated teaching and exhortation. And Revelation shows us our future state in all its glory. All of Scripture is profitable for us, all of it will shape our lives in holy ways, all of it will quench our thirst and hunger for happiness through its exaltation of the Son, the Savior sent by the Father and empowered through the Spirit.

As we saturate our lives with the various texts of Scripture, we will experience an increasing closeness with God. He will become our joy and our hope. We will find assurance of our salvation, one of the most coveted and least-attained blessings in the Christian life. So many of us struggle in this area because our lives have not taken their shape from the Bible, and thus we lack assurance that we have been born again. We act and talk much like the lost around us. As a pastor who dealt his entire career with a worldly congregation (as many pastors do), Edwards fought to show his people that the turmoil and distress they experienced in their lives as a result of weak faith could cease. If they would pursue joy in Christ, and study the Word to find it, they would discover fresh assurance of their conversion, robbing Satan of one of his chief tools for undermining individual Christians and the broader ministry of the church.

In his classic text *The Religious Affections*, Edwards discussed this matter in a meaty section on the "twelfth sign of true Christian faith." There, he defined godliness as "light that shines in the soul" and clarified the connection between words and deeds:

And as this is the evidence that Christ has directed us mainly to look at in others, in judging of them, so it is the evidence that Christ has mainly directed us to give to others, whereby they may judge of us; "Let your light so shine before men, that others seeing your good works, may glorify your Father which is in heaven" (Matthew 5:16). Here Christ directs us to manifest our godliness to others. Godliness is as it were a light that shines in the soul: Christ directs that this light should not only shine within, but that it should shine out before men, that they may see it. But which way shall this be? 'Tis by our good works. Christ don't say, that others hearing your good words, your good story, or your pathetical expressions; but that others seeing your good works, may glorify your Father which is in heaven.

He continued,

> [T]he Apostle [Paul] in the beginning of the [sixth chapter of
> Hebrews], speaks of them that have great common illuminations,
> that have been enlightened, and have tasted of the heavenly
> gift, and were made partakers of the Holy Ghost, and have tasted
> the good Word of God, and the powers of the world to come, that
> afterwards fall away, and are like barren ground, that is nigh unto
> cursing, whose end is to be burned: and then immediately adds in
> the 9th verse (expressing his charity for the Christian Hebrews, as
> having that saving grace, which is better than all these common
> illuminations): "But beloved, we are persuaded better things of you,
> and things that accompany salvation; though we thus speak." And
> then in the next verse, he tells 'em what was the reason he had such
> good thoughts of 'em: he don't say, that it was because they had given
> him a good account of a work of God upon their souls, and talked very
> experimentally; but it was their work, and labor of love; "For God is
> not unrighteous, to forget your work, and labor of love, which ye have
> shewed towards his name, in that ye have ministered to the saints,
> and do minister." (*Works* 2, 407–8)

Having carefully spelled out how true faith manifests itself in
good works, Edwards then covered how an active faith, one that
conforms to the gracious contours of God's Word, produces
assurance:

> [T]he Scripture also speaks of Christian practice as a distinguish-
> ing and sure evidence of grace to persons' own consciences. This
> is very plain in 1 John 2:3: "Hereby we do know that we know him, if
> we keep his commandments." And the testimony of our consciences,
> with respect to our good deeds, is spoken of as that which may give
> us assurance of our own godliness; "My little children, let us not love
> in word, neither in tongue, but in deed . . . and in truth. And hereby

we know that we are of the truth, and shall assure our hearts before him" (1 John 3:18–19). And the apostle Paul, in Hebrews 6 speaks of "the work and labor of love," of the Christian Hebrews, as that which both gave him a persuasion that they had something above the highest common illuminations, and also as that evidence which tended to give them the highest assurance of hope concerning themselves; ver. Hebrews 6:9, etc.: "But beloved, we are persuaded better things of you, and things that accompany salvation, though we thus speak. For God is not unrighteous, to forget your work, and labor of love, which ye have showed towards his name; in that ye have ministered to his saints, and do minister. And we desire that every one of you do show the same diligence, to the full assurance of hope, unto the end." So the Apostle directs the Galatians to examine their behavior or practice, that they might have rejoicing in themselves in their own happy state; "Let every man prove his own work; so shall he have rejoicing in himself, and not in another" (Galatians 6:4). (*Works* 2, 420–21)

In these selections, the pastor communicated principally that holy living produces assurance, and assurance produces joy. Life according to God's design, then, is not simply *right*, but is *rich*, full of the highest pleasure of the world, namely, happiness resulting from the favor of God. Contrary to how so many of us perceive self-examination, as a stringent, joyless, depression-inducing affair, Edwards teaches us that examining our lives will actually lead to "rejoicing" and leave us in a "happy state" due to an awareness of the love and good works the Spirit has worked within us. It will also give us fresh recognition of our sins and a renewed resolve to fight them.

THE NEED TO STUDY OUR SOUL

As mentioned, however, most of us view self-examination as something negative. Because our feelings are sensitive and our hearts are proud, we hesitate to assess ourselves honestly. We do not want the floorboards of our hearts pulled up. Though it maims us, we want to keep our sin hidden. In reality, though, we are only hurting ourselves and those around us, because we are allowing sin to rule us. Self-examination, then, is a crucial practice, for it brings our sin to light and allows grace to shine in our hearts and uncover what we've buried. Our duty, then, is to make our conscience our friend, to listen to it as a trusted confidant, knowing that if it is submitted to God, it will guide us on the right path, and give us happy assurance in Christ.

TRACING THE GOOD LIFE

The good life had a definite shape, as Edwards showed throughout his writings. God did not create us, save us, and then leave us to do whatever we wished. He gave us a way of holiness to follow. He gave us a Bible with teaching to guide us. He gave us a conscience to lead us to holiness despite the presence of sin in our hearts. In all of these ways, God has given the good life a certain form, a definite shape, that He desires all His children to emulate. Edwards repeatedly emphasized, though, that this way of life did not squelch true joy—it produced it. It did squelch a certain kind of pleasure, a worldly, narcissistic, law-breaking pleasure, but it produced a better, lasting delight. True freedom and joy did not for Edwards proceed from egoistic hedonism, as our culture tells us, but from freeing obedience to the dictates of Scripture and the direction of God's Spirit.

Edwards showed throughout his writings on the good life that God originally made His people to walk in perfect harmony with Him. Even before the fall of Adam and Eve, this involved living according to His commands and laws. Restored humanity, those who had been regenerated by the Spirit, once again walked with God in harmony, enabled by the Spirit to experience the bliss of obedience. Freed from the power of sin, the children of God tasted all kinds of blessings—divine love, peace, hope, confidence, endurance, comfort, power, and more. They benefited from the guidance of the Word and experienced, as they repented daily of sin, the ongoing pleasantness of a clean conscience.

Edwards proved that the Lord was not harsh to give us direction in His word, but kind. God desired that we experience delight all of our days and graciously created the ideal conditions for a delightful life, which we have called the good life. This life does not run contrary to our best interests, but serves them even as it fulfills the good purposes of the Lord for our lives. It frees us from slavery to our lower, natural appetites and passions incurred by original sin and enables higher, spiritual principles to lead us. It turns us away from self-driven destruction and places us on a holy journey that is sometimes quite challenging but rewarding both here and in the afterlife. This, and not any other version, is the good life, the life God intends for us.

Living the Good Life

Honor the Lord through Sincere, Passionate Obedience

Ours is not an age that prizes obedience. We have grown up in an anti-authoritarian culture in which the watchword is something like "Do what pleases you and don't judge others." Some Christians have imbibed this spirit as well and seem to think that their faith has no room for God's laws, commandments, or directions for living.

This mindset, which emphasizes faith and the heart over obedience and the mind, alters the biblical picture of the Christian life. In true biblical religion, heart and mind go together and faith fuels obedience. Past generations of Christians have, it is true, gone overboard with rules and laws and have sometimes seemed to reduce the robust life offered us in the gospel to a set of commands. We should reject such a mindset—though we should also remember that the Bible includes many commands and guidelines for the believer to follow.

Once the Holy Spirit converts our fallen hearts, we are called to devote ourselves to lives of holiness and obedience. This does not mean that we cannot also pursue joy. As we have seen in Edwards's writings, we must pursue joy, and in fact, we will find the fullness of joy when our hearts seek to worship the Lord in what the Apostle Paul called "the obedience of faith" (Rom. 1:5, 16:26). Thus, we should never divide holiness from happiness. We must not let the culture determine our understanding of God's character and His law. His law, after all, is not some arbitrary code of conduct, but is both the expression of His character and His beneficent will for mankind.

As with so many other points of application, we need churches that prioritize holiness to encourage us in this direction; we need close friends who keep us accountable and push us on to good works; and we need a close personal walk with the Lord that will allow us to cultivate a rich, happy, holy walk with God. The difference between formalized Christianity, Christianity that looks fine but really is just an exercise to perform without any real passion, and the good life can boil down to sincerity and passion. If we would taste the goodness of God, then we need to sincerely, not half-heartedly, pursue the Lord. This means that we don't simply pray to do it; that we don't just read the sacred text; that we don't simply show up to church, but that we do all these out of a sincere, earnest, passionate desire to love the Lord. The world mocks sincerity, but it is inseparable from true faith and the good life.

Seek Assurance through Godliness

In our day, we often hear statements like, "Well, I'm a believer, but I'm not really into religion." "I love Jesus, but I don't believe in all these rules." "Yeah, I trust God, but the whole church thing gets way overblown." In these and many other such statements, people with a lax faith excuse themselves from true Christian living. This is a tragedy. They may have a basic belief in God, but they are without salvation and thus trick themselves into thinking they are eternally secure when they are not. Or, they may truly be saved, but dishonoring the Lord through a half-hearted, passionless, unholy lifestyle.

True believers in this situation, as with all of us who profess Christ, need to act upon the Edwardsean idea that godliness will generally provide clarity and assurance of our faith (see 1 John 5, for example). Those who constantly doubt their Christian profession need to know that only a godly life, coupled with the witness of the Holy Spirit and the encouragement of a church, will produce true confidence in Christ. None of us will obtain perfection (or anything close to it) until heaven, but the Lord has designed our faith to gain rich assurance when it is driven by an obedient, God-centered heart.

Part 4

True Christianity

Chapter 19

THE PROBLEM OF NOMINAL CHRISTIANITY IN EDWARDS'S DAY

In the former part of this great work of God amongst us, till it got to its height, we seemed to be wonderfully smiled upon and blessed in all respects. Satan (as has been already observed) seemed to be unusually restrained: persons that before had been involved in melancholy, seemed to be as it were waked up out of it; and those that had been entangled with extraordinary temptations, seemed wonderfully to be set at liberty; and not only so, but it was the most remarkable time of health, that ever I knew since I have been in the town. (*Works* 4, 205)

This was Jonathan Edwards's assessment of his town's spiritual health in 1735. Just a little while after this happy state, however, a period of decline and despair struck the community. "In the latter part of May," Edwards wrote, "it began to be very sensible that the Spirit of God was gradually withdrawing from us, and after this time Satan seemed to be more let loose, and raged in a dreadful manner" (*Works* 4, 206). The great promise of the 1735 revival waned as the town gradually settled into a spiritual malaise. Many of the people lost their vision and their zeal, despite maintaining their church membership and even professing to be believers. So it was that Edwards discovered the foe he would battle for decades: nominal Christianity, meaning Christianity in name only, without vibrant faith to accompany it.

Nominal Christianity was a big problem in an eighteenth-century environment dominated by the church. Whether they wanted to or not, people paid taxes to support their local minister (and would do so for another century, roughly). The social conventions of the day called for faithful church attendance and at least the appearance of godliness. A good number of folks followed the strictures of colonial Christianity from a heart of genuine obedience and worship. Despite stereotypes to the contrary, these men and women no doubt loved the stout theology and actional piety demanded by their uncompromising Puritan sermonizers. They wanted to know the Lord; they wanted to kill their sin; they loved being challenged to grow in their daily walk with Christ. There were many folks of this type in Edwards's day, and there are many of this kind in our time, believers who hunger to put off the old man and put on the new (see Col. 3).

But others did not share the zeal of the true church. They were spiritually lukewarm. They had no heart-love for the things of God. They professed to know the true God, but did not display zeal for His Word and His gospel. At one time, they might have seemed to exude genuine interest in the Lord, but after a while, the light dimmed and the fire ebbed. What was left over was a heart—in many cases—that was worse off than before, hardened to the beauty and power of divine truth, bitter over the church's insistent call to holiness. As we will see—and have already covered some chapters ago—a number of nominal Christians would not only bedevil Edwards's pastorate, but would help to push him out of the Northampton church. No small matter, this.

Edwards's own situation was unique to his day. We're long

past the age of petticoats and bewigged preachers. Yet though his age had its own unique contours, we can certainly understand the challenge of nominal Christianity in the twenty-first century. Just like Edwards, we face the problem of spiritual lukewarmness, of people professing to be a Christian but failing to live, speak, think, and act like one on a consistent basis. This ongoing challenge to the true church can lead to discouragement and frustration for faithful believers. But though Edwards knew his own struggles to engage nominalism, he points us to a better way than snarky asides and social media hot takes. Edwards's response to half-hearted faith was fundamentally biblical and theological. So must ours be.

In this chapter, we will look primarily at Edwards's analysis of this problem, an ongoing one he faced: the lukewarmness of professing Christians. We will look at a sermon entitled "Living Unconverted Under Eminent Means of Grace," move to a substantial selection from the *Faithful Narrative of the Surprising Work of God*, and then examine sermons entitled "Many Mansions" and "True Grace Distinguished from the Experience of Devils." Through this analysis, we will gain wisdom into how Edwards thought about the problem of nominalism and how he addressed it. We'll see that the initial step in fighting nominalism is to identify and critique it. So begins our response to a problem that only God can ultimately conquer.

"LIVING UNCONVERTED" UNDER A GODLY MINISTER

Edwards knew the face of nominal Christianity well. He grew up in a pastor's home and possessed keen abilities of discernment from an early age. He was not fooled by cultural Christianity, different as it would have looked in his day, when most New England residents attended church and would have assented to the basic doctrines of the faith. Though one might think this kind of setting ideal to the spread of true faith, Edwards was painfully aware of the lack of vibrant Christian living among the Northampton residents, a point he made abundantly clear in the very first sermon he preached as pastor in 1729. Memorializing his recently deceased grandfather, Solomon Stoddard, Edwards rebuked many of his parishioners in "Living Unconverted Under Eminent Means of Grace," a sermon based on Jeremiah 6:29–30. The people of Northampton had benefited immensely from Stoddard's ministry, Edwards pointed out, though their lives displayed far less of the benefits than they should have:

> There have [been] few places that have enjoyed such eminent powerful means of grace as you of this place have enjoyed. You have lived all your days under a most clear, convincing dispensation of God's word. The whole land is full of gospel light, but this place has been distinguishingly blessed of God with excellent means for a long time under your now deceased minister.

Edwards then turned up the heat, making his subject matter personal:

> And it argues a dismal degree of obduracy and blindness, that persons could stand it out under such a ministry. In what a clear and awakening manner have you hundreds of times had your danger and misery in a natural condition set before you! How clearly have you had the way of salvation shown to you, and how movingly have you had the encouragements of the gospel offered to you!
>
> Such as can live all their days under such means of awakening and of conversion, and have stood it out and have been proof against such preaching, are undoubtedly of exceeding hard hearts. They that are still unawakened, doubtless their hearts are much harder than if they had not lived under such great advantages. Powerful preaching, if it don't awaken, it hardens more than other preaching.

The pastor concluded the point with a vivid warning:

> Those means are now gone; you'll have them no more. You have
> stood it out until the bellows are burnt. You had the preaching, the
> calls and warnings of your eminent deceased minister till he was
> worn out in calling and warning and exhorting of you. God was so
> gracious, and so loathe that you should perish, that he continued
> his ability of preaching to wonderment. But the founder melted in
> vain as to you. He did not cease blowing till the bellows were worn
> out, as it were burnt out, in vain, trying if he could not extract
> some true silver from amongst the lead. He was very loathe to give
> you over till he had persuaded, and God seemed loathe to give you
> over by continuing of him so long to call upon you and warn you.
> But how many wicked are there that are not yet plucked away? (*Works*
> 14, 367–69)

Edwards sought to awaken his spiritually sleeping hearers by reminding them of the great advantage they had long enjoyed in
sitting under a faithful preacher like Stoddard. Not many people
"have enjoyed such eminent powerful means of grace as you,"
challenged a young Edwards. What had this forceful preaching met with? Among other things, declared Edwards, "a dismal
degree of obduracy and blindness" such that Stoddard preached
"till he was worn out in calling and warning and exhorting of you."
Edwards could not have been more direct. If the lukewarm of
Northampton did not soon repent of their half-hearted Christianity, they would lose all opportunity to repent, and the gospel they
respected but never fully embraced would disappear from view.

The lukewarm members of Edwards's congregation made a
common mistake. They committed themselves to the trappings of
religion: respectable decorum, nice clothes, a pleasant churchly
demeanor, and a quiet communal life. They would not, however,
curb their appetites, mortify their secret sins, invest themselves in

gospel work, and serve the church with their whole heart. Many of them undoubtedly took pride in the communal eminence of Stoddard, enjoying their association with such an important pastor in an age when pastors ruled their communities, but it seems that they ultimately failed to look beyond Stoddard's status to consider the import of his message.

THE PASTOR'S PERSONAL EXPERIENCE WITH SPIRITUAL DECLINE

The problem of nominal Christianity in Stoddard's day persisted in Edwards's own. His initial sermon shows that he was committed to fighting this scourge of the church. In the midst of this difficult work in the mid-1730s, he witnessed one of the more bountiful seasons of his ministry. Through the faithful preaching of the Word and a few key events, including the conversion of an influential young woman, a revival broke out in Northampton and surrounding towns, sweeping many into the church. It was a joyous time.

The fruits of revival soon gave way to a wave of doubt and apathy in Northampton. The pastor believed that the devil was urging some who had come under conviction to commit suicide. As noted in his revival report *A Faithful Narrative of the Surprising Work of God*, published in 1737, one Northampton man who had long struggled with depression did take his life. Following this,

> multitudes in this and other towns seemed to have it strongly suggested to 'em, and pressed upon 'em, to do as this person had done. And many that seemed to be under no melancholy, some pious persons that had no special darkness, or doubts about the goodness of their state, nor were under any special trouble or concern of mind about anything spiritual or temporal, yet had it urged upon 'em, as if somebody had spoke to 'em, "Cut your own throat,

now is good opportunity: *now, NOW!*" So that they were obliged to fight with all their might to resist it, and yet no reason suggested to 'em why they should do it.

Following these scary occurrences, the fires of revival died out, according to Edwards:

> After these things the instances of conversion were rare here in comparison of what they had before been. . . . But religion remained here, and I believe in some other places, the main subject of conversation for several months after this. And there were some turns, wherein God's work seemed something to revive, and we were ready to hope that all was going to be renewed again: yet in the main there was a gradual decline of that general, engaged, lively spirit in religion, which had been before.

The pastor went on to express encouragement about the effects of the revival, though he noted ominously that some of them might fade with time:

> I can't say that there has been no instance of any one person that has carried himself so that others should justly be stumbled concerning his profession; nor am I so vain as to imagine that we han't been mistaken concerning any that we have entertained a good opinion of, or that there are none that pass amongst us for sheep, that are indeed wolves in sheep's clothing; who probably may some time or other discover themselves by their fruits. (*Works* 4, 206–9)

Edwards's foresight proved true. Though many people who came to faith in the revival prospered spiritually, others fell away, leaving Edwards to battle discouragement and doubts about his own pastoral ability and faithfulness.

This section from the *Faithful Narrative* helps us to

understand Edwards and his day better, for it encapsulates one of the pastor's recurring experiences throughout his ministry. Indeed, this was not the only time in his career that the Northampton pastor watched as the joy of spiritual awakening gave way to discouragement and malaise. Even in the happiest moments of his career, it seems, Edwards often had to confront religious declension.

SEEKING EARTHLY MANSIONS OVER HEAVENLY MANSIONS

Edwards sometimes grew openly frustrated with the spiritual lukewarmness that he saw in his people. We glimpse a bit of his frustration in a sermon called "Many Mansions" based on John 14:2 and delivered in 1737 after his church, by the instigation of the town leadership, began reordering the pew seating system on the basis of familial wealth. Formerly, the church had ordered its pews according to communal reputation, based on age and "civic usefulness." The new system, structured along financial concerns, infuriated Edwards. In his sermon preached just after the new system took hold, Edwards warned his people of the consequences of this decision:

> Take warning by these warnings of providence to improve your
> time, that you may have a mansion in heaven. We have a house
> of worship newly erected amongst us, which now you have a seat
> in, and probably are pleased with the ornaments of it; and though
> you have a place among others in so comely an house, you know
> not how little a while you shall have a place in this house of God.
> Here are a couple snatched away by death that had met in it but
> a few times, that have been snatched out of it before it was fully
> finished, and never will have any more a seat in it. You know not
> how soon you may follow. And then of great importance will it be
> to you to have a seat in God's house above.

Edwards then devoted attention to the young people of his congregation, who in his eyes were apt to esteem worldly things like social rank:

> Let our young people therefore take warning from hence, and don't [act] such fools as to neglect seeking a place and mansion in heaven. Young persons are especially apt to be taken with the pleasing things of this world. You are now, it may be, much pleased with hopes of your future circumstances in this world, much pleased with the ornaments of that house of worship that you with others have a place in. But, alas, do you not too little consider how soon you may be taken away from all these things, and no more forever have any part in any mansion, or house, or enjoyment, or business under the sun. Therefore let it be your main care to secure an everlasting habitation for hereafter. (*Works* 19, 743–44)

The pastor concluded by exhorting congregants who were nursing their wounds over their newfound seating location to take sight of another realm, where this foolish decision would not matter in the least:

> And if there be any that ben't seated in their seats, because they are too low for 'em, let them consider that it is but a very little while before it will [be] all one to you, whether you have sat high or low here. But it will be of infinite and everlasting concern to you, where your seat is in another world. Let your great concern be while in this world, so to improve your opportunity in God's house in that world, whether you sit high or low, as that you may have [a] glorious and distinguished mansion in God's house in heaven, where you may be fixed in your place in that eternal assembly in everlasting rest. Let the main thing that you prize in God's house be not the outward ornaments of it, [or] an high seat in it, but the word of Christ, and God's ordinance in it. And spend your

time here in seeking Christ, that he may prepare a place for you in
his Father's house; that so when he comes again to this world, he may
take you to him; that where he is, there you may be also. (*Works* 19,
746)

In retrospect, the whole affair seems rather silly and surprising
given the unique position of the Northampton church. Here was
a people given a rich pulpit ministry by the Lord and considerable financial ability to promote the work of the kingdom, and
yet they fought and fussed over the ideal location of their poste-
riors. In such a climate, Edwards pushed his people to serve the
church, not use it for social climbing and status-building: "Let
the main thing that you prize in God's house be not the outward
ornaments of it, [or] an high seat in it, but the word of Christ,
and God's ordinance in it."

As the pastor saw it, the professing Christian with lukewarm
faith seeks the outward things of religion and asks the church to
serve them. The true Christian, however, takes joy not primarily
in what the church does for them, but in what God is doing in
and through the church. Even in his day, Edwards had to fight
nominal faith on a considerable scale. Many in Edwards's own
church had the latter mindset. Neither a state church nor a godly
pastor could ensure that church members knew the Lord. As is
often the case, many were too busy making much of themselves
to make much of the Savior.

THE SHAPE AND NATURE OF TRUE GRACE

Edwards did not content himself with exposing the behaviors
that marked a nominal Christian. He also worked hard to uncover
the specious beliefs of worldly church members and labored to
strip away pretenses of belief with careful arguments and biblical
reasoning. In a notable sermon preached in 1752 on James 2:19,

"True Grace Distinguished from the Experience of Devils," he showed that even devils had knowledge of spiritual things and experienced emotions resulting from spiritual realities. Believers who grounded their faith in mere biblical knowledge, and in the simple experience of various emotions related to their professed faith, had no more cause to assure themselves of their conversion than did the most wicked devil of Satan's realm.

Edwards first discussed in "True Grace" how head knowledge—which he called "speculative knowledge"—of biblical doctrines does not signal the presence of saving faith. Satan himself possesses such knowledge, said the pastor:

> We may hence infer, that no degree of speculative knowledge of things of religion, is any certain sign of saving grace. The devil, before his fall, was among those bright and glorious angels of heaven, which are represented as morning stars, and flames of fire, that excel in strength and wisdom. And though he be now become sinful, yet his sin has not abolished the faculties of the angelic nature; as when man fell, he did not lose the faculties of the human nature. (*Works* 25, 613)

Edwards offered the following gripping words as a summation of this teaching: "The devil is orthodox in his faith; he believes the true scheme of doctrine; he is no Deist, Socinian, Arian, Pelagian, or Antinomian; the articles of his faith are all sound, and what he is thoroughly established in" (*Works* 25, 617). Indeed, one could know any number of hefty theological concepts, as Satan does, and still not possess saving faith:

> Therefore it is manifest, from my text and doctrine, that no degree of speculative knowledge of things of religion, is any certain sign of true piety. Whatever clear notions a man may have of the attributes of God, and doctrine of the trinity; the nature of the

two covenants, the economy of the persons of the trinity, and the part which each person has in the affair of man's redemption; if he can discourse never so excellently of the offices of Christ, and the way of salvation by him, and the admirable methods of divine wisdom; and the harmony of the various attributes of God in that way; if he can talk never so clearly and exactly of the method of the justification of a sinner, and of the nature of conversion, and the operations of the Spirit of God, in applying the redemption of Christ; giving good distinctions, happily solving difficulties, and answering objections; in a manner tending greatly to the enlightening the ignorant, to the edification of the church of God, and the conviction of gainsayers; and the great increase of light in the world: if he has more knowledge of this sort than hundreds of true saints, of an ordinary education, and most divines; yet all is no certain evidence of any degree of saving grace in the heart. (*Works* 25, 616)

Though we may possess theological knowledge and even a strong drive to know the Word, Edwards calls us to check our hearts and the hearts of our fellow church members. Is doctrine merely fodder for debate? Do we simply store up biblical concepts like impersonal data? Edwards prompts us to ask these questions in order that we might avoid a faith consisting only of believed but impersonal truths.

The Northampton pastor also challenged emotive faith, teaching that no emotional state, however strongly felt, could guarantee that a sinner possessed saving faith. Fear of judgment, for example, might well result from a real understanding of divine wrath, but without any interior response of faith,

there are many terrors, that some persons, who are concerned for their salvation, are the subjects of, which are not from any proper awakenings of conscience, or apprehensions of truth; but from melancholy, or frightful impressions on their imagination; or some groundless apprehensions, and the delusions, and false suggestions of Satan. But if they have had never so great, and long-continued terrors, from real awakenings, and convictions of truth, and views of things as they are; this is no more than what is in the devils, and will be in all wicked men, in another world. However stupid and senseless most ungodly men are now, all will be effectually awakened at last: there will [be] no such thing as slumbering in hell. (*Works* 25, 618)

Edwards's sketch of the terrors of judgment demonstrated that fearing God's wrath did not mark a person as a true believer. But neither did a desire to be free of that judgment prove the existence of saving faith in the heart:

The devils, doubtless, long for deliverance from the misery they suffer, and from that greater misery which they expect. If they tremble through fear of it, they must, necessarily, earnestly desire to be delivered from it. Wicked men, are in Scripture, represented as longing for the privileges of the righteous, when the door is shut, and they are shut out from among them: they come to the door, and cry, "Lord, Lord, open to us." Therefore, we are not to look on all desires, or all desires that are very earnest and vehement, as certain evidences of a pious heart. There are earnest desires of a religious nature, which the saints have, that are the proper breathings of a new nature, and distinguishing qualities of true saints: but there are also longings, which unregenerate men may have, which are often mistaken for marks of godliness: they think they hunger and thirst after righteousness; and have earnest desires after God and Christ, and long for heaven; when indeed, all is to be resolved into desires of salvation, from self-love; and so is a longing which arises from no higher principles, than the earnest desires of devils. (*Works* 25, 624–25)

One can fear God and His judgment with the full extent of one's being and still not know the Lord, according to Edwards. Mere recognition of God's existence and His hatred for sin and willingness to punish it does not in any way justify or save the sinner. This, after all, is the conviction of devils. They "long for deliverance from the misery they suffer" (see Mark 5:1–13, for example). They are, of course, unconverted, but they live in abject fear of God's punishment of sin, as do so many people who will not, for whatever reason, repent of their sinful ways.

On the other hand, a vague pleasure in the things of religion, however orthodox, did not necessarily signal a converted heart, either. In the section below, Edwards discusses how an unregenerate sinner could, acting out of a natural love for oneself, find happiness in religion and religious causes. In fact, even a devil, Edwards asserted, could act in this way:

> If your love to God, has its first source from nothing else than a supposed immediate divine witness, or any other supposed evidence, that Christ died for you in particular, and that God loves you; it springs from no higher principles than self-love; which is a principle that reigns in the hearts of devils. Self-love is sufficient, without grace, to cause men to love those that love them, or that they imagine love them, and make much of them; Luke 6:32, "For if ye love them which love you, what thank have you? For sinners also love those that love them." And would not the hearts of devils be filled with great joy, if they, by any means, should take up a confident persuasion that God had pardoned them, and was become their friend, and that they should be delivered from that wrath which they now are in trembling expectation of. If the devils go so far as you have heard, even in their circumstances, being totally cast off, and given up to unrestrained wickedness, being without hope, knowing that God is, and ever will be their enemy, they suffering his wrath without mercy: how far may we

reasonably suppose they might go, in imitation of grace and pious experience, if they had the same degree of knowledge, as clear views, and as strong conviction, under circumstances of hope, and offers of mercy; and being the subjects of common grace, restraining their corruptions, and assisting and exciting the natural principles of reason, conscience, etc.? (*Works* 25, 632)

Having established his point that devils could, given a certain set of circumstances, exercise a certain brand of religiously oriented behavior, Edwards then listed the natural convictions devils might hold, all of which line up with orthodox Christian theology and experience:

Such great conviction of conscience; such a sense of the importance of eternal things; such affecting views of the awful majesty, greatness, power, holiness, justice, and truth of God, and such a sense of his great grace to the saints, if they, or anything like 'em, should be in the heart of a sinner, in this world; at the same time that he, from some strong impression on his imagination, of Christ appearing to him, or sweet words spoken to him, or by some other means, has suddenly, after great terrors, imbibed a strong confidence, that now, this great God, is his friend and father, has released him from all the misery he feared, and has promised him eternal happiness: I say, such things would, doubtless, vastly heighten his ecstasy of joy, and raise the exercise of natural gratitude (that principle from whence sinners love those that love them), and would occasion a great imitation of many graces, in strong exercises. Is it any wonder then, that multitudes under such a sort of affection, are deceived? (*Works* 25, 632–33)

In this passage, Edwards stretches the bounds of what a devil might actually believe theologically, though his point is abundantly clear: a person living under the influence of common grace (as we all do) and acting out of some form of self-love (as we all do) could easily take pleasure in the doctrines and experience of Christianity without actually knowing the Lord in a salvific sense. The truths of Christianity can appear beautiful on a surface level to the unconverted heart. They may elicit emotion and thus affect a person's outward demeanor, just as a child's smile, or a strong ethical conviction, or the promise of hope in a distressing situation may do the same without converting the heart. A person may out of a knowledge of biblical doctrine live a happy and hopeful life, trusting in God's providence, living gratefully in some sense for Christ's sacrifice. However, unless this knowledge is personally applied in repentance of sin and wholehearted faith in the person and work of Jesus Christ, it does not save us from sin and judgment (see James 2:18–26).

CONFRONTING NOMINAL CHRISTIANITY

As this chapter has shown, Jonathan Edwards sought to wake up lax professors of faith and show them that though they considered themselves truly saved for one reason or another, they stood on far shakier ground than they might have thought. His experience, painful as it often was, taught him that nothing could prevent widespread nominal Christianity—not a theocentric church, not a devout pastor-shepherd, not even biblically fueled revival. Sanctioned by Satan, the nominal Christian possessed all too many resources to deceive themselves about their true spiritual state, whether biblical knowledge, fear of judgment, religiously minded happiness, or other things. It is likely that these are the kinds of attributes many of the nominal Christians in our churches possess. They fear the Lord, and go to church, and do religious things, believing on some level that their involvement procures forgiveness and salvation.

In their encounter with true Christianity, these people taste something of the sweetness of religious devotion and biblical truth, though they do no more than sample these good things. They are not so convicted by judgment as to repent of their sin, and they are not so gripped by the glory of divine grace that they embrace Christ. They may know biblical doctrine, even to the point of being able to make a case for a certain scriptural teaching, but this truth has not transformed them. What needs to bore into the heart sits lightly on the conscience, skimming the surface but never penetrating to the soul.

Moving from Edwards's era to ours, the nominal Christian is something like a movie watcher who observes the story of Christianity as it plays out in the lives of true Christians. He comprehends the plot, shrinks back at the scary parts, and grows happy when the good guys win, but he never enters in. He pauses the story when he likes, fast forwards the parts he doesn't enjoy, and watches the scenes he prefers over and over again, shaping his perception of the story by his own preferences. Then, when he sees fit, he stops it altogether. Through it all, he is unaware that just as the story fails to claim him, he is himself unclaimed by the story. He is a mere witness to a transforming reality that will soon pass him by.

Embracing True Christianity

Challenge People to Leave the Trappings of Religion

A central struggle in Edwards's fight against lukewarm Christianity was the love exhibited by many in his church for the trappings, but not the substance, of religion. Though the circumstances have changed, the issue remains. This is especially true in a day when many American Christians have witnessed unprecedented evangelical influence in many areas of cultural life—politics, entertainment, literature, social institutions, and more. This kind of "success" can create a culture in which people bask in the glow of Christianity without actually coming into contact with the true Light.

Without lapsing into hostile wariness about all of our activities, we need to look out for signs in our individual and church lives that show that we enjoy the trappings of the faith more than its substance. In Edwards's day, many people took more pride in their position in the pew than in their faith in Christ. The same can happen today. We can revel in our lush surroundings, and bask in the attention of fellow members, and spend all kinds of time and attention on our own concerns, forgetting the kingdom cause before us. This is what happened in Northampton—people became more focused on themselves than on the mission of the gospel. The same can happen to us today if we are not careful.

Though our present situation may discourage us in certain ways, we can take some comfort in the fact that a pastor like Jonathan Edwards struggled just like we do. Deep piety, hefty preaching, and a brilliant mind cannot in themselves guarantee that a church will grow spiritually (or numerically), just as a CEO mentality, personal charm, and quick wit offer us no assurance of "success." Though we should take pains in our churches and homes to identify false faith and advance the truth, we must know that the Lord in His mysterious providence may or may not reward our work with lasting change and true revival.

Find No Comfort in Knowledge, Emotion, or Impressions Alone

As Edwards memorably showed, we cannot find confidence in spiritual knowledge, emotions, or impressions by themselves. Even a devil can theoretically possess any one of these things and be as far from grace and God as can be. We should of course encourage the development of biblical and theological knowledge, scripturally guided affections, and spiritual impressions and views based on the Bible. But these things in themselves cannot save a person and thus cannot assure a person. As we will see in the chapter to come, only the Lord's converting work can do this.

Different people will land in different categories here. Some will credit their faith to knowledge, others to feelings, others to impressions or views. When we hear such testimony, we need to push deeper, examining whether faith does exist in this one who claims Christ, or whether the experience of faith goes no deeper than simple knowledge of the truth, emotion of the heart, or vague senses of the intuition.

Chapter 20

EDWARDS'S ANSWER TO NOMINAL CHRISTIANITY

Out with certainty, in with mystery. One of the key philosophical trends of the last century has been the shift from certainty to skepticism. Many thinkers, reacting against the intellectual arrogance of philosophers who emphasize the ability of the human mind to know things exhaustively, have emphasized paradox and mystery. People today still talk about "truth" and other foundational principles of life, but they do so in chastened language that communicates a lack of ultimate assurance about their subject. "Well, yeah, I think that's true, but it's true for me—I'm not trying to judge anyone or anything like that."

Many Christians have adopted aspects of this way of thinking. "Well, yeah, I'm a Christian, and I believe in the gospel, but that's just my personal opinion." Aware that the current age does not look kindly on certainty, many Christians publicly downplay the intensity of their belief in God. They talk and think about their faith as more of a personal choice than a divine call.

In the last chapter, we looked at what Edwards said was *not* Christianity. In this chapter, we look at what Edwards believed was true Christianity. In doing so, we examine a section from "The Reality of Conversion," another from *Freedom of the Will*, excerpts from "Justification by Faith Alone" and "A Divine and Supernatural Light," and several passages from *Distinguishing Marks of a True Work of the Spirit of God* and *Treatise on the Religious Affections*. In sum, we see that while Edwards took pains to establish what true Christianity was not (as seen in chapter 20), he also took special care to sketch out an exciting portrait of true Christianity that will, now as then, help us to recover a richly biblical understanding of conversion and the change it effects.

CONVERSION IS REAL

The starting point for a discussion of Edwards's view of conversion has to be this: he believed in it. He believed in the quickening work of the Holy Spirit and its visible effect. Against those who argued that Christian conversion was a myth, a fairy tale, Edwards amassed numerous arguments for its authenticity in his sermon "The Reality of Conversion," based on John 3:10–11. There, he advanced the central claim that

> There is no kind of love in the world that has had such great, visible effects in men as love to Christ has had, though he be an unseen object, which [is] an evidence of a divine work in the hearts of men, infusing that love into them. Thus the voice of reason, Scripture and experience, and the testimony of the best of men do all concur in it, that there must be such a thing as conversion. (Kimnach, 89)

In the midst of nominal believers whose actions caused many to doubt the realness of Christianity, Edwards declared boldly that conversion is real. It is not a psychological eccentricity. It is not an invention of religious types who want to control others. Salvation, Edwards said, proceeds as a "divine work." Salvation happens.

THE HARMONY OF MIND AND WILL

The second step in a proper understanding of Edwards's view of authentic conversion relates to his view of the human will. Though a highly technical discussion, this matter boils down to a basic principle that informs our understanding of how a sinner comes to embrace the truth of the gospel. Some in Edwards's day separated the decision of the mind from the act of the will, arguing that the will did not necessarily follow the "dictates" of the mind. Edwards refuted this argument at length in his *Freedom of the Will*:

> Things that exist in the view of the mind, have their strength, tendency or advantage to move or excite its will, from many things appertaining to the nature and circumstances of the thing viewed, the nature and circumstances of the mind that views, and the degree and manner of its view; which it would perhaps be hard to make a perfect enumeration of. But so much I think may be determined in general, without room for controversy, that whatever is perceived or apprehended by an intelligent and voluntary agent, which has the nature and influence of a motive to volition or choice, is considered or viewed as good; nor has it any tendency to invite or engage the election of the soul in any further degree than it appears such. For to say otherwise, would be to say, that things that appear have a tendency by the appearance they make, to engage the mind to elect them, some other way than by their appearing eligible to it; which is absurd. And therefore it must be true, in some sense, that the will always is as the greatest apparent good is. (*Works* 1, 142)

This passage, though weighty, shows how closely the mind and heart are linked, and how essential it is that one fill one's mind with truth. What our mind fixates on will in turn "move or excite" our wills. In simpler terms, what we see as desirable, as pleasurable, as best, we will want.

This simple but important point clarifies conversion. We do not haphazardly come to faith, choosing to believe the gospel without intellectual assent. We believe in the gospel because we consider its claims in our minds, judge them to be right and good and beautiful, and then decide to give them our assent. Conversion, then, involves the full measure of our minds, as does our subsequent transformation (Rom. 12:1–2).

THE INFLUENCE OF THE HOLY SPIRIT

The Holy Spirit accomplished this work, which is a third prong of an Edwardsean understanding of conversion. As covered in *Part 3*, Edwards believed that Adam and Eve fell away from God. When they did so, God removed the Spirit, the gift of His grace known as the "superior" or "spiritual" principles, from the human heart. Adam and Eve then followed their "natural" principles, their bodily appetites and desires, and disobeyed God, cursing the human race to be ruled by their natural and "inferior" principles by birth.

All of this changed, however, when the Holy Spirit moved in a human heart. The Spirit excited repentance in the sinner and became a "spring of new nature," as the pastor put it in his classic treatise *The Religious Affections*:

> The Spirit of God is given to the true saints to dwell in them, as his proper lasting abode; and to influence their hearts, as a principle of new nature, or as a divine supernatural spring of life and action. The Scriptures represent the Holy Spirit, not only as moving, and occasionally influencing the saints, but as dwelling in them as his temple, his proper abode, and everlasting dwelling place (1 Corinthians 3:16; 2 Corinthians 6:16; John 14:16–17). And he is represented as being there so united to the faculties of the soul, that he becomes there a principle or spring of new nature and life. (*Works* 2, 200)

The Holy Spirit caused the human heart to flare with life as the spiritual principles, the superior graces and gifts of God, took hold:

> From these things it is evident, that those gracious influences which the saints are subjects of, and the effects of God's Spirit which they experience, are entirely above nature, altogether of a different kind from anything that men find within themselves by nature, or only in the exercise of natural principles; and are things which no improvement of those qualifications, or principles that are natural, no advancing or exalting them to higher degrees, and no kind of composition of them, will ever bring men to; because they not only differ from what is natural, and from everything that natural men experience, in degree and circumstances; but also in kind; and are of a nature vastly more excellent. And this is what I mean by supernatural, when I say, that gracious affections are from those influences that are supernatural. (*Works* 2, 205)

Possessing the Holy Spirit, Edwards noted, made a person "spiritual." The Holy Spirit made all the difference. He convinced the sinner's mind of the truthfulness of God, His Word, and His gospel message. In doing so, He regenerated the wicked heart and came to dwell spiritually in the new convert. He does not flit in and out of our hearts like a drifting traveler, roaming here and there. He lives in the believer, taking residence in the heart, giving us "gracious affections" that are "vastly more excellent" than our natural affections.

Edwards's vivid descriptions of the Spirit's work remind us that conversion, though involving our deepest mental processes, is driven by a Person. By the Spirit's work, we find faith in a personal, triune God. We are thus converted not by an abstract theological principle, but by a living, active person.

THE VIVIFYING CONVICTIONS OF THE REDEEMED HEART

If we accept that our wills follow our minds, and that the Spirit saves our souls, how are we to understand the actual faith that God implants within us? Exactly what separates the converting work of God's Spirit from ordinary religious devotion? In his sermon "Justification by Faith Alone," Edwards gave a summation of the gospel that separates it from all other messages and schemes that ground salvation in human effort. Conversion happens the instant a person truly repents of their sin and puts their faith in the atoning death and life-giving resurrection of Jesus Christ:

> When Christ had once undertaken with God, to stand for us, and put himself under our law, by that law he was obliged to suffer, and by the same law he was obliged to obey: by the same law, after he had taken man's guilt upon him, he himself being our surety, could not be acquitted, till he had suffered, nor rewarded till he had obeyed: but he was not acquitted as a private person, but as our head, and believers are acquitted in his acquittance; nor was he accepted to a reward for his obedience as a private person, but as our head, and we are accepted to a reward in his acceptance. The Scripture teaches us, that when Christ was raised from the dead, he was justified; which justification as I have already shown, implies, both his acquittance from our guilt, and his acceptance to the exaltation and glory that was the reward of his obedience: but believers, as soon as they believe are admitted to partake with Christ in this his justification: hence we are told that he was "raised again for our justification" (Romans 4:25). (*Works* 19, 191)

This paragraph is perhaps the most important in the book. It provides one of the most concise summaries of the gospel Edwards gave in his ministry. It contains the raw material of the gospel, the truths that sinners must believe to be saved. Though we have discussed and will consider numerous essential matters related to conversion and true Christianity, there can be no real understanding of these truths unless one identifies the Bible's gospel message as the only means to conversion (see John 3; Rom. 3–5). In the death of Christ for the salvation of the wicked, we discover the heart of salvation and the core content of true Christianity. Jesus has "taken man's guilt upon him" at the cross, dying in our place as a substitute to save us from hell and absorb the wrath of God for our sin. Because of His gift, one greater than any other we can conceive, "we are accepted" by God "to a reward," eternal life with God. This is the gospel. This is the foundation of Christian faith, the center of Edwards's preaching, and the point from which all other discussion of conversion flows.

In order to taste salvation, one must believe this gospel and not merely assent to it. Edwards spoke to this matter in numerous places, but rarely with more elegance and clarity than in his sermon "A Divine and Supernatural Light." In this sermon, he speaks of a fourth plank we might identify in his conversion theology, the "true sense" of holy things that marks the converted heart and that only comes from the influence of the Spirit:

> A true sense of the divine and superlative excellency of the things of religion; a real sense of the excellency of God, and Jesus Christ, and of the work of redemption, and the ways and works of God revealed in the gospel. There is a divine and superlative glory in these things; an excellency that is of a vastly higher kind, and more sublime nature, than in other things; a glory greatly distinguishing them from all that is earthly and temporal. He that is spiritually enlightened truly apprehends and sees it, or has a sense of it. He don't merely rationally believe that God is glorious, but he has a sense of the gloriousness of God in his heart. There is not only a rational belief that God is holy, and that holiness is a good thing; but there is a sense of the loveliness of God's holiness. There is not only a speculatively judging that God is

gracious, but a sense how amiable God is upon that account; or a sense of the beauty of this divine attribute. (*Works* 17, 413)

In one of the most famous passages from all of his writings, Edwards went on to elegantly show how this "true sense" differs from a mere intellectual conviction:

> Thus there is a difference between having an opinion that God is holy and gracious, and having a sense of the loveliness and beauty of that holiness and grace. There is a difference between having a rational judgment that honey is sweet, and having a sense of its sweetness. A man may have the former, that knows not how honey tastes; but a man can't have the latter, unless he has an idea of the taste of honey in his mind. So there is a difference between believing that a person is beautiful, and having a sense of his beauty. The former may be obtained by hearsay, but the latter only by seeing the countenance. There is a wide difference between mere speculative, rational judging anything to be excellent, and having a sense of its sweetness, and beauty. The former rests only in the head, speculation only is concerned in it; but the heart is concerned in the latter. When the heart is sensible of the beauty and amiableness of a thing, it necessarily feels pleasure in the apprehension. It is implied in a person's being heartily sensible of the loveliness of a thing, that the idea of it is sweet and pleasant to his soul; which is a far different thing from having a rational opinion that it is excellent. (*Works* 17, 414)

The difference between a nominal faith that merely mimics biblical Christianity and true faith is this "true sense" that the pastor-theologian speaks of. The phrase itself compels our attention, pairing as it does conviction, "true," and emotion, "sense." Christianity as Edwards saw it—and as the Bible pictures it—involves the sum total of one's mind and one's heart. Head-knowledge without passion reduces Christianity to a collection of interesting propositions. Though he did not cover it here, heart-knowledge without truth reduces Christianity to yet another religious experience. If the two combined, though, an ideal balance could be struck.

When a person believes the gospel message, the things of Christianity, of the Bible, and of church that once seemed so ordinary compared to really interesting things—whether celebrities or sports or movies or whatever else—now possess a "glory greatly distinguishing them from all that is earthly and temporal." In Edwards's biblical view, the person seized by the Spirit cannot see Christianity any longer in earthly terms. Like a butterfly that emerges from a cocoon, the converted sinner sees Christianity and its doctrines as things of beauty. Everything changes at this point for the redeemed person. Life overflows with God's goodness and beauty. The existence that once had no center—or that had a destructive one—now revolves around the person of Jesus Christ, whose work suddenly leaps off every page of the Bible and pours into every corner of life, calling the Christian to experience the joyful process of conformity to the divine will.

THE MARKS OF TRUE CONVERSION
Love for Christ

Edwards did not end his doctrine of conversion at this enlivening point, however. In his 1741 text *Distinguishing Marks of a True Work of the Spirit of God,* Edwards laid out a number of negative and positive signs that distinguished a true work of God from a false one. Though Edwards focused in this text on revivals more broadly, his words apply to individuals seeking to discern whether they know the Lord. Because we looked in the last chapter at several negative signs, aspects of religion that even devils might practice, we look here at the positive signs that indicate the presence of saving faith in the human heart.

The first of these signs was a "raised esteem" for Jesus Christ:

> When that spirit that is at work amongst a people is observed to
> operate after such a manner, as to raise their esteem of that Jesus
> that was born of the Virgin, and was crucified without the gates of
> Jerusalem; and seems more to confirm and establish their minds
> in the truth of what the Gospel declares to us of his being the Son
> of God, and the Saviour of men; 'tis a sure sign that that spirit is
> the Spirit of God. This sign the Apostle gives us in the 1 John 4:2
> and 1 John 4:3 verses, "Hereby know ye the Spirit of God; every
> spirit that confesseth that Jesus Christ is come in the flesh, is of
> God; and every spirit that confesseth not that Jesus Christ is come
> in the flesh, is not of God." This implies a confessing, not only
> that there was such a person that appeared in Palestine, and did
> and suffered those things that are recorded of him, but that that
> person was Christ, i.e. the Son of God, the Anointed of God to
> be Lord and Saviour, as the name Jesus Christ implies. That thus
> much is implied in the Apostle's meaning, is confirmed by the 1
> John 4:15 verse, where the Apostle is still on the same subject of
> signs of the true Spirit: "Whosoever shall confess that Jesus is the
> Son of God, God dwelleth in him, and he in God." (*Works* 4, 249)

The point of this first sign is that when the Spirit moves in a
person's heart and awakens them to faith and repentance, their
view of Jesus changes. The Spirit "raise[s] their esteem" of Jesus
and causes them to see that He is the Christ, "the Anointed
of God to be Lord and Saviour." This recognition is not merely
factual, of course, but involves both head and heart. This clarifies true Christianity. The nominal believer *respects* Jesus, but
does not revere or exalt Him. The true Christian takes delight
in Jesus, a delight that is often palpable and contagious. When
a person claims saving faith, then, we should expect to see a
"raised esteem" for Jesus Christ, the author of our redemption.

THE MARKS OF TRUE CONVERSION
Hatred of Sin

The second sign of a "true work" is an increased hatred for sin, and defeat of sinful practices:

> When the spirit that is at work operates against the interest of Satan's kingdom, which lies in encouraging and establishing sin, and cherishing men's worldly lusts; this is a sure sign that 'tis a true, and not a false spirit. This sign we have given us in the 1 John 4:4 and 1 John 4:5 verses: "Ye are of God, little children, and have overcome them; because greater is he that is in you, than he that is in the world. They are of the world, therefore speak they of the world, and the world heareth them."

The pastor elaborated on this contention:

> So that we may safely determine, from what the Apostle says, that the spirit that is at work amongst a people, that is observed to work after such a manner as to lessen men's esteem of the pleasures, profits and honors of the world, and to take off their hearts from an eager pursuit after these things; and to engage them in a deep concern about a future and eternal happiness in, that invisible world, that the Gospel reveals; and puts them upon earnest seeking the kingdom of God and his righteousness; and convinces them of the dreadfulness of sin, the guilt that it brings, and the misery that it exposes to: I say, the spirit that operates after such a manner, must needs be the Spirit of God. (*Works* 4, 250–51).

This point, like the others, is both profound and simple. One of the clear signs of a work of God is increased hatred for sin. When the Spirit descends upon a human heart, He "lessen[s] men's esteem of the pleasures, profits and honors of the world," showing them "the dreadfulness of sin, the guilt that it brings," and the "misery" that accrues to the unrepentant. One's eyes are suddenly opened to see the dreadfulness of one's condition. Where before one had spotted weaknesses and flaws, but always had excuses at the ready to cover up those personal blemishes, now the Spirit shows the sinner just how degraded and evil he is. He realizes that he is wicked, separated from God, and that he must immediately kill sin, lest it kill him, and seek "the kingdom of God and his righteousness."

THE MARKS OF TRUE CONVERSION
Love for the Word

The third sign of a "true work" is a love for the Bible. Edwards tied this love for Scripture not to simple literary appreciation for its contents, but to a Spirit-given hunger and thirst for the Word of God:

> That spirit that operates in such a manner, as to cause in men a greater regard to the Holy Scriptures, and establishes them more in their truth and divinity, is certainly the Spirit of God. This rule the Apostle gives us in the 1 John 4:6 verse: "We are of God; he that knoweth God heareth us: he that is not of God, heareth not us: hereby know we the spirit of truth and the spirit of error." "We are of God"—that is, "we the apostles, are sent forth of God, and appointed of him, to teach the world, and to deliver that doctrine, those instructions that are to be their rule; therefore he that knoweth God heareth us, etc." The Apostle's argument in the verse equally reaches all that in the same sense are of God, that is, all those that God has appointed and inspired to deliver to his church its rule of faith and practice; all the prophets and apostles, whose doctrine God has made the foundation on which he has built his church, as in Ephesians 2:20; all the penmen of the Holy

Scriptures. The Devil never would go about to beget in persons a
regard to that divine Word, which God hath given to be the great and
standing rule for the direction of his church in all religious matters
and concerns of their souls, in all ages. (*Works* 4, 253)

Many people respect the Bible. It is known as a "holy book," a
sacred text. But few people view it as the actual Word of God,
that which God Himself "has appointed and inspired to deliver
to his church its rule of faith and practice" as "the great and
standing rule for the direction of his church." The Devil, according to Edwards, never impresses upon the human heart that the
Bible possesses unparalleled "truth and divinity"; this only the
Holy Spirit can do. Thus, where a person's heart flames with love
and holy "regard" for the Scriptures, the Spirit has worked.

THE MARKS OF TRUE CONVERSION
Love for Truth and the Things of God

The fourth sign that marked the presence of a "true work" was
a heightened love for truth and the things of God. Edwards
continued,

As for instance, if we observe that the spirit that is at work, makes
men more sensible than they used to be, that there is a God, and that
he is a great God, and a sin-hating God; and makes them more to
realize it, that they must die, and that life is short, and very uncertain;
and confirms persons in it that there is another world, that they have
immortal souls, and that they must give account of themselves to
God; and convinces them that they are exceeding sinful by nature
and practice; and that they are helpless in themselves; and confirms
them in other things that are agreeable to sound doctrine: the spirit
that works thus, operates as a spirit of truth: he represents things
as they are indeed: he brings men to the light; for whatever makes

> truth manifest, is light; as the Apostle Paul observes, Ephesians 5:13,
> "But all things that are reproved are made manifest by the light; for
> whatsoever doth make manifest is light." (*Works* 4, 254–55)

An awareness and responsiveness to divine truth was a clear
signal that the Lord had moved in human hearts. So where
people came to see "that there is a God" and that He is "great"
and "sin-hating," and that they themselves have "immortal souls"
and "must give account of themselves to God," the Spirit was
working true conversion. As Edwards rightly noted, the Spirit
does not lead believers into error. Therefore, when we hear news
of conversion, whether mass or individual, we need to listen for
resonances of the truth in the testimony of the convert. Do they
love the truth more? Do they love God more? Do they subscribe
to sound doctrine and root their faith in it? Or is their faith based
only on little more than sensations, experiences, impressions,
and personal feelings? In our work to lift up biblical Christianity
in our churches, we must emphasize that the children of God
love His truth and abide in it.

THE MARKS OF TRUE CONVERSION
Love for Believers

The final positive sign in Edwards's taxonomy of the Spirit's "true
work" was love for one's fellow Christians. He declared,

> If the spirit that is at work among a people operates as a spirit of
> love to God [and] man, 'tis a sure sign that 'tis the Spirit of God.
> This sign the Apostle insists upon from the 1 John 4:7 verse to the
> end of the chapter: "Beloved, let us love one another; for love is of
> God, and everyone that loveth is born of God, and knoweth God.
> He that loveth not, knoweth not God, for God is love, etc." Here
> 'tis evident that the Apostle is still comparing those two sorts of

persons that are influenced by the opposite kinds of spirits; and mentions love as a mark by which we may know who has the true spirit. But this is especially evident by the 1 John 4:12 and 1 John 4:13 verses: "If we love one another, God dwelleth in us, and his love is perfected in us. Hereby know we that we dwell in him, and he in us, because he hath given us of his Spirit." (*Works* 4, 255)

Many people who profess Christ lose their footing on this final point. They may well appreciate fellow church members and contribute in some way to their well-being, but they have not been filled by the Lord with a holy love for fellow Christians, and thus they do not serve them. Spirit-given love that transcends social, political, religious, or geographic commonality produces sacrifice for the good of one's fellow Christians, as Galatians 6:10 instructs (this sacrificial service will regularly extend to unbelievers as well). True conversion will cause stable couples to take in young Christians hungry for discipleship. It will lead Christians to give generously to missionaries and fellow believers (see 2 Cor. 8). It will drive older believers to spend time mentoring younger ones (see Titus 2).

As Scripture teaches, the healthy church, one filled with true believers, bursts at the seams with love, whether communicated from older women to young moms struggling with the challenges of raising multiple tiny children, or from college students intentionally spending time with elderly members, or from a happily married couple reaching out to another couple struggling with sin (see 1 Cor. 13). In these and many other ways, the true Christian, gifted with love for fellow Christians, pushes beyond themselves and their natural self-centeredness to bless the people around them—people with whom they may have nothing in common besides a mutual love of Christ (Gal. 3:27).

This is not a common standard by which people measure salvation today. If you ask a number of Christians how they know that they are saved, very few of them will reference the church and describe how they love people of all types now because of their unity in Christ. Edwards's words, however, direct us to closely involve the church in our doctrine of assurance. The way one cares for one's fellow members says more about our testimony of conversion than we might initially think. True Christians serve their fellow members out of love. This is a crucial mark of a saved soul and a missing element in many of our assemblies.

EMBODYING THE CONVERTED LIFE

The preceding offers valuable assistance to the modern church as we wrestle with the problem of nominal Christianity. Each of Edwards's crucial contributions informs our own understanding of the biblical testimony on conversion. In sum, he shows us that the Christian life is the personal experience of God's grace and goodness. Though all of us will wrestle with sin until we go on to glory, the true Christian bears marks of conversion and offers the world a picture of a very different way of life. Though we live in a different age from Edwards's, we would be wise to recover these marks in our churches as we stand for true Christianity.

We conclude with this powerful summation from Edwards's *Distinguishing Marks*:

> Therefore when the spirit that is at work amongst a people tends this way, and brings many of them to high and exalting thoughts of the divine Being, and his glorious perfections; and works in them an admiring, delightful sense of the excellency of Jesus Christ; representing him as "the chief among ten thousands, altogether lovely" [Canticles 5:10, Canticles 5:16], and makes him precious to the soul; winning and drawing the heart with those motives and incitements to love which the Apostle speaks of in that passage

of Scripture we are upon, viz. the wonderful, free love of God in giving his only begotten Son to die for us, and the wonderful dying love of Christ to us, who had no love to him, but were his enemies; as vss. 1 John [4]:9 and 1 John [4]:10, "In this was manifested the love of God towards us, because that God sent his only begotten Son into the world, that we might live through him. Herein is love; not that we loved God, but that he loved us, and sent his Son to be the propitiation for our sins." (*Works* 4, 256)

Embracing True Christianity

Seek the "True Sense"

As we prioritize conversion in our circles, we need to emphasize that there is a vast difference between a mere profession of faith and a "true sense" of God's grace in Christ. It is by no means wrong to encourage people to respond to the gospel in a certain way. But we must take care that we do not confuse our hearers. Things like walking an aisle or raising a hand do not save one's soul. Only the "true sense" of the gospel, the sense that convinces the mind and awakens the heart, is salvific. We want people to taste this "true sense" of living faith that comes from genuine repentance from sin and love for Christ and His atoning work. We desire that sinners would not just come to church when it suits them, but that they would know the joy of a Spirit-filled life.

What can we do to create this kind of atmosphere? We can start by defining and celebrating true conversion. If we offer sinners a vague, fuzzy, coddling Christianity, that is what they will respond to and live by, and many of them will not encounter the God of vibrant Christian faith. If we publicly exalt God and His work in Christ, we will greatly help our efforts to promote the

true sense of converting grace. We want to see people who rein-
force their confession of Christ by exhibiting love for God, hatred
for sin, reverence for the Bible, a desire for truth, and unity with
believers of all types and kinds.

Chapter 21

POWERFUL EXAMPLES
OF TRUE CHRISTIANITY

The world is full of evil people. Their choices and actions are often devastating. If a person feeds their natural propensity for evil, they can wreak incredible havoc. History bears this out in abundance. We do not need to rack our brains to come up with examples of people who, having yielded fully to their wickedness, caused untold pain and suffering for many. In Hitler's Germany, Stalin's Russia, and Mao's China, we find examples of this terrible reality. Of course, beyond the ringleaders, the movement personalities, were untold people who had also committed their lives to the propagation of evil, not good. We do not and never will know many of their stories. History has absorbed their evil lives.

There are others from the past who have heard a different call. Some of this group are famous—people like Martin Luther, John Calvin, or John Wesley. These people gave themselves to a greater cause in a public arena. Others, however, lived quieter lives. In their own small corner of the world, they blazed a righteous course. Some taught Sunday school all of their lives and spent their own money on their students as they pointed them to Christ week by week. Others gave sacrificially to missions, skipping vacations to send another missionary to the field. Some

Christians fought for racial and social justice in their communities, sharing the good news of Jesus even as they stood up for the
oppressed when no one else would. Though these anonymous
Christians received little earthly acclaim for their faithfulness to
Christ, their good deeds are known to the Father.

In this chapter, we turn from Edwards's core conversionist
beliefs to look at two personal examples of true Christianity as
he conceived it. We discuss less and marvel more in this chapter as we look back at David Brainerd's work among the Native
Americans from *The Life and Diary of David Brainerd* and the
testimony of Abigail Hutchinson in the midst of terminal illness
from *A Faithful Narrative of the Surprising Work of God*. These
examples encourage us even as they call us to stand out for God
in this sinful world.

THE MISSIONARY HEART OF DAVID BRAINERD

We recall from Part 1 that David Brainerd was a young missionary to various Native American tribes whom Edwards took under
his wing after Brainerd ran into trouble while in school at Yale,
Edwards's alma mater. From an early age, Brainerd believed in
the necessity of conversion, a conviction that landed him in trouble when he accused a Yale tutor of being unconverted. Though
his zeal could get the best of him, Brainerd exhibited strong piety
and a passion for the gospel. For this reason, he clicked well with
Edwards. Edwards supported and mentored Brainerd, functioning as a father figure as Brainerd navigated the challenges of
cross-cultural ministry to the Native Americans in Kaunaumee,
New York; Easton, Pennsylvania; and Cranbury, New Jersey.
After Brainerd died at a young age in 1749, likely from tuberculosis, Edwards published his diary under the title *The Life
and Diary of David Brainerd*. The book became a contemporary

success and a historic piece of missionary literature that has inspired thousands of Christians and missions workers.

In our brief coverage of Brainerd's life and witness, we look chiefly at his love for the lost and his personal devotion to the Lord. At the same time, Brainerd struggled all his life with depression, a conflict that surfaces throughout his diary in sections like this:

> Wednesday, May 18. My circumstances are such that I have no comfort of any kind but what I have in God. I live in the most lonesome wilderness; have but one single person to converse with, that can speak English: Most of the talk I hear is either Highland Scotch or Indian. I have no fellow Christian to whom I might unbosom myself and lay open my spiritual sorrows, and with whom I might take sweet counsel in conversation about heavenly things, and join in social prayer. I live poorly with regard to the comforts of life: most of my diet consists of boiled corn, hasty pudding, etc. I lodge on a bundle of straw, and my labor is hard and extremely difficult; and I have little appearance of success to comfort me. The Indian affairs are very difficult; having no land to live on, but what the Dutch people lay claim to, and threaten to drive them off from; they have no regard to the souls of the poor Indians; and, by what I can learn, they hate me because I come to preach to 'em. But that which makes all my difficulties grievous to be born is that "God hides his face from me." (*Works* 7, 207)

Brainerd had resolved to take the gospel of Jesus Christ to a people many colonists neglected to their shame—the Native Americans (or "Indians" as he calls them). He had little shelter, little support, and little encouragement. He had a bright mind and a passionate heart, but he was not the kind of person one might pick out of a lineup to lead a great work of God.

As this quotation reflects, Brainerd fought relentlessly with his demons, and nearly succumbed to them at numerous points in his early missionary efforts. For month after month in his first few years of witness, he tells of days given over to sorrow and discouragement from the frustrations of failed missionary work. He had chosen to evangelize a pagan people who had no acquaintance with Christ. The darkness of their lives brought him immense pain. Fellowship was scarce. He had an interpreter, but found it difficult to connect with him over spiritual things. To summarize much of his early efforts, he saw no fruit, no tangible evidence of God's converting grace.

Despite his weaknesses and difficulties, however, he persevered out of devotion to the Lord. He kept trying to preach the gospel, even when he faltered in doing so:

> Friday, December 14. Near noon, went to the Indians; but knew not what to say to them, and was ashamed to look them in the face: I felt I had no power to address their consciences, and therefore had no boldness to say anything. Was, much of the day, in a great degree of despair about ever doing or "seeing any good in the land of the living." (*Works* 7, 278)

Days like this nearly sent Brainerd home. But after over a year of sowing the gospel seed, the Native Americans stopped ignoring him and began to take him seriously:

> Saturday, June 29. Preached twice to the Indians; and could not but wonder at their seriousness and the strictness of their attention.—[Journal. Saw (as I thought) the hand of God very evidently, and in a manner somewhat remarkable, making provision for their subsistance together, in order to their being instructed in divine things. For this day and the day before, with only walking a little way from the place of our daily meeting, they killed three deer, which were a seasonable supply for their wants, and without which, it seems, they could not have subsisted together in order

to attend the means of grace.] Blessed be God that has inclined their hearts to hear. And oh, how refreshing it is to me to see them attend with such uncommon diligence and affection, with tears in their eyes and concern in their hearts! In the evening, could not but lift up my heart to God in prayer, while riding to my lodgings: And blessed be his Name, had assistance and freedom. Oh, how much "better than life" is the presence of God! (*Works* 7, 301)

After a long period of spiritual drought, the Lord now honored Brainerd's work by opening the hearts of the lost. This continued as the work gained speed:

August 5. After a sermon had been preached by another minister, I preached and concluded the public work of the solemnity from John 7:37, and in my discourse addressed the Indians in particular, who sat by themselves in a part of the house; at which time one or two or them were struck with deep concern, as they afterwards told me, who had been little affected before: others had their concern increased to a considerable degree. In the evening (the greater part of them being at the house where I lodged) I discoursed to them and found them universally engaged about their soul's concern, inquiring what they should do to be saved. And all their conversation among themselves turned upon religious matters, in which they were much assisted by my interpreter, who was with them day and night.

This day there was one woman, that had been much concerned for her soul ever since she first heard me preach in June last, who obtained comfort, I trust, solid and well grounded: She seemed to be filled with love to Christ, at the same time behaved humbly and tenderly, and appeared afraid of nothing so much as of grieving and offending him whom her soul loved. (*Works* 7, 306)

As a group, the Native Americans were awakening. Concern for their souls spread from person to person, such that Brainerd and his interpreter had to devote many hours to spiritual counsel. Brainerd had even seen some profess faith, including the woman he mentions above, who "seemed to be filled with love to Christ." Brainerd's perseverance was paying off.

THE REWARDS OF BRAINERD'S PERSEVERANCE

The work which once seemed in danger of dying out in abject failure now flared to life with such dynamism that Brainerd could scarcely manage it. One summer day's investment loomed large in the missionary's mind:

> August 16. Spent considerable time in conversing privately with sundry of the Indians. Found one that had got relief and comfort after pressing concern, and could not but hope, when I came to discourse particularly with her, that her comfort was of the right kind.
>
> In the afternoon, preached to them from John 6:26–34. Toward the close of my discourse, divine truths were attended with considerable power upon the audience, and more especially after public service was over, when I particularly addressed sundry distressed persons.

This preaching caused quite a response among Brainerd's hearers:

> There was a great concern for their souls spread pretty generally among them: But especially there were two persons newly awakened to a sense of their sin and misery, one of whom was lately come, and the other had all along been very attentive, and desirous of being awakened, but could never before have any lively

view of her perishing state. But now her concern and spiritual distress was such, that I thought I had never seen *any* more pressing. Sundry old men were also in distress for their souls; so that they could not refrain from weeping and crying out aloud, and their bitter groans were the most convincing as well as affecting evidence of the reality and depth of their inward anguish. God is powerfully at work among them! True and genuine convictions of sin are daily promoted in many instances, and some are newly awakened from time to time; although some few, who felt a commotion in their passions in days past, seem now to discover that their hearts were never duly affected. I never saw the work of God appear so independent of means as at this time. (*Works 7*, 314–16)

Brainerd's faithful preaching of the gospel paid off. His zeal for the gospel and concern for souls, marks of true Christianity, led him to push through hardship and repeatedly witness to the Native Americans. Because he did so, he saw the Lord work in miraculous ways among this people. Dozens came to faith under Brainerd's watch, with the awakening among the lost reaching such a height that the missionary commented that he "never saw the work of God" show itself "so independent of [human] means." In true Edwardsean fashion, Brainerd observed that many people experienced deep "distress for their souls" as "true and genuine convictions of sin" spread to many, including some who had thought themselves saved but now realized "that their hearts were never duly affected." The true preaching of the Word had led to true marks of conversion, sweeping away both pagan lostness and nominal Christianity among the people.

The young man died not long after this exciting event before he reached thirty years of age. He never fully defeated depression, and he knew his struggles, but he died a victorious Christian, one who had given his life to promote the gospel and who had, despite considerable personal weaknesses, persevered in his own walk with Christ until the end. He did not die then in fame or earthly glory. In time, however, his example would help inspire a worldwide evangelical missions movement that led thousands of people from a wide range of denominations to carry the gospel to millions separated from God. Though he found happiness in the Edwards home and in a sweet kinship with Jerusha Edwards, Brainerd was a lonely soul who doggedly went into the wild to witness to pagan tribes. In a manner that speaks volumes today, he picked up his cross and carried it, stopping only when illness and exhaustion ended his earthly labor.

As we pursue true Christianity, we should seek to be believers who have a Brainerd-like commitment to the gospel of Christ and who are willing to lay down their lives to reach those estranged from God in places near and far. All who do so will, like Brainerd, leave a testimony that cannot help but inspire others to do the same in a world desperate for hope.

THE TOUCHING ACCOUNT OF ABIGAIL HUTCHINSON'S DEVOTION

Edwards found inspiring examples of true Christianity not only in missionaries on the field but in members of his own flock. In his Northampton congregation, Jonathan Edwards witnessed many dramatic conversions. Few, however, impressed themselves on his soul more than the salvation of Abigail Hutchinson, a young woman who suffered from a terminal illness. In his *Faithful Narrative of the Surprising Work of God,* Edwards recounted Hutchinson's conversion and subsequent love for God with moving prose. Edwards began with the young woman's background:

She was of a rational understanding family: there could be nothing in her education that tended to enthusiasm, but rather to the contrary extreme. 'Tis in no wise the temper of the family to be ostentatious of experiences, and it was far from being her temper. She was before her conversion, to the observation of her neighbors, of a sober and inoffensive conversation; and was a still, quiet, reserved person. She had long been infirm of body, but her infirmity had never been observed at all to incline her to be notional or fanciful, or to occasion anything of religious melancholy. She was under awakenings scarcely a week, before there seemed to be plain evidence of her being savingly converted. (*Works* 4, 192)

After her brother spoke to her about the gospel, Abigail became frightened about her spiritual condition. She could not shake thoughts about her sin, according to Edwards, and thus came to a crisis point in her spirituality:

Her great terror, she said, was that she had sinned against God. Her distress grew more and more for three days; until (as she said) she saw nothing but blackness of darkness before her, and her very flesh trembled for fear of God's wrath: she wondered and was astonished at herself, that she had been so concerned for her body, and had applied so often to physicians to heal that, and had neglected her soul. Her sinfulness appeared with a very awful aspect to her, especially in three things, viz. her original sin, and her sin in murmuring at God's providence, in the weakness and afflictions she had been under, and in want of duty to parents, though others had looked upon her to excel in dutifulness. On Saturday, she was so earnestly engaged in reading the Bible and other books that she continued in it, searching for something to relieve her, till her eyes were so dim that she could not know the letters. Whilst she was thus engaged in reading, prayer, and other religious exercises, she thought of those words of Christ, wherein he warns us not to be as

the heathen, that think they shall be heard for their much speaking
[Matthew 6:7]; which, she said, led her to see that she had trusted to
her own prayers and religious performances, and now she was put to
a non-plus, and knew not which way to turn herself, or where to seek
relief. (*Works* 4, 192–93)

A few days later, Abigail found rest from her fear and doubt. She
turned to the comforting voice of Scripture, finding encouragement for her penitent heart:

On the Sabbath day she was so ill that her friends thought it not
best that she should go to public worship, of which she seemed
very desirous: but when she went to bed on the Sabbath-day night,
she took up a resolution that she would the next morning go to
the minister, hoping to find some relief there. As she awaked on
Monday morning, a little before day, she wondered within herself
at the easiness and calmness she felt in her mind, which was of
that kind which she never felt before; as she thought of this, such
words as these were in her mind: "The words of the Lord are pure
words, health to the soul and marrow to the bones." And then
these words came to her mind, "The blood of Christ cleanses [us]
from all sin" [1 John 1:7]; which were accompanied with a lively sense
of the excellency of Christ, and his sufficiency to satisfy for the sins of
the whole world. She then thought of that expression, "'tis a pleasant
thing for the eyes to behold the sun" [Ecclesiastes 11:7]; which
words then seemed to her to be very applicable to Jesus Christ. By
these things her mind was led into such contemplations and views of
Christ, as filled her exceeding full of joy. (*Works* 4, 193)

Now that Abigail had discovered the satisfaction and relief that
comes through repentance and faith in the name of the Savior,
she devoted herself to living for the Lord with the time she had
left. It was not long.

Abigail made the most of her days, focusing herself on the grace of God, witnessing to whomever she could, living happily despite her inability to eat solid food and sustain her body. Edwards recorded a number of evidences of the young woman's changed heart, some of which are deeply moving:

> At the last time on Wednesday morning, while in the enjoyment of a spiritual view of Christ's glory and fulness, her soul was filled with distress for Christless persons, to consider what a miserable condition they were in: and she felt in herself a strong inclination immediately to go forth to warn sinners; and proposed it the next day to her brother to assist her in going from house to house; but her brother restrained her, by telling her of the unsuitableness of such a method. She told one of her sisters that day that she loved all mankind, but especially the people of God. Her sister asked her why she loved all mankind. She replied because God had made them. After this, there happened to come into the shop where she was at work, three persons that were thought to have been lately converted; her seeing them as they stepped in one after another into the door so affected her, and so drew forth her love to them, that it overcame her, and she almost fainted: and when they began to talk of the things of religion, it was more than she could bear; they were obliged to cease on that account. (*Works* 4, 194)

Abigail demonstrated clear signs of conversion. Primarily, she had a grave concern for unrepentant sinners, one of the strongest marks of true Christianity. Many people can pretend to have love for God. They can say the right things and go to the right events. But far fewer nominal believers will express concern for the eternal fate of the lost. Lukewarm believers will not want to think about such things, for doing so will raise the question of their own salvation. Abigail's evangelistic heart showed that she loved the Lord. Such concern is an important mark of true Christianity.

Abigail's delight centered on the God she loved. In a manner common among associates of Edwards, she sometimes lost herself in contemplation of the divine, experiencing blissful joy in the Lord:

> She had many extraordinary discoveries of the glory of God and Christ; sometimes, in some particular attributes, and sometimes in many. She gave an account that once, as those four words passed through her mind, "wisdom," "justice," "goodness," and "truth," her soul was filled with a sense of the glory of each of these divine attributes, but especially the last; "truth," said she, "sunk the deepest!" And therefore as these words passed, this was repeated, "Truth, truth!" Her mind was so swallowed up with a sense of the glory of God's truth and other perfections, that she said it seemed as though her life was going, and that she saw it was easy with God to take away her life by discoveries of himself. Soon after this she went to a private religious meeting. . . . Afterwards she was greatly affected, and rejoiced with these words, "Worthy is the Lamb that was slain" [Revelation 5:12]. (*Works* 4, 194–95)

Even though Abigail's faith was young, she had acquired a theocentric worldview from the start. She had no affinity for the trappings of religion. The desperation of her physical condition intensified her love for the Lord, sharpening it in a powerful way. In her waning hours, Abigail had a "sense and view of the glory of God all the time." The dying young woman's strength began to fail, but her affection for Christ did not. Though we must not idealize her, we can admire her and honor her by letting her example fuel our own love for the Lord.

Abigail gave perhaps her most moving demonstration of trust in the Savior in her final days. In words that must have been difficult to write, Edwards described the final deterioration of her condition and the beauty of her faith. The final account is richly edifying:

> Her illness in the latter part of it was seated much in her throat; and swelling inward, filled up the pipe so that she could swallow nothing but what was perfectly liquid, and but very little of that, and with great and long strugglings and stranglings, that which she took in flying out at her nostrils till she at last could swallow nothing at all. She had a raging appetite to food, so that she told her sister, when talking with her about her circumstances, that the worst bit that she threw to her swine would be sweet to her: but yet when she saw that she could not swallow it, she seemed to be as perfectly contented without it, as if she had no appetite to it. Others were greatly moved to see what she underwent, and were filled with admiration at her unexampled patience. At a time when she was striving in vain to get down a little food, something liquid, and was very much spent with it, she looked up on her sister with a smile, saying, "O Sister, this is for my good!" At another time, when her sister was speaking of what she underwent, she told her that she lived an heaven upon earth for all that. She used sometimes to say to her sister, under her extreme sufferings, "It is good to be so!" Her sister once asked her why she said so. "Why," says she, "because God would have it so: It is best that things should be as God would have 'em: it looks best to me." (*Works* 4, 197)

Abigail persevered in her faith until the very end, painful as it was:

> She was very weak a considerable time before she died, having pined away with famine and thirst, so that her flesh seemed to be dried upon her bones; and therefore could say but little, and manifested her mind very much by signs. She said she had matter enough to fill up all her time with talk, if she had but strength. A few days before her death, some asked her whether she held her

integrity still, whether she was not afraid of death. She answered to this purpose, that she had not the least degree of fear of death. They asked her why she would be so confident. She answered, "If I should say otherwise, I should speak contrary to what I know: there is," says she, "indeed a dark entry, that looks something dark, but on the other side there appears such a bright shining light, that I cannot be afraid!" She said not long before she died that she used to be afraid how she should grapple with death; but, says she, "God has shewed me that he can make it easy in great pain." Several days before she died, she could scarcely say anything but just yes, and no, to questions that were asked her, for she seemed to be dying for three days together; but seemed to continue in an admirable sweet composure of soul, without any interruption, to the last, and died as a person that went to sleep, without any struggling, about noon, on Friday, June 27, 1735. (*Works* 4, 198)

Hundreds of years later, we feel the pain of this young woman's death. Her life plays out on paper as something like a tragedy. A young life, so full of joy and beauty, taken at its most promising point, just when faith had caught fire. On closer examination, though, we see that the Lord had a special plan for Abigail. Her calling was not to live long, but to live well. Abigail experienced the delights of true conversion and drew all eyes to God's work.

We do well to take note of how she suffered. So many of us allow ourselves to grow depressed over matters far smaller than a terminal disease. We complain, whether directly or through passive-aggressive speech, forgetting the testimony of people like Abigail Hutchinson. Her example calls us to emulate her and to bear up under suffering and use it to glorify God. To do so, we will have to shift our outlook on this life. Many of us, after all, do not have a terminal illness to bring us face to face with our faith. But if we would evaluate our lives to see what marks of conversion we possess, we would set ourselves up to live life with abandon and leave a testimony like Abigail Hutchinson, who pursued and tasted the riches of true Christianity, and whose memory calls others to do the same.

INCARNATING TRUE CHRISTIANITY

Conversion, as we saw in the last chapter, is real. But not only in a theological sense, such that we can formulate and understand it. Conversion has a definite look and feel. It does not mute one's natural personality or even sweep away all one's sins. But it does make a person new. Examples of people like David Brainerd and Abigail Hutchinson prove this, as do many others from Edwards's writings and from our own experiences. Brainerd and Hutchinson are not "all-stars," after all, but humble, ordinary people saved by the grace of God who lived extraordinary lives due to their pursuit of the Savior. Their lives modeled the doctrines taught by the Northampton pastor, showing us today that his picture of Christianity is not unreachable but is within our own grasp as well.

We have not looked at the lives of these two to idolize them. Instead, we have seen what true Christianity can look like when the heart and mind embrace the gospel and allow it to reshape human existence. The gospel comes to us as a message, but it transcends simple propositions and statements. It is a living force, and when it meets with a repentant, committed heart, it makes all things new (2 Cor. 5:17). Physical beauty and the trappings of wealth may naturally draw our eyes, but the beauty of holiness, sparked from true conversion initiated by the power of the Holy Spirit, shines with a brilliance not seen in anything else in this world.

The lives of David and Abigail ended long ago, but their examples live on. They urge us today to recognize the power of true conversion and the potency of a life devoted in entirety to the work of God. Both of these young people struggled with physical weakness and sickness. Neither had an easy road. But where so

many of us give in to our sin and quit when we encounter obstacles, these two persevered, seeking the face of God. They are
examples for us, Christians whom we must remember as we seek
true conversion and holy passion in our own ordinary, conflicted,
possibility-filled lives.

Embracing True Christianity

Embody Vibrant Christianity in Trial or Comfort

The preceding biographies offer us encouragement. As we have
seen at other places in our study of Edwards's life and work, the
individual committed to God can do great things for Him. This
applies to all types of persons. We do not need to be a theological giant, a pastor, or to be free of physical weakness or various
forms of illness. Both of the people studied in this chapter suffered daily from bodily sickness. The work of the kingdom, we
see, is very different from the world of business or politics. God
uses people of all types and takes special pleasure in glorifying
His name through the weak: "God chose what is weak in the
world to shame the strong," wrote the Apostle Paul in the first
century, and the same truth applies today (1 Cor. 1:27). Though
we so often think that we need to choose the same people to
lead us that the world would choose—the strong, charming,
highly intelligent, and ambitious—we must remember that the
Lord frequently uses the weak and lowly to do great things for
Him. The gospel welcomes and enfranchises all people. Those
whom others would shun have often played a leading role in the
advancement of the kingdom—a crucial truth that we must not
forget. The weak are not disadvantaged when it comes to displaying the strength of true Christianity. The absence of abundance
allows them to display Christ all the more.

Chapter 22

EDWARDS'S DISMISSAL AND THE CONTEMPORARY CALL TO TRUE CHRISTIANITY

In an ideal world, good always wins. We see this in many popular movies. Despite great obstacles, the hero generally defeats the bad guys, rescues the girl, and saves the planet. Order and peace return, celebration ensues, and everyone lives happily ever after.

But real life plays by different rules. Sometimes good—and people working for good—wins out, and sometimes it doesn't. From a Christian perspective, sometimes our virtuous undertakings go well and sometimes they fall short. There is no guarantee in this fallen world that God's people will always prevail or that people living in error will magically adopt truth once it is presented to them. In His providence, God does what He deems is best, producing effects in our lives that we do not always desire and sometimes cannot figure out.

The case of Jonathan Edwards and his congregation fits this premise to a tee. Edwards was his era's most famous pastor, and Northampton was a prominent town with a well-known assembly, the First Church. Yet the Northampton church fired Edwards twenty years into his pastorate, dismissing him for how he handled the Communion Controversy, which we discussed briefly in chapter 7.

We will look more closely at this affair in this chapter, observing that this struggle emerged from Edwards's deep concern over nominal Christianity in his church. Conversion was never theoretical for the pastor; it was always practical, a matter of first concern. We conclude by returning to the present day. Aware that each of us has faults and weaknesses, we will suggest several steps that the modern church might take to renew itself. Our Edwardsean solution will propose a number of points that Christians today can use in their quest to promote true Christianity.

THE COMMUNION CONTROVERSY

Edwards had long disliked the Northampton church's policy on communion that his grandfather, Solomon Stoddard, had instituted. Stoddard, who had pastored the church for fifty-five years before Edwards, saw the sacrament as a "converting ordinance" and thus welcomed all who professed faith and lived decently to take the cup and bread. Edwards had disagreed with his grandfather on this point for decades before he went public with his own view—that only those who lived holy lives could take the sacrament. Edwards spoke of his initial hesitancy to change the policy in 1749:

> I have formerly been of [Stoddard's] opinion, which I imbibed from his books, even from my childhood, and have in my proceedings conformed to his practice; though never without some difficulties in my view, which I could not solve: yet, however, a distrust of my own understanding, and deference to the authority of so venerable a man, the seeming strength of some of his arguments, together with the success he had in his ministry, and his

great reputation and influence, prevailed for a long time to bear down my scruples. (*Works* 12, 169)

In the 1740s, however, Edwards felt he could no longer allow people to take communion who refused to demonstrate by their lifestyle their profession of faith. The pastor did not want to limit communion only to the most spiritually vibrant people in his congregation; he merely wanted to emphasize true conversion in a biblical manner and allow people to take it who lived in a godly way. Edwards thought that this position, grounded in a strong scriptural argument, had the high ground. Instead, the new policy soon crumbled beneath his feet, taking him with it.

Edwards outlined his views in *Lectures on the Qualifications for Full Communion in the Church of Christ*. There, he advanced his view that only professing Christians with evident piety should take the sacrament:

> 'Tis plain by the Scripture, and 'tis owned on all sides, that those who are admitted to the communion of the Christian church must be visible saints. All allow that, which is at once granting the very point in question, for to be visible saints is to be visibly godly men. To be a saint is to be a godly man, and to be visibly a saint is to be visibly a godly man; and to be visibly so is to be so in appearance to the eyes of men: it is to be a godly man as far as men can see and judge.

Undercutting the counter-argument that no one could truly know a person's spiritual state, Edwards offered a clear refutation, pointing out that authentic belief naturally produced evident piety:

> Visibility has relation to reality. Everything that is visibly gold is not real gold, but that which is gold visibly is real gold to

appearance and acceptance. 'Tis so in everything. There are visibly good men and really good men; there are visibly honest men and really honest men. Now there are more men that are visibly honest men than are really so, but he that is visibly an honest man is to appear, or as to what is visible to others, really an honest man. So he that is visibly another man's child [is, to appearance, that man's child]. So he that is visibly a saint is, to appearance and to the eye and judgment of men, really a saint. (*Works* 25, 357)

The controversy over spiritual requirements for communion bled over into church membership. When a young man came to him in 1748 seeking admission to the church, Edwards requested a narrative of his conversion. This emphasis went hand in hand with his views on communion, recently made public. As with communion, Edwards believed that church membership and its privileges were for true Christians, not those professing faith but not living it. When some protested this decision and his position on the Lord's Supper, Edwards, probably unwisely, published not one but two books outlining and defending his understanding of the subject. His argument for pure church membership mirrored his argument for true believers' communion:

'Tis most manifest by the Scripture, and what none denies or disputes, that none ought to be admitted into the Christian church but professing Christians. But they that make no profession of godliness, they are not professors of the Christian religion in the Scripture sense. The Christian religion is the religion of Christ, or the religion that Jesus Christ came to teach. But the religion that Christ taught consisted mainly in true piety of heart and life. Indeed, the custom of the present day has called something else the religion of Christ besides this: 'tis customary to call the doctrines of Christianity the Christian religion. But that is nothing to the purpose; the question is what the Scripture represents as the Christian religion, what the Bible informs us is the religion of Jesus Christ.

Christianity was a "heart religion," said Edwards, not a code of ethics or body of abstract doctrines that one committed to and then forgot:

> The Scripture teaches that the religion of Jesus Christ is heart religion, a spiritual religion. The worship that Christ came to teach was worshipping in spirit and in truth. Now in order to men's professing the religion of Jesus Christ, men must profess that which is the religion of Jesus Christ. But if men profess only the doctrines of religion and the outward services, and leave out what is spiritual, the thing that they profess is not the religion of Jesus Christ, because the most essential things that belong to his religion are left out. To profess a very small part of Christianity only, is not to profess Christianity. (*Works* 25, 359)

The result of a relaxed policy on church membership that did not prioritize a vibrant Christian walk would prove disastrous not only to the church but to Christianity more broadly:

> To make a public profession of common, superficial religion at the same time that a man don't pretend to the internal, is in effect to make an open profession of being lukewarm, and so more hateful to Christ than a heathen. And who can believe that Christ, by his own institution, has appointed such a profession as this to be the terms of being received into his church and family and to his table as his friends and children? (*Works* 25, 360)

Edwards's arguments possessed clarity and force, but many did not receive them well. The controversy begun over communion and extended over membership stretched over many months, with people from all over New England listening for details of the Edwards–First Church divide. In the end, Edwards failed to rally enough supporters to his side. With several previous conflicts in the background that still simmered between Edwards and his detractors, the church fired him on June 22, 1750.

As mentioned in chapter 7, these events disordered Edwards's life and brought many trials to his family. He continued to minister in Northampton for a time as the interim pastor, but no happy resolution came of his situation.

The pastor's stance on true Christianity cost him dearly. Yet in Edwards's mind, this issue was of such importance that he was willing to put everything—his reputation, his pastorate, his personal comfort—on the line. He believed that in advocating for believer's communion, he was helping to win the lost and stamp the church as the holy outpost of God. He took personal responsibility for the advancement of true Christianity. His conception of the pastorate, articulated in his farewell sermon to the church, sheds light on his actions in the controversies over communion and membership:

> Ministers are set as guides and teachers, and are represented in Scripture as lights set up in the churches; and in the present state meet their people from time to time in order to instruct and enlighten them, to correct their mistakes, and to be a voice behind them, saying, "This is the way, walk in it" [Is. 30:21]; to evince and confirm the truth by exhibiting the proper evidences of it, and to refute errors and corrupt opinions, to convince the erroneous and establish the doubting. (*Works* 25, 466)

With his conception of the church, Edwards could not countenance lukewarm practice in the areas of communion or membership. With his conception of his own role as shepherd of his members' souls, he could not stand by as people idled spiritually, allowing the gospel to go in one ear and out the other, as if the good news of God were nothing more than a passing thought. The gospel as Edwards saw it was a searing light that bore into sinful humanity and forever altered it. Upon this conception of the gospel and Christianity Edwards banked all of his pastoral ministry. Other factors emerged that complicated the Northampton situation, but at base, the communion controversy boiled down to different understandings of Christianity. Though he at times fanned the flames of controversy with his manner of handling disagreements, in this matter Edwards took a sound position. Biblical fidelity on this point did not translate to congregational unity, however, leaving one of history's most faithful pastors to retreat to the wilderness.

EMBRACING TRUE CHRISTIANITY

Though Edwards never returned to the same kind of pulpit ministry he had in Northampton, his pastoral and theological legacy lives on. We have traced his doctrine of conversion, peppering it with examples from his life and the lives of others to show that it was no figment of his spiritual imagination. We now seek to apply the insights and practical experience of Edwards to our modern context. Though this is by no means an exhaustive proposal, it is a call to arms to Christians everywhere to seek true conversion and the vivifying life it creates.

A THEOCENTRIC APPROACH TO LIFE, MINISTRY, AND THE GOSPEL

At the center of Edwards's understanding of conversion was his view of God. God had the preeminence—He created life, He founded the church, He saved souls, He deserved obedience and faith. Edwards's ministry centered not around pragmatic questions, but around a dominant concern that all that he would do and say would bring glory to God and advance His kingdom. God, not statistics or personal reputation, occupied center stage in his mind. Edwards knew that he did not need to please man; he needed to please God. He followed the theocentric trail wherever it led him, even when it led into territory that threatened to harm his ministry due to the lack of scriptural understanding in his church. When he lost his job, he did not blame God. His zeal for a ministry that honored the Lord persisted through great trial. Life was not about him, after all. It centered around God and His glory. This outlook grounded Edwards in happy seasons and buoyed him in times of difficulty.

In the deepest part of his soul, Edwards believed that the Lord had called him to labor for true conversion. Theocentric ministry in the name of Christ to a fallen world meant that sinners had to learn about their desperate state. This meant calling hostile sinners to account, a matter to which the Northampton pastor devoted considerable attention. Edwards spent great amounts of time and energy pleading with nominal Christians, who hid beneath a surface Christianity, to recognize the self-deception of their hearts. Edwards could not pretend that all was well in his church and go blithely about his business while members of his church scrambled to sit in more impressive pews and approached the communion table with nothing but a veneer of godliness. Edwards rose to meet these challenges. He did so even when it could—and did—cost him everything.

What can we learn from Edwards's approach today? Looking back to the first chapter, the world in which we live and minister is very similar to Edwards's. Though America as a nation makes few claims about any kind of Christian identity today, many of our churches have drawn people who for one reason or another claim conversion but whose lives fail to measure up to true Christianity (as we saw in chapter 19). In such a setting, with all kinds of financial and social pressures, it is difficult for many pastors to imagine confronting their people with the need to be converted and to reckon with lukewarm Christianity. But this is precisely what lukewarm Christians need. If the material from chapter 19 shows us anything, it is that many professing Christians are floundering. They know basically nothing about the Bible or Christianity, they struggle to attend church, they hold beliefs in direct contradiction to the Scripture, and they neither witness nor have even the most basic success in educating their children in the things of God. This is a frightening situation.

A theocentric ministry demands that our Christian leaders shake off all of the distractions and lesser cares of their vocation and, in the most fundamental sense, rededicate their ministries to the Lord. The historic model of the pastor-theologian offers us an excellent antidote to our weakened pastorates in which theology is a bad word and preaching is group therapy. We don't advocate for a theocentric ministry merely so that people will get right with God. Ministry, as with all of Christianity, is fundamentally about God. It is derived from and dependent upon His Word. The Scripture is authoritative over everything and it is sufficient for all of ministry. It is the mind and counsel of the Almighty given to us to form and direct our ministry in His name.

A BELIEF IN THE CENTRALITY OF THE GOSPEL-DRIVEN CHURCH

The work of Edwards shows that he believed in the centrality of the local church. He saw it as the place where true Christianity took visible shape and God incarnated His gospel. He took church membership seriously and labored to create a situation in which all who belonged to his congregation and observed the sacraments held true love for Christ in their hearts. He gave himself to the work of the church and labored to spread the riches of the biblical witness before his people. In sum, Edwards loved the church and drove himself hard to bless and build it.

We need today to recover an Edwardsean understanding of the church. We need to see it as the outpost of God, and we need our ministers to see themselves as "lights set up in the churches" to point people to God. We need to see the church as the place where true Christians live and work, calling those outside to the light of the gospel that emanates from their assembly. We need our churches to teach the full counsel of Scripture so that believers will know the Bible and be able to incorporate it into their lives. We need our teaching and preaching to center around the gospel to the point that unbelievers visiting our churches have trouble staying in unrepentant sin. Though we want unbelievers and nominal Christians to feel welcome in our churches and loved by our people, we do not want them to be able to play fast and loose with God. We want them to come into constant contact with the gospel such that they will realize their desperate plight and reckon with their sin. We want them to know, above all, that the church is not just another organization, another club to join and profit from, but is a holy movement of God's Spirit that calls people not to be served, but to serve, to lay down their lives in order to glorify God and fulfill His purpose for humanity (following Christ's example—see Matt. 20:28 and Mark 10:45).

A CONCERN FOR NOMINAL CHRISTIANS OF SPECIFIC TYPES

Edwards did not simply lash out against nominal Christianity. He came against it from various angles, addressing specific temptations and circumstances. We saw this demonstrated in his handling of the pew controversy, where he challenged wealthy older members not to find their identity in social status and younger people in the congregation not to think that they could find contentment and safety in material things. Edwards applied such discernment and pastoral sensitivity to the problem of lukewarm faith in numerous places in his sermons. He gave nominal Christianity a face and a name, helping his people to identify and counter it in the process.

We must emulate the Northampton pastor and address lukewarm Christianity wherever we find it, including among the young and unmarried, those who are middle-aged, and even older members who belong to the church but know precious little of true Christianity. With young singles, we need to cement the idea that Christianity is not worth the fullness of one's heart and mind because a particular church happens to be cool or interesting, but because it offers them the chance to experience the joys of the cruciform life and the defeat of sin, death, and hell. Christianity is relevant because it is true, not because of its cultural trappings. The gospel offers true delight, true liberation, and true hope as nothing else does. It brings young hearts and minds that hunger for authenticity and beauty into the embrace of the divine.

With middle-aged people who feel stuck in a malaise of life, we need to emphasize the great purpose every life has before God. Christ's redemption, applied to the soul of mankind, will not allow for a half-hearted life, a wasted stewardship of one's talents and abilities. In the gospel, all find significance and purpose, and all find the cure for a lifetime of sins and failures that justly offend a holy God. With older members who may see their membership more as an association than a calling, we must repeatedly go back to basics and teach that Christianity is not a duty to perform or a worthy organization to join. It is an opportunity to die to self, live with the risen Christ, and serve His people. It is altogether different from anything else on this earth.

THE BEAUTY OF CHRIST AND THE HORROR OF SIN

The final major focus that we may pick up from Edwards was his theological concern to exalt the beauty of Christ and to unmask the horror of sin. In his preaching and theologizing, Edwards repeatedly placed these parallel ideas at the forefront of his understanding of Christianity. As seen in chapters 20 and 21, he took great care to point out the prevalence of deception even as he detailed the way that the "true sense" of conversion inflamed the penitent heart with love for Christ. Biblical faith, in the end, begins and ends with a simultaneous love for the Savior and a hatred of sin. Without either component, faith never leaves the ground. If we profess to love Jesus Christ but never deal with our sin, we are lost, unforgiven by the Father, and will not enter heaven. If we hate our sin but never run to Christ to receive His atoning grace, we have no remission of sins and we will not see eternal life. The Spirit must propel each of these doctrines into the sinful heart and mind if we are ever to know the grace of God and the glory of true Christianity.

We need to seize these twin emphases in our churches today and make them part of the fabric of our ecclesial life. True Christianity is neither solely sorrow over sin nor simply joy in Christ; it is both, married together, residing in the human heart, which personally receives, believes, and acts on these truths. In churches that all too often drift from these foundational realities to ground their identities in other teachings—whether a political identity, a social cause, or a way of living—we need the dual emphasis on sin's influence and Christ's atonement. Remembering the evil of our depravity and the need to fight it ensures that we will not rest easy in our faith, growing soft and lazy, while rooting ourselves in adoration of Christ warms our hearts to love Him and rise above the temptations of this world.

POSSIBLE QUESTIONS TO
ASK OUR NOMINAL FRIENDS

Before we conclude, we offer a series of questions that Christians, churches, and pastors may use in conversations with people who profess faith but struggle to commit themselves wholly to the Lord. These questions are not intended to hurt or wound but rather to help nominal Christians discern the true state of their heart in order that they might experience salvation.

- Do you love God? In your heart, do you desire to follow Him, worship Him, and obey Him?
- Do you love the Bible? Do you want to follow the One whom it reveals, Jesus Christ, and follow His commandments?
- Do you love living out and sharing the gospel? Do you monetarily support other Christians in need?
- Do you love Christians?
- Do you enjoy church and draw nourishment from it?
- Does the matter of eternity concern you? Do you live as if eternity is real?
- Does the Bible shape your ethics and morals? Or do you just go with what you feel at a gut level? When there is conflict between your natural inclinations and what the Bible says, which side wins?

CHALLENGING NOMINAL CHRISTIANITY

We began this part on true Christianity with a look at the current state of marriage. We noted, in short, that it has fallen on hard times. We then commented that there is a far deeper form of adultery and half-hearted commitment that plagues our world today—spiritual lukewarmness. Just as some spouses today go through the motions of marriage, pretending to love the person with whom they have covenanted, some professing Christians join churches without any personal love for the gospel.

This is a hard situation, but may the example and teaching of Jonathan Edwards challenge us to press on and to seek true conversion and authentic Christianity in our lives and churches. We desire not to accommodate nominal Christianity—but to address it with the gospel. We seek to call people who profess to love God to do just that: to love Him. If we hope for our world to gain a fresh love for marriage, how much greater is our hope for nominal Christians to truly take Christ as their Lord?

The time is short; the hour draws nearer when the risen King will return to earth and claim His people for Himself. At His coming, He will judge the lukewarm, the nominal believer, spewing them from His mouth, casting them aside. As Edwards did, then, we call to all who will hear to seek the Son while He may be found, to feel the weight of sin's burden, and to cast themselves on the mercy of God. Now, while we still have time, let us prepare ourselves and flee the darkness of this world for the light that will soon break like the dawn.

Part 5

Heaven & Hell

Chapter 23

THE DISAPPEARANCE
OF THE AFTERLIFE

Those—dying then,
Knew where they went—
They went to God's Right Hand—
That Hand is amputated now
And God cannot be found—

The abdication of Belief
Makes the Behavior small—
Better an ignis fatuus
Than no illume at all—

(Norton, 2383)

Edwards did not write these words. They were composed by
Emily Dickinson. Dickinson, one of America's greatest poets
of the nineteenth century, wrote the brief and untitled poem
in a different cultural climate than Edwards's. The American
colonies had become a nation. The Industrial Revolution had
transformed daily life. Most pertinent to the poem, many pastors
had embraced the popular academic spirit that effectively deem-
phasized the historic doctrines of orthodox Christianity.

The Christian faith as experienced by many church members had changed, too. Where Christians had once emphasized the glories of heaven and the terrors of hell, many professing believers in Dickinson's era suffered an apparent "abdication of Belief." They no longer subscribed to the awesome truths of immortality. Instead, they busied themselves with the things of this world. Dickinson, though not an avid churchgoer herself, lamented this situation and the impoverished moral behavior it produced.

The same problem that Dickinson observed many years ago belongs to our age. Many believers and churches do not reflect deeply on the age to come. Evangelicalism as a whole seems to have shifted focus from the life to come to life in this world. This has the unfortunate consequence of diminishing the importance of ultimate realities.

The call to preach the need for salvation and the prospect of the afterlife proceeds from the Scripture. In one section from the book of Ezekiel, the Lord thunders to Ezekiel, His prophet, to do just this, warning him of the dire consequences of failure on this point:

> So you, son of man, I have made a watchman for the house of Israel. Whenever you hear a word from my mouth, you shall give them warning from me. If I say to the wicked, O wicked one, you shall surely die, and you do not speak to warn the wicked to turn from his way, that wicked person shall die in his iniquity, but his blood I will require at your hand. But if you warn the wicked to turn from his way, and he does not turn from his way, that person shall die in his iniquity, but you will have delivered your soul. (Ezek. 33:7–9)

Though the passage does not mention heaven and hell, it shows that the Lord holds His shepherds and prophets responsible for declaring His message of salvation. The prophets were divinely called to warn the people of God of the reality of judgment and the need to reconcile themselves to their Creator and Judge. The prophet did not choose whether or not to highlight these things. The people, for their part, were not free to pick and choose which parts of the prophet's message they liked best.

Much has changed since Ezekiel's day, when every person could not help but come face to face with both their mortality and the truth of the afterlife. We feel this shift keenly in the West, where various factors push against biblical teaching on the afterlife. In the broader culture, hell, especially, is a relic of a severe past, an idea that few people seriously entertain. Heaven, on the other hand, retains popularity, though what heaven actually looks like in the minds of many has changed dramatically. In Christian circles, though many believers retain belief in heaven and hell, the practical reality is that this earth often has more significance for many of us than does the afterlife.

To begin to rectify this situation, we must first understand how we have arrived at this place. We will do so in this chapter. We will briefly tour our cultural history, examining how belief in the afterlife has changed and decreased over the last few centuries. After we have traced the decline of belief in the afterlife, we will turn to Edwards's writing and thinking in pursuit of a biblical eschatological vision. The pastor-theologian devoted a great deal of attention to the afterlife and penned numerous pieces that called for his audience to reckon with the prospect of eternity in either heaven or hell. These pieces, whether sermons to his congregation, theological treatises, or letters to his children, illustrate his convictions and will revive our own. Through study of them, we will see that Edwards wrote and preached on the need to prepare one's soul for death not because he was a kill-joy, but because he loved his people deeply and wanted them to avoid wrath and taste eternal life.

A BRIEF CULTURAL HISTORY OF BELIEF IN THE AFTERLIFE

Our remarks on this point can only be brief as we provide a sketch of the decline of belief in hell in our society. As we will see, the story of widespread loss of faith in the afterlife parallels the larger story of cultural unbelief.

As noted in the introduction, the vast majority of people in the history of the world believed in a dualistic afterlife. For much of the last two millennia in the West, Catholicism and Protestantism have held sway over the minds and hearts of the common people. Though these two strands of Christianity have significant differences, each has traditionally taught that heaven and hell exist. Taking this teaching from the Bible, church leaders passed it on to their followers, who in turn accepted the teaching as truth. They had no perception as many of us do that they were choosing one worldview option among many. Rather, the biblical teaching as mediated by their church leaders was fact, and they were required by God to believe His Word.

Popular views of hell in the Middle Ages, for example, were often visceral and horrifying, far removed from our sanitized modern conceptions, as historian Piero Camporesi shows:

> The "sepulchre of hell", "with its fetid corpses which were indis-
> solubly linked to hundreds of others", this "rubbish heap of rotting
> matter devours the dead without disintegrating them, disintegrates
> them without incinerating them, and incinerates them in everlasting
> death", worked like a peculiar self-feeding incinerator which simul-
> taneously disintegrated and regenerated the rubbish which flowed
> from the rotten world, and paradoxically transformed the ephemeral
> into immortal, elevating the rejects and garbage into eternal, glorious
> trophies of divine justice. It was like a "rubbish heap filled with little
> worms" whose contents are continually regenerated and reintegrated in
> an incomprehensible cycle of sublimated destruction. (Camporesi, 55)

Pictures like this played in the minds of the masses for ages. Unlike our era, when many Christians shut hell from their minds, in previous days most people would have heard sermons illustrating the horrors of the realm of the damned.

Everything began to change in the sixteenth, seventeenth, and eighteenth centuries, however. Some thinkers, following trends begun in the Renaissance, began to openly question the authority of the Bible, the existence of God, and the reality of heaven and hell. In Europe, especially in influential France, the number of "heretics" swelled as highly intelligent philosophers— called "philosophes"—launched attacks against the dogma of the Catholic Church. The Church, not used to having its teaching questioned so boldly in public, reacted strongly against the philosophes, which won the thinkers great approval from their peers. In time, through the power of the printing press, the Enlightenment's ideas spread from country to country and city to city.

As history shows, the Enlightenment accomplished nothing less than a sea change in the West. Coupled with factors like rising health standards and increased social prosperity due to the rise of markets, many common folk began to wonder whether Christianity was worth all the moral trouble, with all of its constraints and denunciations, and whether heaven and hell might be little more than an invention of the church. Camporesi vividly describes this shift:

> Together with the growing infrequency of famine and the extinction of that other divine punishment, the plague, the European desire for life, which was reflected in the demographic increase and the rebirth of Christian hope in the form of a less absolute and tyrannical, less cruel and severe justice, laid the foundations, under the long influence of rationalism, for deism, pantheism, and for an anti-dogmatic historical criticism and skepticism; it even led to the dismantling of the dark city of punishment and to

> the gradual emptying—through the filter of a deliberate mental
> reform—of the life—prison of the damned. (Camporesi, 103–4)

The teaching of the Enlightement philosophers caused many people to question beliefs long established as truth, even as changing living conditions allowed people to gradually liberate themselves from otherworldly teachings. Freshly emboldened, many people distanced themselves from Christianity and its view of the afterlife in the eighteenth and nineteenth centuries. In the academy, which grew especially strong in the nineteenth century, higher criticism of the Bible caught on, and soon scholars were debunking whole books of the sacred text. It became fashionable among leading thinkers to disbelieve the Bible. Yet, this was by no means the only religious trend of this period; Christian revivals broke out frequently, and Baptists and Methodists surged in popularity in this age. Even in Europe, stories of the demise of Christianity were in places greatly exaggerated. Yet a shift had taken place, one that altered the West definitively.

We also need to look specifically at what has happened in America in the last 200 years to erode belief in the Christian afterlife. Theologian Al Mohler notes that in the nineteenth century in America, "Deists and Unitarians had rejected the idea of God as judge. In certain circles, higher criticism had undermined confidence in the Bible as divine revelation, and churchmen increasingly treated hell as a metaphor" (*Hell Under Fire*, 24–25). A new wing of Christianity rose to prominence in America in this time. Liberal Christianity explicitly retained certain elements of Christian teaching while rejecting others, including belief in an errorless Scripture, a wrathful God, a substitute sacrifice paying the blood penalty for sin, and hell. These views spread from New England—once the bastion of biblical Christianity in America—to various corners of the country, including many cities and centers of academic life.

The seed of doubt planted in the nineteenth century yielded a forest of skepticism in the twentieth. Mohler weighs in incisively:

> Theologically, the century that began in comfortable Victorian eloquence quickly became fertile ground for nihilism and *angst*. What World War I did not destroy, World War II took by assault and atrocity. The battlefields of Verdun and Ypres gave way to the ovens of Dachau and Auschwitz as symbols of the century.
>
> At the same time, the technological revolutions of the century extended the worldview of scientific naturalism throughout much of the culture of the West, especially among elites. The result was a complete revolution in the place of religion in general, and Christianity in particular, in the public space. Ideological and symbolic secularization became the norm in Western societies with advanced technologies and ever-increasing levels of economic wealth. Both heaven and hell took on an essentially this-worldly character. (*Hell Under Fire*, 26)

The specter of secularism assaulted Christianity on numerous fronts, as the above makes clear. The great wars of the first part of the twentieth century swept away the tenuous Christian commitment of many Europeans and Americans. Weakened Christianity, Christianity without an omnipotent and all-wise God, a glorious Savior laying His life down to save His people, and eternal life and death, proved no match for the "ovens of Dachau and Auschwitz." Horror at the scope and spectacle of human suffering overwhelmed loosely held religious commitment.

With little connection to the rock-solid biblical foundation that nurtures the soul and buttresses the mind, modern man searched for a salve, a worldview that could give solace in the midst of mass destruction. His quest led him to various outlets. He found some relief in technology and the promise of scientific discovery. He nursed his spiritual wounds in the burgeoning psychological movement. He gave himself over to nihilism. He spent himself in hedonistic excess. In each of these outlets, he embraced a world-centered ideology and lost sight of the wonder of heaven and the horror of hell. Man, a spiritual creature bearing the imprint of eternity, morphed into a soulless being with no attachment to a concrete afterlife.

The Christian faith has suffered in the wake of these developments. Many Christian leaders have allowed the major cultural trends to shape the way they think about and live the Christian faith. Mohler suggests that in our day,

> sin has been redefined as a lack of self-esteem rather than as an insult to the glory of God. Salvation has been reconceived as liberation from oppression, internal or external. The gospel becomes a means of release from bondage to bad habits rather than rescue from a sentence of eternity in hell. (*Hell Under Fire*, 40)

Historian D. P. Walker concurs in his treatment of the modern view of hell:

> Eternal torment is nowadays an unpopular doctrine among most kinds of Christians; the God of love has nearly driven out the God of vengeance; vindictive justice has had to take refuge among the advocates of hanging; and it is no longer considered respectable to enjoy the infliction of even the justest punishment. (Walker, 262)

Philosopher A. J. Conyers points out that heaven is also out of vogue today:

> We live in a world no longer under heaven. At least in most people's minds and imaginations that vision of reality has become little more than a caricature, conjuring up the saints and angels

of baroque frescoes. And in the church only a hint remains of the power it once exercised in the hearts of believers. (Conyers, 11)

The Christian church is losing its grasp on heaven and hell. As is clear from this testimony, when set against our fast-paced, ever-changing, self-serving world, the afterlife—seemingly so vague and far off—struggles to hold our attention.

WHAT MODERNS BELIEVE ABOUT THE AFTERLIFE

Many who do believe in Christianity have modernized it. We have made our faith about fulfillment and achievement, senti-mentalized love, and earthly progress. We have adopted the consumerist mindset endemic to the West and have substituted the pursuit of plenty for the pursuit of piety. David Wells suggests,

> This experience of abundance which is the result of both extraordinary ingenuity and untamed desire is a telltale sign that we have moved from a traditional society to one that is modern, from a time when God and the supernatural were "natural" parts of life, to one in which God is now alienated and dislocated from our modernized world. In traditional societies, what one could legitimately have wanted was limited. It was, of course, limited because people lived with only a few choices and little knowledge of life other than the life they lived; their vision of life had not been invaded, as ours is, by pictures of beguiling Caribbean shorelines, sleek luxury under the Lexus insignia, time-shares in fabulous places, or exotic perfumes sure to stir hidden passions. (Wells, 42)

Wells's analysis brings us back to where we started: preference. We modern folk live with a mind-boggling array of choices that our ancestors never knew. The family is in Dallas, but do we prefer the weather in Denver? Our parents ran a drug store, but would we prefer dentistry? Should we have kids now, or delay five or six years? Would we like to reinvent our bodies? If so, what would we like to change—a new nose? Different eyelids? Fuller, thicker lips? In these and countless other ways—many of them neutral, a good number of them acceptable, and some of them downright harmful—we encounter the category of choice, never realizing how differently we act and think from our forebears.

When it comes to choices about the afterlife, Americans exercise their "right" with aplomb. A recent Barna poll probing belief in heaven and hell discovered the following results:

> In all, 76% believe that Heaven exists, while nearly the same pro-
> portion said that there is such a thing as Hell (71%). Respondents
> were given various descriptions of Heaven and asked to choose
> the statement that best fits their belief about Heaven. Those who
> believe in Heaven were divided between describing Heaven as
> "a state of eternal existence in God's presence" (46%) and those
> who said it is "an actual place of rest and reward where souls go
> after death" (30%). Other Americans claimed that Heaven is just
> "symbolic" (14%), that there is no such thing as life after death
> (5%), or that they are not sure (5%).
>
> While there is no dominant view of Hell, two particular perspec-
> tives are popular. Four out of ten adults believe that Hell is "a state of
> eternal separation from God's presence" (39%) and one-third (32%)
> says it is "an actual place of torment and suffering where people's
> souls go after death." A third perspective that one in eight adults
> believe is that "Hell is just a symbol of an unknown bad outcome after
> death" (13%). Other respondents were "not sure" or said they that
> they do not believe in an afterlife (16%). (Barna)

This data is backed up by 2015 findings from Pew Research Center (Murphy). Despite widespread alarm about secularization, belief in heaven and hell had barely shifted across the board, from seventy-four percent (heaven) and fifty-nine percent (hell) in 2007 to 7seventy-two percent (heaven) and fifty-eight percent (hell). While the rise of the "Nones" is real—twenty-three percent in 2015 versus sixteen percent in 2007—but widespread belief in the afterlife persists (Lipka). These numbers reflecting belief in the afterlife may seem high given the foregoing commentary, and it is surely true that some form of belief in heaven and hell does persist today. Yet one cannot help but note the uncertainty when respondents attempted to define their views of hell. This is, after all, where the rubber meets the eschatological road. Many will profess to believe in Christian doctrine, but we must look closely at how they define this doctrine to grasp the strength of their belief. At the end of the day, far fewer people than one might think claim belief in heaven and hell as the Bible defines these realms. In addition, we might also note that one cannot separate heaven and hell, as so many seem to think. The Scripture does not give us the option of choosing which realm we want to believe in.

HOW A LOSS OF BIBLICAL BELIEF IN THE AFTERLIFE HAS AFFECTED THE CHURCH

The shifts in cultural thinking about the afterlife have transformed the way many Christians preach. Many pastors wish to reach people for Jesus, but they know that many folks have little patience with heady doctrine or biblical instruction. They choose to preach on more practical matters, areas that most people can readily understand. This kind of approach is understandable, but it has the unfortunate effect of silencing what past Christians have called the "whole counsel" of God, meaning the full sweep of biblical theology. In this kind of environment, preaching can become little more than an advice session or what others have called "group therapy."

Many pastors resist these trends. But where they do not, the people in the pew have little stimulus to think about the afterlife and things of eternal consequence. We are left instead to think much about things of this world. Thus, many of us think little about heaven and a good deal about football, renovating our houses, shopping, or gossip. We rarely talk about hell but often about television and movies. We joke about being "heavenly minded" and shy away from Christians who seem to be, viewing them as odd and out-of-place (indeed, they are). We strive to be cool, hip, fashionable, relevant, and plugged in, unaware of how little these things will matter in eternity. Our mindset, unbeknownst to us, is almost entirely rooted in this world. We have little connection with the life to come, which the Scripture teaches has already begun in us and in our churches (Mark 1:15).

Many of us sense this sad situation and want it to change. We do not want to be so busy, and we do not like what certain aspects of our modern way of life have done to our devotions, our daily thoughts, and our time at church. Many of us want to be more focused on heaven and more faithful in leading people away from hell through gospel proclamation. The problem, though, is that our modern lifestyle has trained us only to think deeply and searchingly about things like heaven and hell when our more pressing concerns have ceased—which is a rare occurrence.

AN EDWARDSEAN SOLUTION TO OUR MODERN DILEMMA

Though the task seems impossible, we have guides who have gone before us and who can help us to recover an eschatological perspective. One of them is Edwards, who devoted tremendous amounts of time and energy to thinking and teaching on heaven and hell. In these final chapters, we will look at his specific views, seeing how very real heaven and hell actually are, and finding our hearts stirred by the biblical material that he powerfully exposits.

EDWARDS'S CULTURAL CONTEXT

In Edwards's eighteenth-century era, the afterlife dominated the thinking of many people, including parents, who sought to ready their children for their eternal destiny. Marsden describes how many parents prepared their children for death:

> Much of Puritan upbringing was designed to teach children to recognize how insecure their lives were. Every child knew of brothers, sisters, cousins, or friends who had suddenly died. Cotton Mather . . . eventually lost thirteen of his fifteen children. Parents nightly reminded their children that sleep was a type of death and taught them such prayers as "This day is past; but tell me who can say / That I shall surely live another day." . . . One of the Edwards children's surviving writing exercises reads, "Nothing is more certain than death. Take no delay in the great work of preparing for death." (Marsden, 26–7)

Popular literature of the day underscored this perspective. Historian Charles Hambrick-Stowe comments on a wildly successful author, Michael Wigglesworth, who wrote a popular book called *The Day of Doom*:

> Wigglesworth exhorted thousands of New Englanders to prepare for death in *The Day of Doom* and his other poems. His prefatory lines explicitly stated that the epic's purpose was "That Death and Judgment may not come / And find thee unprepared." His overriding method in *The Day of Doom* was to instill the fear of Christ as terrible Judge and drive penitents to Him for mercy in this life before it was too late. Terror was a means of grace, but the hoped-for end was escape from terror. "Oh get a part in Christ," Wigglesworth cried, "And make the Judge thy Friend." (Hambrick-Stowe, 239–40)

Such a text would struggle to find even a Christian publisher today, but colonial New England prized literature of a different kind, as Hambrick-Stowe's reports of sales records show: *"The Day of Doom* was the most popular piece of literature in seventeenth-century New England. An unprecedented eighteen-hundred copies were printed in the first edition in 1662, which sold out in the first year. Thereafter the work was reissued repeatedly" (Hambrick-Stowe, 240).

We might wonder what cultural impulse accounted for these hefty sales figures. Colonial citizens of the seventeenth and eighteenth centuries knew a world much different from ours. They had no hospitals. They possessed precious few working remedies for illness. They knew very little about the causes of sickness—germ theory, for example, did not emerge until the mid-nineteenth century. Pregnancy and labor were potentially fearful undertakings: scholars have estimated that one in six children died in colonial America, meaning that most families would mourn the loss of at least one or two children in their lifetime (Marten, 80). Attacks from Native Americans posed a constant threat in many places. American colonists did not study death out of a perverse fascination, but practical necessity. Where we try to cheat death, they prepared themselves to meet it.

EDWARDS'S FOCUS ON THE AFTERLIFE

As was common for a minister of his time, Edwards often confronted death in his preaching. In his sermon "The Importance of a Future State," for example, he discoursed plainly about death, reminding his people of its certain visitation:

> But all other men must die in the ordinary way of separation of
> their souls from their bodies. Men of all ranks, degrees, and orders
> must die: strong [and] weak; kings, princes [and] beggars; rich

[and] poor; good [and] bad. (*Works* 10, 356–7)

Edwards outlined how God had planted eternity in the heart of all people, leaving us with the knowledge in our conscience that this life is not the end of things:

> Now God has implanted in us this natural disposition of expecting a reward or punishment, according as we do well or ill, for this disposition is natural to us: 'tis in our very nature; God had made it with us. And to what purpose should God make in us a disposition to expect rewards and punishments if there are none? (*Works* 10, 357)

Edwards had a plainspoken approach to death and the life beyond. Death, for him, was a fundamental consequence of existence. All people must face it. Accordingly, Edwards sought to prepare his people for the end.

In another sermon, "Death and Judgment," preached to his Native American congregation in Stockbridge, the pastor walked his listeners through the essential matters of life and death:

> In this world, sometimes, wicked men are great kings, and deal very hardly and cruelly with good men, and put 'em to death; and therefore, there must be another world where good men shall all be happy and wicked men miserable. . . .
>
> In another world, God will call 'em to an account [of] what they have done here in this world: how they have improved their time, and whe[ther] they have kept his commandments or no.
>
> He will [hold] them to an account that have heard the gospel preached; [he will ask] whether or no they have repented of their sins and have in their hearts accepted of Jesus Christ as their Savior.
>
> And then all wicked men, and they that would not repent of their

sins and come [to] Christ, will have their mouths stopped and will
have nothing to say. (*Works* 25, 594–95)

The pastor's straightforward approach to the afterlife allowed him
to reach his Native American audience in clear, understandable
language. Sermons like this one revealed how the decisions and
habits of this life had far-reaching consequences for the next. In
the afterlife God would balance the scales of justice.

The pastor's sermons on the afterlife took many forms, some
plain, others soaring in their sweep. In his "Farewell Sermon" to
his Northampton congregation, Edwards painted a hair-raising
picture of the last day that surely grabbed the attention of his
hearers:

> Although the whole world will be then present, all mankind of all
> generations gathered in one vast assembly, with all of the angelic
> nature, both elect and fallen angels; yet we need not suppose,
> that everyone will have a distinct and particular knowledge of each
> individual of the whole assembled multitude, which will undoubtedly
> consist of many millions of millions. Though 'tis probable that men's
> capacities will be much greater than in their present state, yet they will
> not be infinite: though their understanding and comprehension will be
> vastly extended, yet men will not be deified. There will probably be a
> very enlarged view, that particular persons will have of the various parts
> and members of that vast assembly. . . . There will be special reason,
> why those who have had special concerns together in this world, in
> their state of probation, and whose mutual affairs will be then to be
> tried and judged, should especially be set in one another's view.

The last day would mark the end of man's ability to repent. When
all people appeared before the great judgment seat of God, none
could change their stripes, a fact that Edwards brought out in
chilling detail:

But when they shall meet together at the day of judgment . . . they will all meet in an unchangeable state. Sinners will be in an unchangeable state: they who then shall be under the guilt and power of sin, and have the wrath of God abiding on them, shall be beyond all remedy or possibility of change, and shall meet their ministers without any hopes of relief or remedy, or getting any good by their means. And as for the saints, they will be already perfectly delivered from all their before-remaining corruption, temptation and calamities of every kind, and set forever out of their reach; and no deliverance, no happy alteration will remain to be accomplished in the way of the use of means of grace, under the administration of ministers. It will then be pronounced, "He that is unjust, let him be unjust still; and he that is filthy, let him be filthy still; and he that is righteous, let him be righteous still; and he that is holy, let him be holy still" [Revelation 22:11]. (*Works* 25, 466)

With his exegetical insight and vivid imagination, Edwards transported his hearers to the holy ground he described. Behind his foreboding sketch of the day of judgment was a pressing concern that his people prepare themselves for it. Edwards closed his sermon with a hopeful but sober call to seek the Lord while He could be found as a Savior and not a Judge:

Dear children, I leave you in an evil world, that is full of snares and temptations. God only knows what will become of you. This the Scripture has told us, that there are but few saved: and we have abundant confirmation of it from what we see. This we see, that children die as well as others: multitudes die before they grow up; and of those that grow up, comparatively few ever give good evidence of saving conversion to God. I pray God to pity you, and take care of you, and provide for you the best means for the good of your souls; and that God himself would undertake for you, to be your

heavenly Father, and the mighty Redeemer of your immortal souls.
(*Works* 25, 484–5)

The pastor's final words to the Northampton congregation did not
resolve the bitter conflict between Edwards and his detractors.
They did, however, direct the church members to recognize the
fragility of life and to throw themselves on the mercy of Christ.

Edwards did not only preach this message to his congregation. He spoke of it constantly to his children. To live in the
Edwards household was to come into regular contact with the
reality of death and the necessity of gospel preparation for the afterlife. The following letter to Edwards's daughter Esther, dated
May 27, 1755, shows both the tenderness and seriousness of the
father on these matters:

> Dear Child,
>
> Though you are a great way off from us, yet you are not out of our
> minds: I am full of concern for you, often think of you, and often
> pray for you. Though you are at so great a distance from us, and
> from all your relations, yet this is a comfort to us, that the same
> God that is here, is also at Onohquaga; and that though you are
> out of our sight and out of our reach, you are always in God's
> hands, who is infinitely gracious; and we can go to him, and commit
> you to his care and mercy. Take heed that you don't forget or neglect
> him. Always set God before your eyes, and live in his fear, and seek
> him every day with all diligence: for 'tis he, and he only can make you
> happy or miserable, as he pleases; and your life and health, and the
> eternal salvation of your soul, and your all in this life and that which is
> to come, depends on his will and pleasure.
>
> The week before last, on Thursday, David died; whom you knew
> and used to play with, and who used to live at our house. His soul is
> gone into the eternal world. Whether he was prepared for death, we
> don't know. This is a loud call of God to you to prepare for death. You

see that they that are young die, as well as those that are old: David was not very much older than you. Remember what Christ has said, that you must be born again, or you never can see the kingdom of God. Never give yourself any rest, unless you have good evidence that you are converted and become a new creature. We hope that God will preserve your life and health, and return you to Stockbridge again in safety; but always remember that life is uncertain: you know not how soon you must die, and therefore had need to be always ready.

We have very lately heard from your brothers and sisters at Northampton and at Newark, that they are well. Your aged grandfather and grandmother, when I was at Windsor, gave their love to you. We here all do the same.

I am,

Your tender and affectionate father,

Jonathan Edwards.

(*Works* 16, 666–67)

The letter makes clear both that Jonathan took eternity seriously and that he loved his daughter Esther. He expressed that he was "full of concern" for her, and his tone is affectionate throughout. But sentimentality did not overwhelm theology for Edwards. Love at its height involved concern for the soul and ultimate things. Edwards thus went to great lengths to impress upon his little girl that she needed to "always set God before" her if she was to transcend this life and rest eternally with Him in heaven. Surely, she had received many letters and admonitions just like this one. In his fathering, as in his preaching, Edwards communicated that death was close—but so was the God of mercy.

REDISCOVERING THE AFTERLIFE

In our age, the worldviews of too many Christians resemble the nineteenth-century system of belief so eloquently decried in the poem by Emily Dickinson quoted in the introduction. In our day, many of us busy ourselves with this world and the perfection of our existence in it. We have little fire for an otherworldly lifestyle, because we have little connection to the other world. It is generally taken for granted, rarely meditated on, rarely spoken of. The temporality of this life, the fragility of it, is forgotten.

Hope does exist for a recovery of vigorous spiritual belief and practice. In the work and example of Edwards and many other eternity-minded Christians from the past, we find the perspective we need. Edwards lived and worked as if heaven and hell were real, because he knew that they were. Our contact with Edwards's vivid, biblically saturated descriptions of the day of judgment and the age to come chart the way forward. We need to let the biblical testimony on the afterlife seep into our consciences and steep for a while so that we may pursue a new way of thinking and living.

In a world stricken with a plague of narcissism and distractedness, it is essential that we recognize the truth about the afterlife now, while we may ready ourselves for the end. Death and the final judgment swiftly approach us all. In these last days, our only hope is to prepare ourselves for the end by seeking the One who holds eternity in His mighty hand.

Preparing for Eternity

Know How the World Is Shaping Your Thoughts

In an age when many ignore or disdain the Bible's teaching on eternity, the challenge for Christians is to both believe the truth about eternity and then to live in light of it. We may accomplish the first by studying scriptural books like the Minor Prophets, which have much to say about the judgment and the afterlife, the Pauline epistles (1 and 2 Thess., for example), and the book of Revelation. As we study these works with a commentary at hand to help us puzzle through the hard parts, we can also immerse ourselves in strong theology. As one can readily tell, the work of Jonathan Edwards is a great place to start. The Puritans of post-Reformation era England and America focused a great deal on the afterlife (the Puritan paperbacks from Banner of Truth books have much helpful material on this subject). This kind of self-education will help us to refute unsound thinking, even as it expands our own worldview and stokes our imagination to contemplate the life to come.

The gospel is meant to usher in an eschatological life, a life lived with heaven and hell in full view. This life will naturally include many of the good things common to this world, but it has a fundamentally different orientation and frame of reference than the unbelieving life, which is by definition this-worldly. Our challenge, then, is plain—we need to take heaven and hell seriously. We need to glorify God by prioritizing eternity. We need to show the world by the way we live that heaven and hell are real. Belief in the afterlife is not, as so many think, a matter of preference. It is a necessity with eternal consequences. This point will only make sense to unbelievers around us when we Christians, those who have been claimed for all eternity, live with the reality of eternity ever before us.

Chapter 24

THE FRIGHTENING PROSPECT OF HELL

The movie scene is familiar to many of us today. A small figure struggles across a craggy landscape, fighting the force of an evil will as he goes. Accompanied by a trustworthy companion, he follows the lead of an unlikely guide, a strange creature of unearthly skin tone. The figure, of course, is Frodo Baggins, and the story is *The Lord of the Rings* by J. R. R. Tolkien.

The story of this film centers on Frodo's quest for Mordor, the city of evil and death, ruled over by the spirit of Sauron, the dark lord. The *Lord of the Rings* conveys a sense of terrible dread. Mordor is a force for evil, a place of destruction and malevolence, and it is sheer madness for Frodo and his party to approach it. In this cinematic locale, we get a taste of what a realm of darkness might be like. Outside of frightening films, most of us rarely encounter, let alone mull over, such places of suffering and torment. For most people in the broader culture, the hellish place that is Mordor is nothing more than the outworkings of a particularly active imagination.

There is truth to this thought. However, Mordor is based on a real place. Not a place on this earth, of course, but a realm far beyond this world, known to students of the Bible as hell.

The Scripture offers a description of a hell that makes Mordor seem tame by comparison. Led by Jesus, who spoke more than any other single figure about hell, the biblical voices present this realm as a real place where the unrepentant sinner is punished eternally for his sins (see, for starters, Deut. 32; Isa. 66; Dan. 12; Matt. 5, 10, 18, 23; Mark 9; Luke 12; John 5; Gal. 6; Eph. 5; 2 Thess. 1; Rev. 14, 20).

Among eminent preachers of the Christian past, Jonathan Edwards represents an unparalleled guide to the doctrine of hell. This chapter will examine several of Edwards's sermons that consider hell with great depth, insight, and clarity. These include "Warnings of Future Punishment Don't Seem Real to the Wicked," which shows us the dire predicament of the lost mind; *Distinguishing Marks of a Work of the Spirit of God*, which offers a stirring call to preach judgment; "The Torments of Hell Are Exceeding Great" and "Sinners in the Hands of an Angry God," which together offer an apocalyptic picture of hell; and "The Justice of God in the Damnation of Sinners," which shows that God is just in His work of judgment.

TAKING HELL SERIOUSLY

Edwards preached on numerous occasions about the reality of future judgment. It was not the singular emphasis of his career, but neither was it a doctrinal footnote. In his sermon "Warnings of Future Punishment Don't Seem Real to the Wicked," based on God's warning to Lot in Genesis 19:14, we find a sound starting point for our analysis of Edwardsean preaching on hell. Though a grave reality of earthly life, most people, Edwards suggested, thought little about it:

> Now the greater part of men have not a lively sensible apprehen-
> sion of the wrath of God and of eternal punishment; it never was

set before their eyes and brought into clear view. They have very little of a notion what the wrath of God is, and so it don't appear very terrible to them. They have but a faint dull idea of the misery of the damned: and that is the reason that, when they are told of it, it don't terrify them. It seems to them like a fable or a dream that makes very little impression upon their minds. (*Works* 14, 202)

Edwards was right in his day, and he is right in ours. Most people have not engaged in sustained and purposeful reflection on the doctrine of hell. Most have heard little about it. Even those who have come face to face with the doctrine have not had it "brought into clear view" by careful, probing teaching. The natural mind has little motivation to carefully consider the matter, and thus the little knowledge of hell that most people possess doesn't "terrify them" but rather seems more like "a fable or a dream" than a possible conclusion to earthly life.

This lack of attention blinded the lost to the facts about hell. First, said Edwards, the lost had little sense of how they would suffer in hell:

They han't a sensible apprehension of the manner of their punishment. 'Tis a strange punishment that is appointed to the workers of iniquity: it will be a torment inflicted after a new manner, in a way that they never experienced anything like it while they were here in this world. And it is a punishment that wicked men have but a very little notion of. They hear that the wrath of God will be poured out upon them, but they don't know what that pouring out of God's wrath is. They hear that there will be horror of conscience, but they know but very little what that horror of conscience will be. And therefore pouring out of God's wrath, and horror of conscience, don't seem very dreadful to them. They hear that they shall be tormented by devils, but they don't see how; and knowing but little of the manner of the punishment, they ben't much disquieted by fears of it. (*Works* 14, 203)

Unbelievers not only had no sense of how they would suffer in eternity, they had no idea how overwhelming that suffering would be:

> They han't a lively sensible idea of the greatness of the punishment. They hear that it will be intolerable, exceeding dreadful, that [it] will fill their souls with misery, that it will be like fire and brimstone and the like; but they nevertheless seldom think what is meant by these expressions. They never felt none of it, and never saw anybody under this punishment or that ever did endure it, and so they have no notion how dreadful it is—no, not of the hundredth part of the greatness of that misery—and so they are not terrified and affrighted by it.

Further, though they might have heard that judgment would last forever, they had no developed understanding of what eternal judgment would feel like:

> They have no lively sensible apprehension of the eternity of this punishment. They consider but little, and apprehend but very little, what is meant by those words, "eternal," "everlasting," "forever and ever." They know but little what it will be to bear misery forever without change and without end. They don't imagine how it will be when they come to be in hell, to think with themselves, "Here I must be forever and ever; there is no escape; there is no help; there's no comfort." They have very little of an idea how such a despair will sink and oppress them, and will feel like a mountain of lead that will fall upon and crush them. (*Works* 14, 203)

In these passages, Edwards exposed the terrible plight of the unredeemed sinner. Those who reject the gospel have no sense, tragically, of what is coming for them. Even if they acknowledge that they deserve punishment for sin, it often doesn't "seem very dreadful to them." After they hear that hell will be dreadful beyond all comprehension, they still have "felt none of it" and "so they are not terrified" by it. Though they accept that hell is eternal, they "have little of an idea how such a despair," stretching over all the ages, will "fall upon and crush them."

In these ways, we see that the unregenerate mindset opposes biblical logic. It makes no sense. It promises no hope. It makes things worse than they already are, because it leads the sinner to blithely refuse the truth and bury his head in the sand. The thinking of the natural man does not lead to life, to careful reflection on things that matter. It leads only to death.

WHY EDWARDS PREACHED ON HELL

Though the pastor did not often reflect on his reasons for preaching the doctrine of hell, he touched on his motivation in a brief section in his revival classic *The Distinguishing Marks of a Work of the Spirit of God*. His remarks inform the sermons covered in this chapter and instruct modern-day Christians on how to preach hell today.

In *Distinguishing Marks*, Edwards sought to help his fellow Christians think through the false and positive signs of a true work of God. In the course of doing so, he showed that it was folly not to preach about hell, for it was real and would claim every lost soul unless the truth was preached:

> If there be really a hell of such dreadful, and never-ending torments, as is generally supposed, that multitudes are in great danger of, and that the bigger part of men in Christian countries do actually from generation to generation fall into, for want of a sense of the terribleness of it, and their danger of it, and so for want of taking due care to avoid it; then why is it not proper for those that have the care of souls, to take great pains to make men sensible of

it? Why should not they be told as much of the truth as can be? If I am in danger of going to hell, I should be glad to know as much as possibly I can of the dreadfulness of it: if I am very prone to neglect due care to avoid it, he does me the best kindness, that does most to represent to me the truth of the case, that sets forth my misery and danger in the liveliest manner. (*Works* 4, 246–47)

The treatment of the subject is straightforward and sensible. If hell is real, Edwards says, "I should be glad to know as much as possibly I can of the dreadfulness of it." The preacher knew that hell was real and thus viewed it as the "best kindness" to speak of it to lost souls. He felt fully justified in exposing humanity's "misery and danger in the liveliest manner." One did not simply state a sentence about hell and then move off of the subject as fast as possible. To do justice to the subject, one had to bring to light the full horror of the realm of the damned.

Edwards went on in *Distinguishing Marks* to underscore this approach to the subject by relating it to earthly situations of great danger:

I appeal to every one in this congregation, whether this is not the very course they would take in case of exposedness to any great temporal calamity? If any of you that are heads of families, saw one of your children in an house that was all on fire over its head, and in eminent danger of being soon consumed in the flames, that seemed to be very insensible of its danger, and neglected to escape, after you had often spake to it, and called to it, would you go on to speak to it only in a cold and indifferent manner? Would not you cry aloud, and call earnestly to it, and represent the danger it was in, and its own folly in delaying, in the most lively manner you was capable of? Would not nature itself teach this, and oblige you to it? If you should continue to speak to it only in a cold manner, as you are wont to do in ordinary conversation about indifferent matters, would not those about you begin to think you were bereft of reason yourself?

Even though this direct approach made great sense, few took note of its alarm, and fewer still heard it and then warned others of hell:

> This is not the way of mankind, nor the way of any one person in this congregation, in temporal affairs of great moment, that require earnest heed and great haste, and about which they are greatly concerned, to speak to others of their danger, and warn them but a little; and when they do it at all, do it in a cold indifferent manner: nature teaches men otherwise. If we that have the care of souls, knew what hell was, had seen the state of the damned, or by any other means, become sensible how dreadful their case was; and at the same time knew that the bigger part of men went thither; and saw our hearers in eminent danger, and that they were not sensible of their danger, and so after being often warned neglected to escape, it would be morally impossible for us to avoid abundantly and most earnestly setting before them the dreadfulness of that misery they were in danger of, and their great exposedness to it, and warning them to fly from it, and even to cry aloud to them. (*Works* 4, 247)

The point is incontrovertible. When one has seen what hell is like through the testimony of the Scripture, one cannot help but warn others of hellfire. Man, contrary to what he often thinks, is not fine, but is "in eminent danger" that he is "not sensible" of. We who believe the Bible have not seen what hell is actually like, but we have read the New Testament's abundant coverage of it. We are thus called to tell the lost of their condition, to "cry aloud to them" and warn them of hell.

Edwards concluded his discussion of this matter in *Distinguishing Marks* by challenging those who failed to warn sinners of the hellish fate that awaited them. He contrasted their approach with his own:

> Some talk of it as an unreasonable thing to think to fright persons to heaven; but I think it is a reasonable thing to endeavor to fright persons away from hell, that stand upon the brink of it, and are just ready to fall into it, and are senseless of their danger: 'tis a reasonable thing to fright a person out of an house on fire. The word "fright" is commonly used for sudden causeless fear, or groundless surprise; but surely a just fear, that there is good reason for, though it be very great, is not to be spoken against under any such name. (*Works* 4, 248)

Some in Edwards's day did not want to scare or "fright" people. Such preaching was "unreasonable." Yet Edwards, a man of academic distinction and refined sensibility, nonetheless knew that sinners stood "upon the brink" of hell. Though one's natural inhibitions might lead one to avoid scaring people, the certain danger of the sinner called Christians to warn nonbelievers of their imminent fate. Though Edwards would not have endorsed scare tactics, he believed firmly in cultivating a "just fear," a proper biblical fright, of everlasting torment. Because so few people even thought about hell, the danger they faced was "very great." So too was the need for preaching on hellfire.

The logic of the matter required action. Edwards did not adopt his mindset out of mere choice. He believed that he was obligated to tell the lost of their fate. Anything else would render him negligent and seal the damnation of his fellow man, who, instead of concerning himself with ultimate realities, busied himself with the small things of life. The Christian could not waste time. He could not waver about what to say. Judgment was real. Vengeance approached. The only hope of escape was true, vibrant, exhortational preaching on the darkness of hell and the liberating light of the gospel.

THE TORMENTS OF HELL

Edwards went to great lengths in his preaching on hell to bring that realm of terror to life. In his sermon "The Torments of Hell Are Exceeding Great," based on Luke 16:24, Edwards walked his hearers through the theology of judgment, showing the foundations of the doctrine before leaving his audience with several pictures that made the discussion real.

Edwards began the sermon with a brief discussion of wrath. Wrath was not impersonal or abstract for Edwards. As a biblical Christian, he recognized that wrath was personal. It was *God's* own wrath:

> The punishment that is threatened to be inflicted on ungodly men is the wrath of God. God has often said that he will pour out his wrath upon the wicked. The wicked, they treasure up wrath; they are vessels of wrath, and they shall drink of the cup of God's wrath that is poured out without mixture. Revelation 14:10, "The same shall drink of the wine of the wrath of God, which is poured out without mixture." That is, there shall be no mixture of mercy; there shall be no sort of mitigation or moderation. God sometimes executes judgments upon sinners in this world, but it is with great mixtures of mercy and with restraint. But then there will be full and unmixed wrath. (*Works* 14, 304)

The pastor's words provide clarity on a subject that can easily drift into the abstract. Biblical wrath is not impersonal. It is the outpouring of the fury of a person done wrong. From the first bite of the forbidden fruit to the present day, mankind has heaped up sins against God. Because of this, He will one day pour out His wrath, "full and unmixed," without mercy.

Edwards elaborated on the connection between God's character and His wrath, showing how numerous verses in Scripture showed Him to be angry at sin:

> The Scripture uses the same way of arguing to prove the dreadfulness of God's anger, from the greatness of his Being and majesty and power; and therefore we may be sure the argument is good. Psalms 90:11, "Who knoweth the power of thine anger? even according to thy fear, so is thy wrath." "According to thy fear"; that is, according to thy awful majesty and greatness, these fearful attributes. The Psalmist argues here from the greatness of God's majesty that the power of his anger is so great that we can't conceive of it. Again, Ezekiel 22:14, "Can thine heart endure, or can thine hands be strong, in the days that I shall deal with thee?" Where the argument is plainly this: that seeing 'tis God who shall deal with them, therefore their punishment will be intolerable. Again, 2 Thessalonians 1:7–9, "The Lord Jesus shall be revealed from heaven, in flaming fire taking vengeance on them who know not God, and obey not the gospel: who shall be punished with everlasting destruction from the presence of the Lord, and from the glory of his power." Where there is evidently an argument implied, that the punishment and destruction of unbelievers will be exceeding dreadful, because it comes from the presence of the Lord and because it is inflicted by such mighty power. Again, there is the same argument very plain, Hebrews 10:31, "It is a fearful thing to fall into the hands of the living God." (*Works* 14, 306)

Unbelievers sometimes express confidence in their ability to handle the judgment of God. Against such thinking, Edwards plainly pointed out that the teaching of Scripture is that "the power of his anger is so great that we can't conceive of it." Divine anger "will be intolerable and exceeding dreadful." Man cannot bear it; nothing will relieve it; time will not lessen it. For eternity, God will pursue the wicked and exact His justice for their sin. The visitation of wrath on the unrepentant would bring God great glory, Edwards taught. God had no second thoughts about the judgment. He would not struggle or hesitate to carry it out. As Edwards preached in "Torments," He did all things to manifest His glory, including judgment:

> 'Tis God's glory that he is a jealous God as well as that he is an infinitely gracious God. When Moses desired to see God's glory and God answered him by proclaiming his glory, they were both in his mercy and grace, and also his jealousy. His name that he proclaimed to Moses consisted of them two things. Exodus 34:6–7, "And the Lord passed by before him, and proclaimed, The Lord, The Lord God, merciful and gracious, long-suffering, abundant in goodness and truth"; and then in the next verse, "That will by no means clear the guilty; visiting the iniquity of the fathers upon the children, and upon the children's children, unto the third and to the fourth generation." 'Tis God's glory that he is a consuming fire, and he has appointed the damnation of the wicked on purpose to show forth this glory of his. As the Scripture expressly teaches us, Romans 9:22, "What if God, willing to show his wrath, and to make his power known, endured with much long-suffering the vessels of wrath fitted to destruction." (*Works* 14, 307)

In reading such texts, modern readers often wonder about their justice and fairness. A deep and justifiable sadness for the lost washes over us as we read of their eternal destruction. Edwards undoubtedly felt the same way, but his theocentric perspective left his questions tethered to his trust of the Lord. Edwards knew from Scripture that God does all things for His glory. His personal judgment, carried out as a result of His personal wrath, results in His personal glory. The Scripture was clear on this matter.

With this backdrop in place, Edwards next covered the character of sin. In a world where we are trained to explain away sin, Edwards put it into proper perspective in "Torments":

> [R]ebellion against God's authority and contempt of his majesty, which every sin contains, is an infinite evil, because it has that infinite aggravation of being against an infinitely excellent and glorious majesty and most absolute authority. A sin against a more excellent being is doubtless greater than against a less excellent; and therefore, sins against one infinite in majesty, authority and excellency must be infinite in aggravation, and so deserves not a finite, but an infinite punishment, which can be only by its being infinite in duration. And then one sin deserves that the punishment should be to that degree of intenseness as to be the destruction of the creature, because every sin is an act of hostility, and 'tis fit that God's enemies should be destroyed.

The lives of unrepentant sinners heap up just condemnation from a holy and gracious God:

> If every sin, therefore, though comparatively small, deserves eternal death and destruction, how dreadful then is the deserved punishment of wicked men, whose hearts are full of sin, full of inveterate implacable enmity to God and all that is good, and set upon all manner of evil: whose very natures are full of sin as a viper is full of poison, and who have lived all their days in sinful practices; who have committed sin continually, as constantly as they have rose or lay down, or eat or drank, yea, from whom sin has flowed as continually as water from a spring; who have every day been practicing of known sins; that have disobeyed God to his face time after time incessantly; have every day cast contempt

upon God's power, upon his justice and holiness, and affronted his majesty and slighted his mercy; have stopped their ears to commands, to calls and warnings, and instead of growing better, have grown worse and worse the more God commands and calls; who have committed many great sins, have grossly transgressed God's holy law. (*Works* 14, 309–10)

If Edwards showed in his preaching that God's wrath is personal, he also showed that sin on the part of humanity is personal. Sin is an offense committed against God. It is entirely natural; people do it without thinking, even as they do it as the result of sustained planning. As a transgression against God and His holy character, sin calls for God's judgment.

Edwards next offered a number of vivid descriptions of the judgment. First he considered Mark 9:44 (KJV), focusing on the phrase "Where their worm dieth not":

Another metaphor that is used to express this torment, is the worm that never dies. Mark 9:44, "Where their worm dieth not." It is taken from Isaiah 66:24, "And they shall go forth, and look upon the carcasses of the men that have transgressed against me: for their worm shall not die, [neither shall their fire be quenched]." The expression of the worm's not dying in the carcasses of these men alludes to this: when a dead carcass lies upon the face of the earth till it begins to putrefy, it will presently be overrun with worms; the carcass will be filled within and without with worms gnawing upon it. And the expression of their fire's not being quenched alludes to the custom of the heathens, when any of them died, to burn them in a fire and so entomb their ashes. Now the Prophet says, "Their worm shall not die." When a dead carcass lies putrefying upon the earth, after a while the carcass will be consumed and the worms will die, but the worms that shall gnaw upon the carcasses of these men shall not; that is, their souls shall always be tormented. The similitude holds forth exceeding misery: how miserable must a man be, to be alive and yet have his flesh and bowels and vitals all filled with worms continually gnawing upon his body, as they do upon a dead carcass. (*Works* 14, 310–11)

Next, he looked at the fiery destruction of Sodom (Gen. 19:1–29) and how it might parallel hellfire:

> Now when the destruction of Sodom is said to be by the raining of brimstone and fire out of heaven, it seems to have been by miraculous thunder and lightning. The fire of lightning is brimstone and fire, or the burning of a sulfurous matter. It is probable, therefore, that they were destroyed by thick and perpetual flashes of lightning and claps of thunder. 'Tis a way of dying that nature has a peculiar horror of. And what a dreadful picture does it give us of the destruction of hell, that it shall be like perpetual flashes of lightning with amazing claps of thunder upon the heads of the wicked, piercing their souls through and through. Is hell as Sodom was, all full of nothing but fire and brimstone, continual incessant peals of thunder and glaring flashes of lightning upon everyone's head, in everyone's face and through everyone's heart, and that without any cessation, which they shall feel to the utmost and yet live to feel more? It shall not be as when anyone is killed with lightning in this world: he is killed in a moment and neither hears, nor perhaps feels, anything; or if he does, 'tis but for a moment. But in hell, they shall feel it all; they shall feel the dismal pain and rendings of soul that it will cause, and that without ceasing. It will not be one flash of lightning, and then an intermission, and another by and by, but the lightning will be one perpetual glare, and all in the same soul. (*Works* 14, 317)

In each of these descriptions of hell, Edwards showed how the calamities of ancient Sodom offer only a dim foreshadowing of the horrors of hell. On earth, human carcasses are lifeless, but in hell the wicked would feel the "worms continually gnawing upon his body." In Sodom, the wicked were felled in an instant; in hell, "the lightning will be one perpetual glare." As bad as earthly death and judgment proved to be, they were mercifully temporal in a way that hellish judgment would not be.

UNSETTLING IMAGES FROM THE REALM OF DESTRUCTION

Edwards offered the most horrifying depictions of hell in his sermon "Sinners in the Hands of an Angry God," a homily on Deuteronomy 32:35 (KJV): "Their foot shall slide in due time." The sermon is the most famous in American history. It is starkly terrifying, filled with apocalyptic imagery that bears looking into. First, Edwards compared God's vengeance to mighty rivers:

> The wrath of God is like great waters that are dammed for the present; they increase more and more, and rise higher and higher, till an outlet is given, and the longer the stream is stopped, the more rapid and mighty is its course, when once it is let loose. 'Tis true, that judgment against your evil works has not been executed hitherto; the floods of God's vengeance have been withheld; but your guilt in the meantime is constantly increasing, and you are every day treasuring up more wrath; the waters are continually rising and waxing more and more mighty; and there is nothing but the mere pleasure of God that holds the waters back that are unwilling to be stopped, and press hard to go forward; if God should only withdraw his hand from the floodgate, it would immediately fly open, and the fiery floods of the fierceness and wrath of God would rush forth with inconceivable fury, and would come upon you with omnipotent power; and if your strength were ten thousand times greater than it is, yea, ten thousand times greater

than the strength of the stoutest, sturdiest devil in hell, it would
be nothing to withstand or endure it. (*Works* 22, 410–11)

He then pictured God as a bowman with a bead on His target
(Ps. 11:2):

The bow of God's wrath is bent, and the arrow made ready on
the string, and Justice bends the arrow at your heart, and strains
the bow, and it is nothing but the mere pleasure of God, and that of
an angry God, without any promise or obligation at all, that keeps
the arrow one moment from being made drunk with your blood.
(*Works* 22, 411)

In the sermon's abiding image, Edwards compared the sinner to
a spider held back from an open flame by the "mere pleasure" of
the Lord:

The God that holds you over the pit of hell, much as one holds a
spider, or some loathsome insect, over the fire, abhors you, and
is dreadfully provoked; his wrath towards you burns like fire; he
looks upon you as worthy of nothing else, but to be cast into the
fire; he is of purer eyes than to bear to have you in his sight; you
are ten thousand times so abominable in his eyes as the most
hateful venomous serpent is in ours. You have offended him
infinitely more than ever a stubborn rebel did his prince: and yet
'tis nothing but his hand that holds you from falling into the fire
every moment; 'tis to be ascribed to nothing else, that you did
not go to hell the last night; that you was suffered to awake again
in this world, after you closed your eyes to sleep: and there is
no other reason to be given why you have not dropped into hell
since you arose in the morning, but that God's hand has held you
up; there is no other reason to be given why you han't gone to hell
since you have sat here in the house of God, provoking his pure eyes

by your sinful wicked manner of attending his solemn worship: yea, there is nothing else that is to be given as a reason why you don't this very moment drop down into hell. (*Works* 22, 411–12)

In a particularly visceral passage based on Isaiah 63:3, he pictured the Lord as the one who tramples the wicked in a winepress:

How awful are those words, Isaiah 63:3, which are the words of the great God, "I will tread them in mine anger, and trample them in my fury; and their blood shall be sprinkled upon my garments, and I will stain all my raiment." 'Tis perhaps impossible to conceive of words that carry in them greater manifestations of these three things, viz. contempt, and hatred, and fierceness of indignation. If you cry to God to pity you, he will be so far from pitying you in your doleful case, or showing you the least regard or favor, that instead of that he'll only tread you under foot: and though he will know that you can't bear the weight of omnipotence treading upon you, yet he won't regard that, but he will crush you under his feet without mercy; he'll crush out your blood, and make it fly, and it shall be sprinkled on his garments, so as to stain all his raiment. He will not only hate you, but he will have you in the utmost contempt; no place shall be thought fit for you, but under his feet, to be trodden down as the mire of the streets. (*Works* 22, 414)

The collective weight of these images boggles the mind. In our age, when many professing Christians question the doctrine of hell, warm to the unbiblical idea of universal salvation, and re-envision certain texts along annihilationist lines, Edwards's remarkable images lead us back to the plain and dreadful teaching of certain Scripture passages.

The various pictures Edwards paints of hell—as a flood of vengeance, an arrow aimed at the heart, a great furnace over which sinners dangle, and a winepress filled with blood—each draw out an aspect of hell. The Scripture looks at the realm from various angles, all of which contribute to a general conception of it as a place of the most intense suffering. Those of us who have accepted an unbalanced view of God—where God is only loving and gentle and has no place in His character for just wrath—will struggle with these images. We will be tempted to omit or, at the very least, ignore this aspect of His character.

Though we tremble at the scriptural testimony on judgment, we must take care that we do not allow our emotions, however moved by the fate of the lost, to overwhelm the plain teaching of the Bible. As Edwards brings out in a number of sermons, including those covered above, the Scripture presents God's judgment of the wicked as an outworking of His majesty. In a way that is hard for us to comprehend, the fury of God's justice brings glory to God. His justice proceeds from His righteousness, His holy hatred of sin. The existence of wickedness calls into necessity His judgment.

Edwards's own mind boggled at these realities. Yet he knew that the Scripture spoke with piercing clarity about the day of judgment and hell. Even if he did not fully know the mind of God, he knew that the Lord was trustworthy and right. If God was God, then by definition He was holy and just, however much the finite mind might grapple with His decrees. He expressed this belief in his sermon "The Justice of God in the Damnation of Sinners," based on Romans 3:19:

> 'Tis meet that God should order all these things, according to
> his own pleasure. By reason of his greatness and glory, by which
> he is infinitely above all, he is worthy to be sovereign, and that
> his pleasure should in all things take place: he is worthy that he
> should make himself his end, and that he should make nothing
> but his own wisdom his rule in pursuing that end, without asking

leave or counsel of any, and without giving account of any of his matters. 'Tis fit that he that is absolutely perfect, and infinitely wise, and the fountain of all wisdom, should determine everything by his own will, even things of the greatest importance, such as the eternal salvation or damnation of sinners. 'Tis meet that he should be thus sovereign, because he is the first being, the eternal being, whence all other beings are. He is the creator of all things; and all are absolutely and universally dependent on him; and therefore 'tis meet that he should act as the sovereign possessor of heaven and earth. (*Works* 19, 347–48)

As Edwards teaches, the Lord is "absolutely perfect" and "infinitely wise." We are not. We have no right to question God, to make Him bow before us and answer to us. Our response to His holy Word and the wisdom it reveals is obedience and trust. He is the "sovereign possessor" of all; we are but the possessed.

As Edwards's example instructs us, we are called by Him to shirk the foolishness of this world and embrace the truth of Scripture and its doctrines, including the unpopular doctrines of hell and judgment. We are called by Him to preach the truth, including the unfashionable truth regarding damnation and torment. We are called by Him to set the matter in theocentric terms, to show how God is right, that sin is an offense against God, and God is just to punish it. We are called by Him to preach the full scriptural counsel about hell, referencing and explaining the vivid pictures of that realm the Bible provides. We are not called to reshape the faith to make it more palatable to the sinful heart. God requires us to be faithful to His Word and, like Edwards so powerfully did, to preach the whole counsel, including the parts that unsettle us and cause us to pray for mercy for those far off from the Lord.

THE CERTAINTY OF GOD'S JUDGMENT

It is not easy to work one's way through the doctrine of punishment. Yet as Edwards showed, judgment is an important, if secondary, aspect of the ultimate plan of God and the mission of Christ. The second coming in particular will reveal the awesome majesty of the Savior. Sinners who derided Him, denied Him, ignored Him, took Him for granted, hated Him, mocked Him, made Him a joke, used Him as a curse word, reshaped Him in their image, and failed to take His Word seriously will meet a terrible end. To cite the ominous words of the prophet Hosea, those who have sowed to the wind "shall reap the whirlwind" (Hos. 8:7).

More terrible than any mythic journey to Mordor or any other realm, the scriptural testimony on hell commands our sober attention and assent. It implores us to share the gospel with all we can while we still have time. It drives us to pray for the lost so that they may escape the judgment of the Lord. It reminds us of what we have been spared, knowledge that cannot help but bring us to our knees in thanksgiving to God for the atonement of His Son. The biblical doctrine of hell reshapes all our thinking about the future of this world and its inhabitants. Soon, we know, the righteous justice of Christ will sweep over the earth. Soon the visions of Scripture elaborated by Edwards and others will come true. In that day, none will resist the Lord.

Preparing for Eternity

Acknowledge the Reality of Hell

The Bible, especially the New Testament, makes abundantly clear that hell is real, an actual place, and the eternal destination of much of the human race (Matt. 7:14). Scripture speaks much of hell, with Jesus raising the subject more than any other biblical voice (for starters, see Matt. 5:22, 29–30; 18:8–9; 25:46; Mark 9:43–48; Luke 16:23; John 3:36; 5:24; 10:28).

It is important that we modern people recognize the difficulty we naturally have with accepting the reality of hell. We will be tempted by our modern sensibilities to refashion the doctrine, tweak it, apologize for it, dislike it, and reject it. Many of us have accepted tenets of thought that make accepting the whole counsel of Christian doctrine a challenging proposition. Our godless age tempts us to sift biblical truth for the parts we like, instead of allowing God to speak authoritatively into our lives.

We are responsible for declaring the gospel, not for telling people what they want to hear. As is quite clear from American history, preaching a feel-good, personally enhancing message of positive religious thinking can attract quite a crowd. It's not difficult in this country to win a large following with a religious message. It is far more challenging to build a church through faithful preaching of the biblical gospel—the message of redemption from judgment through the atoning death and life-giving resurrection of Christ. If we only aspire to build a nice building, win some hearers, raise some money, and do some positive things, we can tailor our message as we see fit—the specific content will follow the spirit of the times. But if we would see sinners won from hell, lives dramatically changed by the Word, and disciples of Christ raised up, then like Edwards we will need to embrace the gospel, preach the whole counsel of the Word, and seek to make true disciples for the glory of God Almighty.

Preach Hell

Many people read the culture today and conclude, rightly, that preaching hell will turn hearers off. So they emphasize the positive aspects of Christianity and tuck away their belief in hell. While no one would urge believers to preach only judgment to the world, the biblical figures who have gone before us preached a bold message of salvation from judgment (see Acts 2 and 4, for example). It makes little sense, after all, to preach only salvation. Salvation from what, we might ask? From oneself? From psychological problems? From sadness? Well, yes, to all of the above and more. But far more importantly, we need to preach salvation from judgment, specifically, from the day of judgment and the eternal punishment in hell that will follow. In addition, our efforts to massage the message may have little effect and, surprisingly, even impair our attempts to reach the lost.

We preach hell not because of its evangelistic results, of course, but out of a desire to remain faithful to the scriptural gospel. With that said, hell is a potent reality, as Edwards recognized. It has led many to flee to the arms of Christ for salvation. The preaching of Christ, of the apostles, and of countless figures throughout church history testify to the fact that sinners often repent as a result of hearing both the bad news, future condemnation for sin, and the good news, the glorious atonement of Christ. Too many Christians today speak ill of "hellfire and brimstone" preaching. We need to tell the truth about hell with balance and humility; but just as biblical figures did not shy away from preaching God's just punishment of sin, neither should we.

Chapter 25

THE GLORIOUS
PROSPECT OF HEAVEN

Christians are called in the New Testament "strangers and pilgrims," a striking metaphor for the Christian life (1 Peter 2:11
KJV). On this earth, believers are not "residents." They are likened
to an alien race, a nomadic tribe making its way through a wilderness. There is an element of sadness in this description, a note of
yearning. Christians have no true home in this place. Our home
is another realm: heaven.

While we travel, every Christian sees a bit of heaven, finds
its light drawing them closer. Yet few of us have recognized the
full glory of the life to come. In this chapter, we examine Edwards's vision of heaven. We look at the following sermons: "True
Saints, When Absent from the Body, Are Present with the Lord,"
which shows us that heaven is real; "Nothing Upon Earth Can
Represent the Glories of Heaven," "The Pure in Heart Blessed,"
and "The Many Mansions," all of which show various degrees
of our heavenly joy; "Serving God in Heaven," which teaches
that we will serve the Lord in heaven; "Degrees of Glory," which
reveals that our earthly lives resound in eternity; and "Heaven
Is a World of Love," the grandest sermon of them all. We will
not necessarily construct a rigorous argument in this chapter,

but rather present various depictions of heaven from Edwards's material that will reinvigorate us for the journey ahead. In the pastor's awe-inspiring preaching and teaching on heaven, we find fresh faith and courage to journey on through barren wilderness in search of a place of perfect peace and joy.

HEAVEN IS REAL

To understand the Edwardsean conception of heaven, we need to know first of all that the pastor believed that heaven was real. This may sound obvious, but Edwards knew that many Christians struggled to keep this belief in sight. In a sermon now called "True Saints, When Absent from the Body, Are Present with the Lord," based on 2 Corinthians 5:8, Edwards sought to pull his hearers away from their temporal concerns to show them that they would soon rest with the Lord. Death could come for them in an instant, but they did not need to fear it if they trusted in Christ. Heaven awaited:

> When we are absent from our dear friends, they are out of sight; but when we are with them, we have the opportunity and satisfaction of seeing them. So while the saints are in the body, and are absent from the Lord, he is in several respects out of sight; 1 Peter 1:8, "Whom having not seen, ye love: in whom, though now ye see him not, yet believing," etc. They have indeed, in this world, a spiritual sight of Christ; but they see through a glass darkly, and with great interruption: but in heaven, they see him face to face (1 Corinthians 13:12). "The pure in heart are blessed; for they shall see God" (Matthew 5:8). (*Works* 25, 229)

Heaven allowed glorified believers the opportunity to behold their Lord. Edwards helps us to see that heaven, fundamentally, is about fellowship with God. Heaven is the realm of God that contains "all the glory of the Godhead." No matter what unanswered questions we may have—Will we know one another? What will we look like? What will we do?—we may know for certain that the focus of heaven is our God. It is not our desires and whims that will direct things in heaven, but His. However we might imagine the shape of our life to come, we may rest assured that the Lord will order all things perfectly.

In heaven, we will think much about our redemption, Edwards suggested. Contemplation of God's plan of salvation will produce more love for the Lord than we can imagine:

> And when the souls of the saints leave their bodies, to go to be with Christ, they behold the marvelous glory of that great work of his, the work of redemption, and of the glorious way of salvation by him; which the angels desire to look into. They have a most clear view of the unfathomable depths of the manifold wisdom and knowledge of God; and the most bright displays of the infinite purity and holiness of God, that do appear in that way and work: and see in another manner, than the saints do here, what is the breadth and length and depth and height of the grace and love of Christ, appearing in his redemption. And as they see the unspeakable riches and glory of the attribute of God's grace, so they most clearly behold and understand Christ's eternal and unmeasurable dying love to them in particular. And in short they see everything in Christ that tends to kindle and enflame love, and everything that tends to gratify love, and everything that tends to satisfy them: and that in the most clear and glorious manner, without any darkness or delusion, without any impediment or interruption. (*Works* 25, 230)

Though they faced different challenges than we do, Edwards's people experienced the same struggle to embrace heaven that many of us do. They loved their earthly lives. They feared death, wondering occasionally if the promise of heaven would come true. They grieved deeply at the funerals of Christians, sometimes feeling more sadness than joy. Edwards ministered to people who struggled with such issues by reassuring them of the certain home of the Christian. "[W]hen the souls of the saints leave their bodies," he reminded them, they "go to be with Christ" in heaven. There they "do see him as he is." Death signals no lasting tragedy for the believer. One moment we are in our bodies, navigating the complexities of this realm. The next, we are ushered into the presence of Christ.

Upon meeting Christ, Edwards continued, we recognize and worship Him as our "glorious and loving Redeemer." The fact of Christ's substitutionary atonement does not fade into the distance for us in heaven; It grows more beautiful. As the "sun" rises in the morning and brings illumination, so will our ascension to heaven cause the glory of Christ's death and resurrection to shine afresh.

This kind of heavenly happiness will not fade away as it does on earth. Later in "True Saints," Edwards noted that Christians in heaven are "a thousand times" happier than we are because of their intimate association with Jesus:

> On these accounts the saints in heaven must needs be under a thousand times greater advantage than we here, for a full view of the state of the church on earth, and a speedy, direct and certain acquaintance with all its affairs, in every part. And that which gives them much greater advantage for such an acquaintance, than the things already mentioned, is their being constantly in the immediate presence of Christ, and in the enjoyment of the most perfect intercourse with him, who is the King who manages all these affairs, and has an absolutely perfect knowledge of them. Christ is the head of the whole glorified assembly; they are mystically his glorified body: and what the head sees, it sees for the

information of the whole body, according to its capacity; and what the head enjoys, is for the joy of the whole body. (*Works* 25, 237)

In heaven, Jesus is the lodestar. He is the center, the substance, the focus, and His joy is the "joy of the whole body." None will find their happiness diminished in the world to come; all will have perfect delight in His presence. Insights like this from Edwards are worth pondering and soaking up.

HEAVEN IS A GLORIOUS CITY

Some of what makes heaven hard to believe in is that we have not seen it and thus have little sense of what it looks like. In his sermon "Nothing Upon Earth Can Represent the Glories of Heaven," derived from Revelation 21:18, Edwards reminds us that heaven is a city, albeit unlike any we have ever seen:

> Heaven is likened in Scripture to a splendid and glorious city. Many men are ever surprised and amazed by the sight of a splendid city. We need not to be told how often heaven is called the holy city of God. Other cities are built by men, but this city, we are told, was built immediately by God himself. His hands reared up the stately mansions of this city, and his wisdom contrived them. Hebrews 11:10, "For he looked for a city which has foundations, whose builder and maker is God." Other cities that are royal cities, that is, the cities that are the seats of kings and where they keep their courts, are commonly, above all others, stately and beautiful; but heaven, we are told, is the royal city of God, where the King of heaven and earth dwells, and displays his glory. Hebrews 12:22, "The city of the living God." (*Works* 14, 141)

In this city, the realm of perfection, mankind would revel in the greatness of God. Edwards explained this in his sermon, "The

Pure in Heart Blessed," based on Matthew 5:8. The Lord had expressly made the heart of man for heaven by fitting it to become perfectly happy:

> When God gave man his capacity of happiness, he doubtless made provision for the filling of it. There was some good that God had in his eye when he made the vessel, and made it of such dimensions, that he knew to be sufficient to fill it and to contain which the vessel was prepared; and doubtless that, whatever it be, is man's true blessedness. And that good which is found not to be commensurate to men's capacity and natural cravings, and never can equal it, it certainly denotes it not to be that wherein men's happiness consists.

Your heart is not made for this earth, Edwards told his hearers. It was made for another realm. Happiness here is fleeting and insufficient. Happiness in heaven is full and undimmed, never ceasing, always supplied by the love of God:

> But the fountain that supplies that joy and delight which the soul has in seeing God is sufficient to fill the vessel, because it is infinite. He that sees the glory of God, he in his measure beholds that that there is no end of. The understanding may extend itself as far [as] it will; it doth but take its flight out into an endless expanse and dive into a bottomless ocean. It may discover more and more of the beauty and loveliness of God, but it never will exhaust the fountain. Man may as well swallow up the ocean as he can extend his faculties to the utmost of God's excellency. (*Works* 17, 72)

As is clear in this quotation, Edwards believed that happiness, like knowledge, would be progressive in heaven, ever increasing. Yet, this did not lessen the happiness that the glorified believer would experience. All who went to heaven would experience "full satisfaction":

> How blessed therefore are they that do see God, that are come to this exhaustless fountain! They have obtained that delight that gives full satisfaction; being come to this pleasure, they neither do nor can desire any more. They can sit down fully contented, and take up with this enjoyment forever and ever, and desire no change. After they have had the pleasures of beholding the face of God millions of ages, it won't grow a dull story; the relish of this delight will be as exquisite as ever. There is enough still for the utmost employment of every faculty. (*Works* 17, 73)

We often make the pleasures of this world our standard for happiness. Yet even the best and most lasting joys of this world cannot fractionally compare to the goodness of heaven. Living in heaven, Edwards tells us, is like taking "flight out into an endless expanse" and plunging "into a bottomless ocean" of the "beauty and loveliness of God."

None of this will prove "a dull story," as our earthly joys often do. God has made lasting delight in earthly experiences and possessions evasive. We lose happiness easily here. We grow bored with our favorite things. We easily sense something of the ennui of this world, the listlessness, the tendency to break down and stagnate. We will not know such a deadening pattern in heaven. Our enhanced senses will handle as much delight as they possibly can for all of eternity. We will know joy upon joy, delight upon delight, "forever and ever."

MANSIONS FOR ALL

The gold standard of earthly achievement has been, for centuries, a mansion. Though we might initially chastise such a desire,

it seems from the Bible that we were made to desire a heavenly
mansion, a place where we can rest in satisfaction and ease,
as John 14:2 promises. Edwards elaborated on this text in his
sermon "Many Mansions":

> Let all be hence exhorted, earnestly to seek that they may be
> admitted to a mansion in heaven. You have heard that this is God's
> house: it is his temple. If David, when he was in the wilderness of
> Judah, and in the land of Jeshua, and of the Philistines, so longed
> that he might again return into the land of Israel, that he might
> have a place in the house of God here on earth, and prized a place
> there so much, though it was but that of a doorkeeper; then how
> great in happiness will it be to have a place in this heavenly temple
> of God. If they are looked upon as enjoying an high privilege that
> have a seat appointed there in kings' courts, or an apartment in
> kings' palaces, especially those that have an abode there in the qual-
> ity of the king's children; then how great a privilege will it be to have
> an apartment or mansion assigned us in God's heavenly palace, and to
> have a place there as his children. How great is their glory and honor
> that are admitted to be of the household of God. (*Works* 19, 743)

Edwards's words show that God intends for His people to live
satisfied, restful, enjoyable lives in heaven. This is what the mansion signifies—not self-glorifying wealth, but the abundant, generous gift of God to His people. On this earth Christians know
suffering, poverty, and want to varying degrees. It is a sure hope
that in the life to come, the Lord will give us an endless bounty
of goodness and a "high privilege" that has never been known on
this earth (1 Cor. 2:6–10).

We will not hole up in our heavenly mansions, however. In
the world to come, we will gather as the family of God:

Heaven is the house where God dwells with his family. God is represented in Scripture as having a family; and though some of this family are now on earth, yet in so being, they are abroad, or not at home, but all going home. Ephesians 3:15, "Of whom the whole family in heaven and earth is named." Heaven is the place that God has built for himself and his children. God has many children, and the place designed for 'em is heaven. And therefore the saints, being the children of God, are said to be of the household of God. Ephesians 2:19, "Now therefore ye are no more strangers and foreigners, but fellow citizens with the saints, and of the household of God." God is represented as an householder, or the head of a family, and heaven is his house. (*Works* 19, 738)

In heaven, we will dwell together with God. We will gather as a joyful family to celebrate the One who has called us to Himself. We will experience perfect communion and intimate fellowship with one another and with our God. We will make our way to our mansion and take unforeseen delight in the home prepared for us.

SERVING GOD IN HEAVEN

Just because heaven is a place of worship does not mean that it is a tame, lazy, boring realm. According to Edwards's sermon "Serving God in Heaven," a meditation on Revelation 22:3, the ideal realm would feature mankind in his ideal state. This meant action, not passivity:

But man's powers of action were given him for action. God aimed at action, in giving man such capacities of action. And therefore when the reasonable creature is in action, or in the exercise of those powers of action which God hath given it, then 'tis in its more perfect state if its acts are suitable to the rational nature,

and consequently is more happy than in a state of idleness.
(*Works* 17, 254)

In serving the Lord, man was fulfilling the design-plan God had
created for him:

> Therefore, when man serves God, he acts most according to
> his nature. He is employed in that sort of action that is most
> distinguishing of him from the beasts. He acts then in a way most
> according to the end of his formation, and most agreeable to his
> make and formation of the human nature itself. A man never acts
> so rationally as when he serves God. No actions [are] so agreeable
> to reason, and all that are contrary to God's service are contrary to
> reason. And therefore, doubtless, his happiness consists in serving
> God. (*Works* 17, 255)

This illuminates why we naturally gravitate to work. Even without the light of revelation, there is something in the heart of a
person that relishes productivity. Most of us are happiest when
put to good ends. The satisfaction we enjoy in such work fore-
shadows our lives in the age to come, which will be filled with
all kinds of fruitful endeavors in the name of our Lord. Edwards
spelled this out further in "Serving God":

> The saints in heaven will take great delight in serving of [God],
> as they delight in doing that which is just and right. Justice is
> what they delight in; if anything is right and equal, it is sufficient
> to make those spirits that are made perfect to love it and take
> pleasure [in] it. They will see those charms in equity that will cause
> them to have a perfect love to it. Saints' love to equity and justice in
> this world is not perfect. Sometimes a love to other things prevails
> over it. A saint here may be drawn to do those things that are contrary

to it, but it will not be so in heaven, where the soul shall be brought to
its perfect rectitude of nature.

He continued,

> They will be sensible that 'tis most reasonable that God should be
> their ruler, in that he has redeemed them. They will see that all the
> service which they can render to him is but a small recompense
> for that great redemption. They will be sensible then how great the
> redemption was, much more sensible than they are now; for then,
> they will be sensible how terrible the destruction is that they were
> redeemed from, and shall know by experience how glorious the
> happiness which was purchased for them. (*Works* 17, 256)

As Edwards showed, the reality of redemption will not sit lightly
on the minds of the glorified saints. It will drive us to serve the
Lord with fullness of joy. Heaven is a place of service, but not
rote service of the kind we all know well on earth. We will work
for the Lord with the happiest of hearts.

DEGREES OF GLORY IN THE AFTERLIFE

Edwards believed that our earthly lives counted in the afterlife.
In his sermon "Degrees of Glory," based on 2 Corinthians 9:6, he
argued that the believer who pursues the glory of God in this life
will experience greater honor than a lax believer. The pastor set
forth this view early in the sermon:

> The Scriptures declare that God will hereafter reward every man
> according to his works; as Matthew 16:27, "For the Son of man
> shall come in the glory of his Father with his angels; and then he
> shall reward every man according to his works"; and in many other
> places. Now, by this we but justly understand only that Christ

rewards everyone according to the quantity of his works, viz. that
he will reward good to them that have done good, and evil to them
that have done evil; but also that the reward will be in proportion
to men's works. Thus it shall be with the wicked: their punishment will be in proportion to their wicked works; as is abundantly
manifest. Thus we read, it shall be more tolerable for some of
them than others at the day of judgment. And Christ signifies the
different degrees of punishment in hell by the different degrees of
capital punishments among the Jews, in Matthew 5:22. "Whosoever shall be angry with his brother without a cause shall be in
danger of the judgment." And as wicked men shall in this sense be
rewarded according to their works, viz. in proportion, so doubtless will
the godly. Yea, the rewards being according to our works, our labor is
expressly in this sense applied to the godly by the Apostle. 1 Corinthians 3:8, "Now he that planteth and he that watereth are one: and
every man shall receive his own reward according to his own labor."
(*Works* 19, 616)

Though we might instinctively think that every Christian will
occupy the same position in heaven, Edwards argued that it was
not so. He grounded his argument in Scripture:

God has abundantly promised to reward the good works of the
saints in another world. Christ has said that if we do but give a
cup [of cold water only, we shall in no wise lose our reward]. But
how can this be, if it be so that whether they do more good works
or fewer, all that have just the same reward? When a person has
a good work before him to be done, how can he say with himself
to encourage himself to do, "If I do it, I shall be rewarded for it; I
shall in no case lose my reward"; if at the same time it be true that
he shall have as great a reward, if he lets it alone as if he does it;
and he shall have as much future happiness, if he does few good
works as many? There can be no such thing as any reward at all for

good works, unless they are rewarded with some additional degree of happiness. If nothing be added, then there is nothing gained. (*Works* 19, 616–17)

Living with heavenly rewards in mind was not an option, as Edwards found in his study of the Word. It was

a duty expressly commanded. Matthew 6:19–20, "Lay not up for yourselves treasures upon earth, where moth and rust doth corrupt, and where thieves break through and steal: but lay up for yourselves treasures in heaven, where neither moth nor rust doth corrupt, and where thieves do not break through nor steal." By laying up treasure in heaven is not only meant obtain some inheritance there, but to be adding to it; as is evident by the comparison made between this and what is forbidden, viz. laying up treasure on earth. By which Christ don't mean that we should get nothing in this world, but not do as worldly-minded men do, be striving insatiably to hoard up, and keep adding to our worldly good things; but rather strive to add to our inheritance in heaven, and heap up treasure there; labor daily to increase our interest there by doing good works, and abounding in them; as appears by [the] Luke 12:33. "Sell that ye have, and give alms; provide yourselves bags which wax not old, a treasure in the heavens." (*Works* 19, 621–22)

Edwards's argument matches the plain teaching of Scripture. The way that we live on this earth affects our heavenly status. The more that we live for the Lord with the little time that we have here, the more He will reward us in the life to come. Day-to-day life, with moment-by-moment, even second-by-second decisions, counts. It is not all a wash, or all the same to God. The thoughts we think, the programs we choose to watch, the evangelistic conversation we try to have, the cup of cold water we give in the name of Christ, the word of correction we offer a straying believer, the prayer we say as we hurry to work—all of this matters to God. All of it impacts, in a way we do not fully understand now, our eternal standing in heaven.

We do not know exactly how things will shake out. It may very well be that the leaders we admire now must take a back seat to saints we have never heard of in heaven. Our earthly calculus for heavenly standing may prove wrong altogether. We do not know, in the end, where the Lord will seat us in His gallery of worship. We do know, however, that the life we live on this earth matters. Every second of our earthly existence counts.

HEAVEN IS A WORLD OF LOVE

The axis on which heaven turns, according to Edwards in his sermon "Heaven Is a World of Love," is love. In this sermon, one of the pastor's most stirring, his prose spiraled to great heights. The text immediately grabs the reader's attention and permanently affects the way one thinks about heaven. The central idea of "Heaven Is a World of Love" is that God dwells in heaven and fills the realm with the essence of His being, which is love. The text begins on this note:

> Heaven is the palace, or presence-chamber, of the Supreme Being who is both the cause and source of all holy love. God, indeed, with respect to his essence is everywhere. He fills heaven and earth. But yet he is said on some accounts more especially to be in some places rather than others. He was said of old to dwell in the land of Israel above all other lands, and in Jerusalem above all other cities in that land, and in the temple above all other houses in that city, and in the holy of holies above all other apartments in that temple, and on the mercy seat over the ark above all other places in the holy of holies. But heaven is his dwelling place above all other places in the universe. (*Works* 8, 369)

Edwards captures the largeness of God and heaven here. God is gigantic. He is not small or limited. The Lord "fills heaven and earth." Yet heaven "is his dwelling place" in a special way. It is a place where only things that please God may dwell. He will tolerate no sin, no effects of the curse, no beings who do not delight in Him, but only things that are "lovely":

> There are none but lovely objects in heaven. There is no odious or polluted person or thing to be seen there. There is nothing wicked and unholy. Revelation 21:27, "And there shall in no wise enter into it anything that defileth, neither whatsoever worketh abomination, or maketh a lie." There is nothing which is deformed either in natural or moral deformity. Everything which is to be beheld there is amiable. The God, who dwells and gloriously manifests himself there, is infinitely lovely. There is to be seen a glorious heavenly Father, a glorious Redeemer; there is to be felt and possessed a glorious Sanctifier. All the persons who belong to that blessed society are lovely. The Father of the family is so, and so are all his children. The Head of the body is so, and so are all the members. Concerning the angels, there are none who are unlovely. There are no evil angels suffered to infest heaven as they do this world. They are not suffered to come near, but are kept at a distance with a great gulf between them. In the church of saints there are no unlovely persons; there are no false professors, none who pretend to be saints, who are persons of an unchristian, hateful spirit and behavior, as is often the case in this world. There is no one object there to give offense, or at any time to give any occasion for any passion or motion of hatred; but every object shall draw forth love. (*Works* 8, 370)

The identifying characteristic of this otherworldly society is love. In the realm of this world, every relationship is tainted by sin in some way. We experience the love of God and mediate it to others, but even among highly mature Christians, affection is not pure. The heavenly society knows no such weaknesses of love. Proceeding from the Godhead and flowing undiminished into all who reside there, love is the fundamental principle, the defining characteristic of existence:

> With respect to the degree of their love, it is perfect. The love which is in the heart of God is perfect, with an absolute, infinite and divine perfection. The love of the angels and saints to God and Christ is perfect in its kind, or with such a perfection as is proper to their nature, perfect with a sinless perfection, and perfect in that it is commensurate with the capacities of their natures. So it is said in the text, when that which is perfect is come, that which is in part shall be done away. Their love shall be without any remains of a contrary principle. Having no pride or selfishness to interrupt or hinder its exercises, their hearts shall be full of love. That which was in the heart as but a grain of mustard seed in this world shall there be as a great tree. The soul which only had a little spark of divine love in it in this world shall be, as it were, wholly turned into love; and be like the sun, not having a spot in it, but being wholly a bright, ardent flame. There shall be no remaining enmity, distaste, coldness and deadness of heart towards God and Christ; not the least remainder of any principle of envy to be exercised towards any angels or saints who are superior in glory, no contempt or slight towards any who are inferior. (*Works* 8, 375–76)

More comforting and hopeful words one can scarcely find. The Northampton pastor compels his hearers to remember the sweet and sometimes forgotten promises of Scripture. The "mustard seed" that fights to grow here will surely grow into "a great tree" in eternity. The soul that fought to taste the love of God in this earth but battled bitterly against besetting sin, hurtful situations, and desperate circumstances will find its "little spark of divine love" turned into "a bright, ardent flame." Nothing will impair the Christian's love for the Lord, no "enmity, distaste, coldness and deadness of heart," no "principle of envy," no "contempt or slight." The absence of these problems so familiar to us who dwell in a sinful world clarify the wonder and hope of heaven.

It is worth noting that the subject of jealousy occupies a great deal of space in the sermon. Most believers today avoid this issue. It's an uncomfortable sin to confront, both in ourselves and others. In a unique way, jealousy poses the power to altogether destroy love. Where it resides in a heart, it naturally crowds out positive affections. Edwards does not offer any personal reflection on this matter, but as a highly gifted person, it is certain that he faced considerable envy in his life. His words, stemming from personal experience, remind us that the petty rivalries and bitter envy of this world will have no place in the realm to come:

Those who have a lower station in glory than others suffer no diminution of their own happiness by seeing others above them in glory. On the contrary they rejoice in it. All that whole society rejoice in each other's happiness; for the love of benevolence is perfect in them. Everyone has not only a sincere but a perfect good will to every other. Sincere and strong love is greatly gratified and delighted in the prosperity of the beloved. And if the love be perfect, the greater the prosperity of the beloved is, the more is the lover pleased and delighted. For the prosperity of the beloved is, as it were, the food of love; and therefore the greater that prosperity is, the more richly is love feasted. The love of benevolence is delighted in beholding the prosperity of another, as the love of complacence is delighted in viewing the beauty of another. So that the superior prosperity of those who are higher in glory is so far from being any damp to the happiness of saints of lower degree that it is an addition to it, or a part of it. There is undoubtedly an inconceivably pure, sweet and fervent love between the saints in glory; and their love is in proportion to the perfection and amiableness of the objects beloved. And therefore it must necessarily cause delight in them when they see others' happiness and glory to be in proportion to their amiableness, and so in proportion to their love of them. Those who are highest in glory are those who are highest in holiness, and therefore are those who are most beloved by all the saints. For they love those most who are most holy, and so they will all rejoice in it that they are most happy. And it will be a damp to none of the saints to see them who have higher degrees of holiness and likeness to God to be more loved than themselves; for all shall have as much love as they desire, and as great manifestations of love as they can bear; all shall be fully satisfied. (*Works* 8, 375)

Though the human heart, so prone to competition, struggles with this reality, Edwards taught that heaven would include no jealousy over position or honor earned by holy living. Instead, the joy of one would fuel the joy of all:

And when there is perfect satisfaction, there is no room for envy. And they will have no temptation to envy those who are above them in glory from their superiors being lifted up with pride. We are apt to conceive that those who are more holy, and more happy than others in heaven, will be elated and lifted up in their spirit above others. Whereas their being above them in holiness implies their being superior to them in humility; for their superior humility is part of their superior holiness. Though all are perfectly free from pride, yet as some will have greater degrees of divine knowledge than others, will have larger capacities to see more of the divine perfections, so they will see more of their own comparative littleness and nothingness, and therefore will be lowest abased in humility. And besides, the inferior in glory will have no temptation to envy those who are higher. For those who are highest will not only be more beloved by the lower saints for their higher holiness, but they will also have more of a spirit of love to others. They will love those who are below them more than other saints of less capacity. They who are in highest degrees of glory will be of largest capacity, and so of greatest knowledge, and will see most of God's loveliness, and consequently will have love to God and love to saints most abounding in their hearts. So that those who are lower in glory will not envy those who are above them. (*Works* 8, 376)

Heaven must be an unearthly place, if this kind of fellowship characterizes it. The love of the saints for one another, a love that flows from the shared affection of the Godhead, so orders their feelings and thoughts that they rejoice fully and completely in the promotion of another. No "What about me?" plagues the minds of children of God in the realm to come. Where they once felt twinges of jealousy mixed in with their genuine happiness for a fellow Christian, in heaven they will know only pure happiness as the Lord honors others for their faithfulness. The blessing of God given to all will serve as the "food of love" that will feed and heighten the happiness of all. Heaven is a world of love, a place where jealousy, narcissism, self-promotion, and bitterness have no place.

LONGING FOR HEAVEN

All of the preceding promises to awaken our passion for heaven. Considerable trials rise up before us on this earth. Our sin attacks us, and Satan seeks to discourage us from pursuing holiness. The suffering of others can overwhelm us at times and make us feel that our quest is futile. Though we are strangers and pilgrims now, we have great hope. We are redeemed by the Savior. We have seen a vision of a better place where God receives His children. As Edwards described movingly toward the end of "Heaven

Is a World of Love," heaven offers all who are faithful to Christ the opportunity to enter "the Paradise of God":

> And all this in a garden of love, the Paradise of God, where everything has a cast of holy love, and everything conspires to promote and stir up love, and nothing to interrupt its exercises; where everything is fitted by an all-wise God for the enjoyment of love under the greatest advantages. And all this shall be without any fading of the beauty of the objects beloved, or any decaying of love in the lover, and any satiety in the faculty which enjoys love. O! what tranquility may we conclude there is in such a world as this! Who can express the sweetness of this peace? What a calm is this, what a heaven of rest is here to arrive at after persons have gone through a world of storms and tempests, a world of pride, and selfishness, and envy, and malice, and scorn, and contempt, and contention and war? What a Canaan of rest, a land flowing with milk and honey to come to after one has gone through a great and terrible wilderness, full of spiteful and poisonous serpents, where no rest could be found? (*Works* 8, 385)

As we make our way through this life, let us remember: this is what awaits us.

Preparing for Eternity

Believe in Heaven

The main challenge before us is simply this: to believe in heaven. We don't mean any old make-your-own version. We mean the biblical view, one nicely expounded by Edwards in the sermons covered above. Heaven is real. It has a definite character. The book of Revelation in particular teaches us about it. We would do well to study this text to fire our hearts and inform our imaginations about the blessed afterlife. Too often we approach Revelation merely as an apocalyptic puzzle. It certainly is that, but there is also tremendous value in studying heaven to inspire belief in the life to come. What a harvest of happiness awaits us. In heaven, we will take up a mansion prepared for us; we will serve the Lord with our talents and abilities; we will rest in the arms of Christ; we will worship the Lord by singing and praising the resurrected Lamb; we will rejoice as faithful Christians receive the acclamation of Almighty God for their lives. This is not all we will do and be in heaven—we possess limited knowledge of the shape of our lives there. We can see clearly, though, that heaven is a realm where we will worship our majestic God in many different ways. If we find ourselves reducing heaven to any one paradigm, we must remind ourselves of the many-sidedness of the blessed life to come. Doing so will stave off unwarranted disinterest and boredom related to heaven and will provoke eagerness and excitement about it. The multidimensional glory of heaven, flowing from the eternal triune God, will soon bring fully into view what we now see "in a mirror dimly" (1 Cor. 13:12).

Chapter 26

THE TRANSFORMING POWER OF AN ETERNITY-FOCUSED MINDSET

The previous chapter looked at the life of the "stranger and pilgrim," examining what the Christian focuses on as they travel to the world to come. Heaven occupies the mind of the traveler, pushing them on to see their Savior and find their reward. Yet, we might ask, what does this life look like on a daily basis? Are we to live with our heads in the clouds, walking in a daze through our obligations and pastimes? Do we abandon our earthly chores, find a nice hill to sit on, and wait for death?

The biblical figures listed in a passage familiar to many of us, Hebrews 11, offer us a solid answer to our questions. The various heroes listed in this passage all trusted that God would grant them something greater than this world. After celebrating a number of these figures, including Abel, Enoch, Noah, Abraham, and Sarah, the author of the letter tells us that

> if they had been thinking of that land from which they had gone out, they would have had opportunity to return. But as it is, they desire a better country, that is, a heavenly one. Therefore God is

not ashamed to be called their God, for he has prepared for them a city. (Hebrews 11:15–16)

The author later heralds unknown martyrs, men and women now lost to time whose faith made their lives an offering to Christ:

> Some were tortured, refusing to accept release, so that they might rise again to a better life. Others suffered mocking and flogging, and even chains and imprisonment. They were stoned, they were sawn in two, they were killed with the sword. They went about in skins of sheep and goats, destitute, afflicted, mistreated—of whom the world was not worthy—wandering about in deserts and mountains, and in dens and caves of the earth. (Hebrews 11:35–38)

Though these heroes did not know all that we do about heaven, they viewed their earthly experiences through the promise of a blessed afterlife. Their belief in the life to come did not result in a Zen-like, otherworldly mental state that enabled them to shut their eyes to sin and sorrow. Rather, the eschatological (future-oriented), heaven-focused mindset of these heroes formed them into agents of grace, people who followed the call of the Lord through the valley of the shadow of death.

Our era presents the eschatological Christian with unique challenges, a number of which we will briefly identify as we piece together what a heavenly minded Christian life looks like today. In this brief closing chapter, we will offer several suggestions to help us adopt an eschatological mindset in our day. We will blend scriptural analysis, Edwardsean teaching, and contemporary perspective to accomplish this goal. We will look at several ways that heaven-focused thinking affects who we are and how we live, including our identity, family, church, work, and witness.

DEVELOPING IDENTITY

Edwards, like the heroes of the Bible, lived life differently than his peers. He had heaven on the brain. As described in previous chapters, he took frequent trips to the countryside, mulling over the promise of heaven as he rode his horse through brisk breezes and rolling hills. He thought deeply about this earth, but he considered himself a citizen of another land. Edwards's meditation produced not only deep preaching, but a radically different way of life.

His insights, based on the Bible, can do the same for us. At our core, we can reconceive our existences, rooting them in heaven more than earth. What does this mean, practically? It means that we study Scripture, saturate our minds with it, and learn to think in scriptural categories. We need to commit ourselves to putting the Scripture and its teaching on the afterlife constantly before us so that the Holy Spirit can transform our lives. As we read texts on heaven and hell, meditating deeply on them, we will naturally find that we think of heaven as our true home.

This kind of commitment will influence our lives in numerous ways. We will see ourselves as heaven-bound Christians first, not employees, not parents, not politically concerned citizens, not sports fans. Recognizing ourselves as children of God bound for heaven will prevent us from investing ourselves too deeply in earthly matters. We need this kind of grounding. We will live on this earth, at the longest, for a hundred or so years. We will worship God in heaven for eternity. We all know that it is challenging to live for a realm that we cannot see, but really, is this not the paradox of our faith? We love a Savior we have not seen. Can we not live in anticipation of the heavenly realm where the Lord dwells and waits to receive His children?

PRIORITIZING FAMILY

Sometimes we can act as if our family members will not live forever. That may sound strange to Christian readers, but practically, it applies to the way many families live on a day-to-day basis. We need to adopt and apply an eschatological mindset for the sake of those we love. Our spouses, children, and extended family members will spend eternity in either heaven or hell. Remembering this simple reality will prod us out of complacence and cause us to approach all of our family interactions with care and a sense of gravity.

Edwards did not often reflect on the theology of his family, but he left clear evidence of his belief in the importance of marriage. In one sermon, he reflected on how earthly marriage is a picture of the Christ-church union:

> And as the husband provides the wife with food and clothing; so the pastor, as Christ's steward, makes provision for his people, and brings forth out of his treasure things new and old, gives every one his portion of meat in due season, and is made the instrument of spiritually clothing and adorning their souls. And on the other hand, the minister receives benefit from the people, as they minister greatly to his spiritual good by that holy converse to which their union to him as his flock leads them. The conjugal relation leads the persons united therein to the most intimate acquaintance and conversation with each other; so the union there is between a faithful pastor and a Christian people leads them to the intimate conversation about things of a spiritual nature: it leads the people most freely and fully to open the care of their souls to the pastor, and leads him to deal most freely, closely and thoroughly with them in things pertaining thereto. And this conversation not only tends to *their* benefit, but also greatly to *his*. (*Works* 25, 176)

He spoke as well of the love of children, representing the church, for their Head, the Lamb who saved them:

> And on the other hand, they love and honor him with an holy affection and esteem; and not merely as having their admiration raised, and their carnal affections moved, by having their ears tickled, and their curiosity and other fleshly principles gratified by a florid eloquence, and the excellency of speech and man's wisdom; but receiving him as the messenger of the Lord of hosts, coming to them on a divine and infinitely important errand, and with those holy qualifications that resemble the virtues of the Lamb of God. (*Works* 25, 174)

These spiritually-focused comments bear on the way we think of our families today. We should not, for example, cede spiritual care of our children to another person, whether a youth minister, coach, or other authority figure, however gifted they may be. As parents, we need to shepherd our children and raise them in the fear and admonition of the Lord. We need to keep their lives in eternal perspective, carefully choosing what sins and attitudes to tackle at a given time. With unsaved extended family members, we should undertake, however awkward it may be, to share the gospel, realizing that their only hope for heaven is Jesus Christ. This is a key part of the eschatological mindset. It is not the part we want to think much about, but we must do so if we are to honor God's Word.

As the words above show, Edwards wished for the marriage relationship and the parent-child relationship to be character-ized by love. This has import for us in our own familial roles. We should adopt a way of life that will best enable us to care for our family members, particularly our children. Modern consumer-ism pushes us to sacrifice anything and everything for the sake of spending power and the accumulation of goods and experiences.

Family is often sacrificed in the process. Christians who live with eternity in mind will find such a sacrifice impossible. In an individual sense, the most significant responsibility one can have is the care of a child. Every child has a soul; every soul is precious. Those parents who focus on this plain truth will find themselves fundamentally unable to yield primacy of focus and attention to anything but their children. This logic may seem strange to an unbeliever trying to get the most out of this world, but may make great sense to those who have different priorities and hopes for this life.

LOVING CHURCH

The modern era has dramatically reshaped the local church. In a climate flooded with self-help books and life-improvement tips, many churches have shaped themselves more as nurturers of the psyche than outposts of heaven storming the gates of hell. These assemblies oftentimes find receptive audiences, and many of them do preach the gospel and lead people to salvation in Christ. But their posture, their conception of church, leaves much to be desired.

We do well to recall what Edwards said of the church: "Christ deals with his church as a father…He has not contented himself with only saying, 'Be kind one to another,' knowing that a care that lies in everybody's hands equally is like to be neglected, but he has appointed officers, that his children may be fed in both body and soul as their necessities require" (Bailey, 108). These words remind us of the need for local churches to be more than a communal rallying point, a place to celebrate shared heritage and common political views, a conduit for certain social causes, a site of moral formation, or a safe zone for the training of children in certain behaviors and ideas. The church is grounded in truth and led by fearless Bible-loving "officers," as Edwards calls them. God has said more to the church than just "be kind"; He has called the church to be a Word-centered family, and from this rock-solid bond of fellowship to offer the lost a powerful picture of transformation and acceptance. How important this is. Where many around us have no family, the people of God can become their family (Ps. 27:10).

INVIGORATING WORK

The eschatological mindset also refigures our conception of work. All work, as Martin Luther so helpfully emphasized, is God's work. We recall Edwards's words on the "degrees of glory": we should "strive to add to our inheritance in heaven, and heap up treasure there; labor daily to increase our interest there by doing good works, and abounding in them" (*Works* 19, 621–22). What needed zest this is. We should esteem work while always keeping it in proper perspective, unlike so many in our society who fail on this point, and who destroy their souls in pursuit of economic dreams.

As Edwards argued, our earthly lives share a direct connection with our heavenly lives (1 Cor. 10:31). The way we live here directly affects our spiritual maturity and thus our heavenly standing (see Matt. 6:19; James 2). We must reject the anti-work spirit so common in our age, dramatized to great comedic effect in sitcoms and movies, and work with energy and intensity in our callings. All work done for the Lord is important. Every position, every vocation, allows us the opportunity to give God glory, whether we labor as a flower-shop owner, a stay-at-home mother, a bus driver, a corporate lawyer, or a writer. How we do the work given us in God's gracious providence matters greatly to Him (Col. 3:23–24).

RENEWING MINDS

It is impossible to write about Jonathan Edwards and his kind of eternity-focused mindset without making reference to the development of the mind. Edwards knew that his mind was a gift from God, so he devoted great attention to cultivating and strengthening it. He wanted to serve God by thinking well with the time given him. Doing so would deepen all of his life and ministry and thereby bring God more glory—and Jonathan more eternal reward. The ultimate focus of all this thinking, for Edwards? The things of God, as he said: "The wisdom of God was not given for any particular age, but for all ages" (Bailey, 121). So it is that we pursue wisdom, and especially divine wisdom, using our minds not as arbiters of holy truth, but recipients and celebrants of it.

In this spirit, we do well to remember the words of the apostle Paul to the Roman Christians to "be transformed by the renewal of your mind" (Rom. 12:2). We can speed this transformation by reading weighty theological works. In the writings of Augustine, Luther, Calvin, the Puritans, Edwards, and many others from history, we will find much to chew on. We should not confine our reading only to Christian sources but should seek to better understand world and national history, philosophy, and politics. It will help us greatly to find a thoughtful Christian in our church and ask them to help us identify books that will enable us to think more deeply and thus live richer lives that bring God more glory. As we study the Scripture, learn theology, and train ourselves to critique and learn from secular thought, we will expand our understanding of God and His world, grow wiser in how we live and think, and experience the satisfaction of loving God with our mind (Matt. 22:37).

Such a transformed mind relates directly to the privilege of Christian witness. As Christians, we cannot responsibly argue that evangelism falls only to the professionals. To be given the gospel is to be given the joyful task of passing it on. Some will prove more adept at this work than others, but every Christian not only gets to share the gospel, but take up an evangelistic—some would say "missional"—life modeled on the Great Commission of Matthew 28:16–20. This kind of life, which Christians have been practicing for centuries, stems from belief in the afterlife. Christians who do not evangelize have not, for one reason or another, looked closely enough at the content of their faith, which is rooted in eternity.

JONATHAN EDWARDS, ESCHATOLOGICAL CHRISTIAN

We have sketched a vision of an eschatological life. There is much that we could add; our vision is regrettably brief. But we trust that the material of the previous chapters, coupled with the suggestions of this chapter, will provide much food for thought about how Christians may live in light of eternity. We have repeatedly stressed that we are dealing here not merely with some tweaks to an existing way of life, but with a radical, otherworldly existence that looks, feels, and sounds different from a worldly condition. In a remarkable way, Jonathan Edwards saw the significance and seriousness of eternity. His writings reveal a mind captivated by the afterlife and a heart gripped by the fragility of humanity.

In a way that most of us do not, Edwards looked long and hard at heaven and hell. He saw that each was real. He realized that he could not skate lightly over hell, tucking it into a doctrinal statement while never mentioning it or warning sinners about it. He *had* to preach about it, and to do so with textual faithfulness and biblically inspired imagination. Such preaching would not only warn the sinner, but drive him to the inexhaustible well of God's mercy. Hell had an evangelistic power, Edwards knew. The church and pastor who trifled with it, passed it over, or quickly moved over it did so to their own detriment and at the cost of full-bodied gospel witness. On the other hand, heaven had definite character and shape, Edwards saw. It had a glory and depth that few preachers or theologians discovered and communicated. Even as faithful preaching on hell would inspire holy fear in the heart of the sinner, biblical preaching on heaven would set the heart soaring with hope. The great God who filled hell with terror simultaneously set love free to rush over the inhabitants of heaven. In passage after passage, Edwards sought to show his hearers just how marvelous heaven would be, though no words could do it justice. We see, then, that heaven and hell were meant to be preached together, each disclosing the importance of the other, each shedding light on our glorious God.

We need not write or speak like the pastor to honor his legacy and live as eschatological Christians. We do not need to be a pastor. We do not need to work in vocational ministry. We need only to grasp the realities that sit plainly before us and apply them to our lives, or rather, allow them to transform our hearts and minds such that we experience the joy and weight and significance of an eschatological life. We are born with eternity in our hearts, a wise man once declared, but our sin often blinds us to this fact (Eccl. 3:11). We naturally drift to a world-focused mindset, especially in a technological, consumerist, entertainment-obsessed culture like our own. Here, everything that matters ultimately seems of little consequence, while everything of little consequence seems ultimately important. Sin and Satan and the very spirit of this death-cursed world urge us to live as we wish before oblivion overtakes and silences us. The Bible, however, tells a different story, a true one, which we cannot ignore. The afterlife is real. Heaven and hell exist. Our souls will go to one or the other, and the way we live and think in this life bears directly on the realm we end up in.

Among his many writings, few texts demonstrate the Edwardsean eschatological mindset, the kind we so desperately need, better than his letters to his children. Writing to his son

Timothy, Edwards offered a model of the kind of purposeful, eternity-centered, large-God theology we need today:

> That which you met with, in your passage from New York to Newark, which was the occasion of your fever, was indeed a remarkable mine, a dispensation full of instruction, and a very loud call of God to you, to make haste and not to delay in the great business of religion. If you now have that distemper, which you have been threatened with, you are separated from your earthly friends; none of them must come to see you; and if you should die of it, you have already taken a final and everlasting leave of them while you are yet alive, not to have the comfort of their presence and immediate care, and never to see them again in the land of the living. And if you have escaped that distemper, it is by a remarkable providence that you are preserved. And your having been so exposed to it, must certainly be a loud call of God, not to trust in earthly friends, or anything here below. Young persons are very apt to trust in parents and friends, when they are sick, or when they think of being on a deathbed. But this providence remarkably teaches you the need of a better friend, and a better parent, than earthly parents are; one who is everywhere present, and all-sufficient; that can't be kept off by infectious distempers; who is able to save from death or to make happy in death; to save from eternal misery and to bestow eternal life. (*Works* 16, 579)

Reminding his son of the Savior, the father concluded his letter:

> Therefore, there is your only hope; and in him must be your refuge, who invites you to come to him, and says, "He that cometh to me, I will in no wise cast out" [John 6:37]. Whatever your circumstances are, it is your duty not to despair, but to hope in infinite mercy through a Redeemer. For God makes it your duty to pray to him for mercy which would not be your duty, if it was

allowable for you to despair. We are expressly commanded to call upon God in the day of trouble; and when we are afflicted, then to pray. (*Works* 16, 580)

As we have said before, Edwards was no killjoy. He loved his children and delighted in their company, but he also committed himself to the duty of preparing them for eternity. He did this with his offspring, with his wife, and with himself. After he fell ill from a vaccination gone wrong in 1758, the pastor, so ambitious and able, rapidly came near his death. The account of his passing by his doctor, William Shippen, shows that Jonathan took his own counsel seriously. He met his end with eternity fully in view, as Shippen related:

> And never did any mortal man more fully and clearly evidence the sincerity of all his professions, by one continued, universal, calm, cheerful resignation, and patient submission to the divine will, through every stage of his disease, than he; not so much as one discontented expression, nor the least appearance of murmuring through the whole. And never did any person expire with more perfect freedom from pain;—not so much as one distorted hair— but in the most proper sense of the words, he really fell asleep. Death had certainly lost its sting, as to him. (Marsden, 494)

When a Christian lives with eternity in mind, shaping life in view of it, death truly does lose its sting. We see this in the example of Jonathan Edwards. Even as his vision dimmed to darkness, Edwards showed no fear. Through the blood of Christ, he had defeated his enemy and escaped the wrath of God. Through the power of the Spirit, he had lived a holy life and promoted the gospel of grace. As will one day be true of us if Christ tarries, he was going home; the struggles and pains of this earth over, the world of love just coming into sight.

WORKS CITED

The following shortened forms of books by or about Jonathan Edwards are used in the text to indicate the source of quotations.

Bailey, Richard A. and Gregory A. Wills. *The Salvation of Souls: Nine Previously Unpublished Sermons on the Call of Ministry and the Gospel by Jonathan Edwards.* Wheaton, IL: Crossway, 2002.
Cited as "Bailey" in the text.

Barna, George. *Today's Pastors: A Revealing Look at What Pastors Are Saying About Themselves, Their Peers and the Pressures They Face.* Ventura, CA: Regal, 1999.
Cited as "Barna" in the text.

Barna Group. "Americans Describe Their Views About Life After Death." *Barna Group,* October 21, 2003. https://www.barna.com/research/americans-describe-their-views-about-life-after-death/.
Cited as "Barna Group" in the text.

Camporesi, Piero. *The Fear of Hell: Images of Damnation and Salvation in Early Modern Europe.* University Park, PA: Penn State University Press, 1991.
Cited as "Camporesi" in the text.

Conyers, A. J. *The Eclipse of Heaven: Rediscovering the Hope of a World Beyond.* Downers Grove, IL: InterVarsity Press, 1992.
Cited as "Conyers" in the text.

Hambrick-Stowe, Charles. *The Practice of Piety: Puritan Devotional Disciplines in Seventeenth-Century New England.* Chapel Hill, NC: UNC Press, 1983.
Cited as "Hambrick-Stowe" in the text.

Kimnach, Wilson H., Kenneth P. Minkema, and Douglas A. Sweeney, eds. *The Sermons of Jonathan Edwards: A Reader.* New Haven: Yale Univ. Press, 1999.
Cited as "Kimnach" in the text.

Lipka, Michael. "A Closer Look at America's Rapidly Growing Religious 'Nones.'" *Pew Research Center* website, May 13, 2015.
Cited as "Lipka" in the text.

Marsden, George. *Jonathan Edwards: A Life.* New Haven: Yale Univ. Press, 2003.
Cited as "Marsden" in the text.

Marten, James. *Children in Colonial America.* New York: NYU Press, 2006.
Cited as "Marten" in the text.

Minkema, Kenneth P. "Jonathan Edwards's Defense of Slavery." *Massachusetts Historical Review* 4 (2002): 23–59.
Cited as "Minkema" in the text.

Morgan, Christopher W. and Robert A. Peterson. *Hell Under Fire: Modern Scholarship Reinvents Eternal Punishment.* Grand Rapids: Zondervan, 2004.
Cited as "*Hell Under Fire*" in the text.

Murphy, Caryle. "Most Americans Believe in Heaven … and Hell." *Pew Research Center* website, November 10, 2015.
Cited as "Murphy" in the text.

Norton Anthology of American Literature, vol. 1. New York: W. W. Norton & Company, 1979.
Cited as "*Norton*" in the text.

Stark, Rodney. *What Americans Really Believe.* Waco: Baylor University Press, 2008.
Cited as "Stark" in the text.

Sweeney, Douglas A. *Jonathan Edwards and the Ministry of the Word: A Model of Faith and Thought.* Downers Grove: IVP Academic, 2009.

Walker, D. P. *Decline of Hell: Seventeenth-Century Discussions of Eternal Torment.* Chicago: University of Chicago Press, 1964.
Cited as "Walker" in the text.

Wells, David. *Above All Earthly Pow'rs: Christ in a Postmodern World.* Grand Rapids: Eerdmans, 2005.
Cited as "*Above All Earthly Pow'rs*" in the text.

————. *The Courage to Be Protestant: Truth-lovers, Marketers, and Emergents in the Postmodern World.* Grand Rapids: Eerdmans, 2008.
Cited as "*Courage to Be Protestant*" in the text.

Zahnd, Brian. "Sinners in the Hands of a Loving God." *Brian Zahnd* website. July 8, 2015.
https://brianzahnd.com/2015/07/sinners-in-the-hands-of-a-loving-god.
Cited as "Zahnd" in the text.

BOOKS IN THE YALE UNIVERSITY PRESS
WORKS OF JONATHAN EDWARDS SERIES

In the text, the volumes are listed in the following format: (*Works* 1, 200). The "1" refers to the series volume; the "200" refers to the page number in the given volume.

Edwards, Jonathan. *Freedom of the Will*, ed. Paul Ramsey, *The Works of Jonathan Edwards*, vol. 1. New Haven: Yale, 1957.

————. *Religious Affections*, ed. John Smith, *The Works of Jonathan Edwards*, vol. 2. New Haven: Yale, 1959.

————. *Original Sin*, ed. Clyde A. Holbrook, *The Works of Jonathan Edwards*, vol. 3. New Haven: Yale, 1970.

————. *The Great Awakening*, ed. C. C. Goen, *The Works of Jonathan Edwards*, vol. 4. New Haven: Yale, 1972.

————. *Scientific and Philosophical Writings*, ed. Wallace E. Anderson, *The Works of Jonathan Edwards*, vol. 6. New Haven: Yale, 1980.

————. *The Life of David Brainerd*, ed. Norman Pettit, *The Works of Jonathan Edwards*, vol. 7. New Haven: Yale, 1984.

————. *Ethical Writings*, ed. Paul Ramsay, *The Works of Jonathan Edwards*, vol. 8. New Haven: Yale, 1989.

————. *A History of the Work of Redemption*, ed. John F. Wilson, *The Works of Jonathan Edwards*, vol. 9. New Haven: Yale, 1989.

————. *Sermons and Discourses, 1720–1723*, ed. Wilson Kimnach, *The Works of Jonathan Edwards*, vol. 10. New Haven: Yale, 1992.

————. *Typological Writings*, ed. Wallace E. Anderson and David Watters, *The Works of Jonathan Edwards*, vol. 11. New Haven: Yale, 1993.

_____. *Ecclesiastical Writings*, ed. David Hall, *The Works of Jonathan Edwards*, vol. 12. New Haven: Yale, 1994.

_____. *Sermons and Discourses, 1723–1729*, ed. Kenneth E. Minkema, *The Works of Jonathan Edwards*, vol. 14. New Haven: Yale, 1997.

_____. *Notes on Scripture*, ed. Stephen Stein, *The Works of Jonathan Edwards*, vol. 15. New Haven: Yale, 1998.

_____. *Letters and Personal Writings*, ed. George S. Claghorn, *The Works of Jonathan Edwards*, vol. 16. New Haven: Yale, 1998.

_____. *Sermons and Discourses, 1730–1733*, ed. Mark Valeri, *The Works of Jonathan Edwards*, vol. 17. New Haven: Yale, 1999.

_____. *The "Miscellanies," 501–832*, ed. Ava Chamberlain, *The Works of Jonathan Edwards*, vol. 18. New Haven: Yale, 2000.

_____. *Sermons and Discourses, 1734–1738*, ed. M. X. Lesser, *The Works of Jonathan Edwards*, vol. 19. New Haven: Yale, 2001.

_____. *Sermons and Discourses, 1739–1742*, ed. Harry S. Stout and Nathan O. Hatch with Kyle P. Farley, *The Works of Jonathan Edwards*, vol. 22. New Haven: Yale, 2003.

_____. *Sermons and Discourses, 1743–1758*, ed. M. X. Lesser, *The Works of Jonathan Edwards*, vol. 25. New Haven: Yale, 2006.

_____. *Sermons and Discourses, 1743–1758*, ed. M. X. Lesser, *The Works of Jonathan Edwards*, vol. 25. New Haven: Yale, 2006.

RECOMMENDED RESOURCES ON JONATHAN EDWARDS

For the premier collection of Edwards's own writing, see *The Works of Jonathan Edwards*, vol. 1–26, Yale University Press. Access these works—and 73 more in digital form—in their entirety free of charge at http://edwards.yale.edu.

For secondary sources, we recommend the following.

FOR INTRODUCTORY READING

Byrd, James P. *Jonathan Edwards for Armchair Theologians*. Louisville, KY: Westminster John Knox Press, 2008.

Finn, Nathan A. and Jeremy Kimble. *A Reader's Guide to the Major Writings of Jonathan Edwards*. Wheaton, IL: Crossway, 2017.

McDermott, Gerald R. *Seeing God: Jonathan Edwards and Spiritual Discernment*. Vancouver: Regent College Publishing, 2000.

Nichols, Stephen A. *Jonathan Edwards: A Guided Tour of His Life and Thought*. Phillipsburg, NJ: Presbyterian & Reformed, 2001.

Ortlund, Dane C. *Edwards on the Christian Life: Alive to the Beauty of God*. Wheaton, IL: Crossway, 2014.

Storms, Sam. *Signs of the Spirit: An Interpretation of Jonathan Edwards' Religious Affections*. Wheaton, IL: Crossway Books, 2007.

Stout, Harry S. *The Jonathan Edwards Encyclopedia*. Grand Rapids: Eerdmans, 2017.

FOR DEEPER READING

Crisp, Oliver D. and Douglas A. Sweeney, eds. *After Jonathan Edwards: The Courses of the New England Theology*. Oxford: Oxford University Press, 2012.

Gura, Philip F. *Jonathan Edwards: America's Evangelical*. New York: Hill & Wang, 2005.

Kimnach, Wilson H., Kenneth P. Minkema, and Douglas A. Sweeney, eds. *The Sermons of Jonathan Edwards: A Reader*. New Haven: Yale University Press, 1999.

Lesser, M. X. *Reading Jonathan Edwards: An Annotated Bibliography in Three Parts, 1729–2005*. Grand Rapids: Eerdmans, 2008

Marsden, George. *Jonathan Edwards: A Life*. New Haven: Yale University Press, 2003.

McDermott, Gerald R., ed. *Understanding Jonathan Edwards: An Introduction to America's Theologian*. New York: Oxford University Press, 2009.

Moody, Josh. *Jonathan Edwards and Justification*. Wheaton, IL: Crossway, 2012.

_____. *The God-Centered Life: Insights from Jonathan Edwards for Today*. Vancouver: Regent College Publishing, 2007.

Murray, Iain H. *Jonathan Edwards: A New Biography*. Edinburgh: Banner of Truth Trust, 1987.

Piper, John. *God's Passion for His Glory: Living the Vision of Jonathan Edwards*. Wheaton, IL: Crossway Books, 1998.

_____, and Justin Taylor, eds. *A God Entranced Vision of All Things: The Legacy of Jonathan Edwards*. Wheaton, IL: Crossway Books, 2004.

Smith, John E., Harry S. Stout, and Kenneth P. Minkema, eds. *A Jonathan Edwards Reader*. New Haven: Yale University Press, 1995.

Strachan, Owen. *Always in God's Hands: Day by Day in the Company of Jonathan Edwards*. Carol Stream, IL: Tyndale Momentum, 2018.

Sweeney, Douglas A. *Edwards the Exegete: Biblical Interpretation and Anglo-Protestant Culture on the Edge of the Enlightenment*. New York: Oxford University Press, 2015.

_____. *Jonathan Edwards and the Ministry of the Word: A Model of Faith and Thought*. Downers Grove, IL: InterVarsity Press, 2009.

Vanhoozer, Kevin and Owen Strachan. *The Pastor as Public Theologian: Reclaiming a Lost Vision*. Grand Rapids, MI: Baker Academic, 2015.

ACKNOWLEDGMENTS

We would like to thank Drew Dyck, Adam Dalton, and Kevin Emmert of Moody Publishers. Drew and Adam, along with several other folks, had the idea to condense the five volumes of the *Essential Edwards Collection* into one. This is the latest in a long line of very good ideas by Moody editors—we think here of Dave Dewit, who originally proposed the series concept. Kevin offered numerous helpful edits that only strengthened the work.

We would like to thank John Piper for graciously providing a series foreword, and for his ongoing work to champion a distinctly Edwardsean vision of the affections, the grandness of God, and the importance of doxological living.

We are deeply thankful for the love of our wives, Bethany Strachan and Wilma Sweeney. Without their support and sacrifice, we could not have written this book. As Jonathan excelled in marrying the godly Sarah, so we have gained far more from these women of Christ than we deserve.

We greatly appreciate the leadership and support of our institutional presidents, Drs. Jason Allen (of Midwestern Baptist Theological Seminary) and David Dockery (of Trinity Evangelical Divinity School). In thankfulness for Dr. Dockery's long line of faithfulness, commitment to excellent Christian scholarship, and promotion of what Edwards called Christ-centered "true religion," we dedicate this book to him.

Above all, we thank the God who has made us, saved us, and remade us for his own glory. The opportunity to remanate even a sliver of his excellency is a precious gift indeed.

ENCOUNTER GOD. WORSHIP MORE.

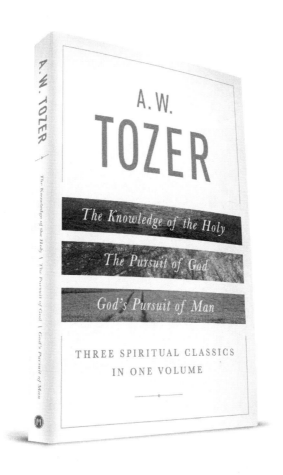

**MOODY
Publishers®**

From the Word to Life®

Considered to be Tozer's greatest works, *The Knowledge of the Holy*, *The Pursuit of God*, and *God's Pursuit of Man* are now available in a single volume. In *Three Spiritual Classics*, you will discover a God of breathtaking majesty and world-changing love, and you will find yourself worshipping through every page.

978-0-8024-1861-6

STUDY THE BIBLE WITH PROFESSORS FROM MOODY BIBLE INSTITUTE

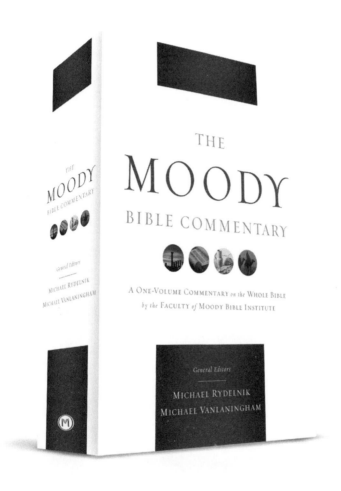

A MOODY CLASSIC

MOODY
Publishers®

From the Word to Life®

In an age of limited travel and isolated nations, C.H. Spurgeon preached to over 10,000,000 people. In this classic work, Spurgeon most clearly presented the message of salvation, a great witnessing tool and inspiring book for on fire followers.

978-0-8024-5452-2 | also available as an eBook

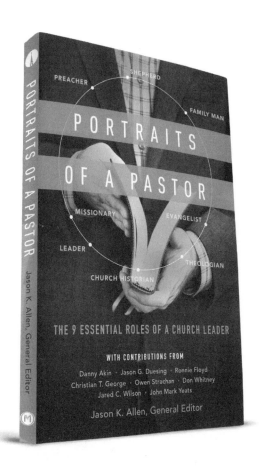